FUNNY WEATHER

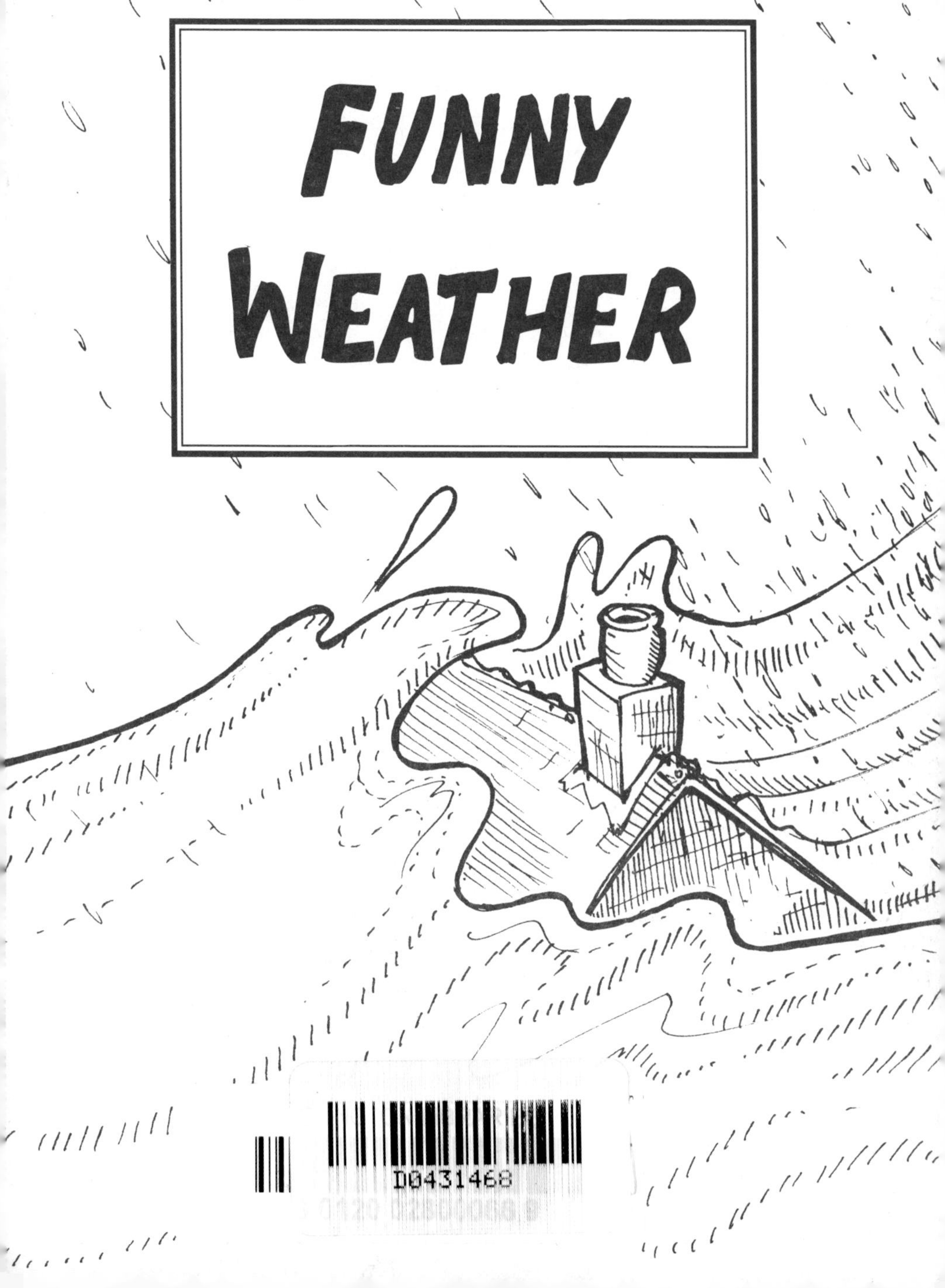

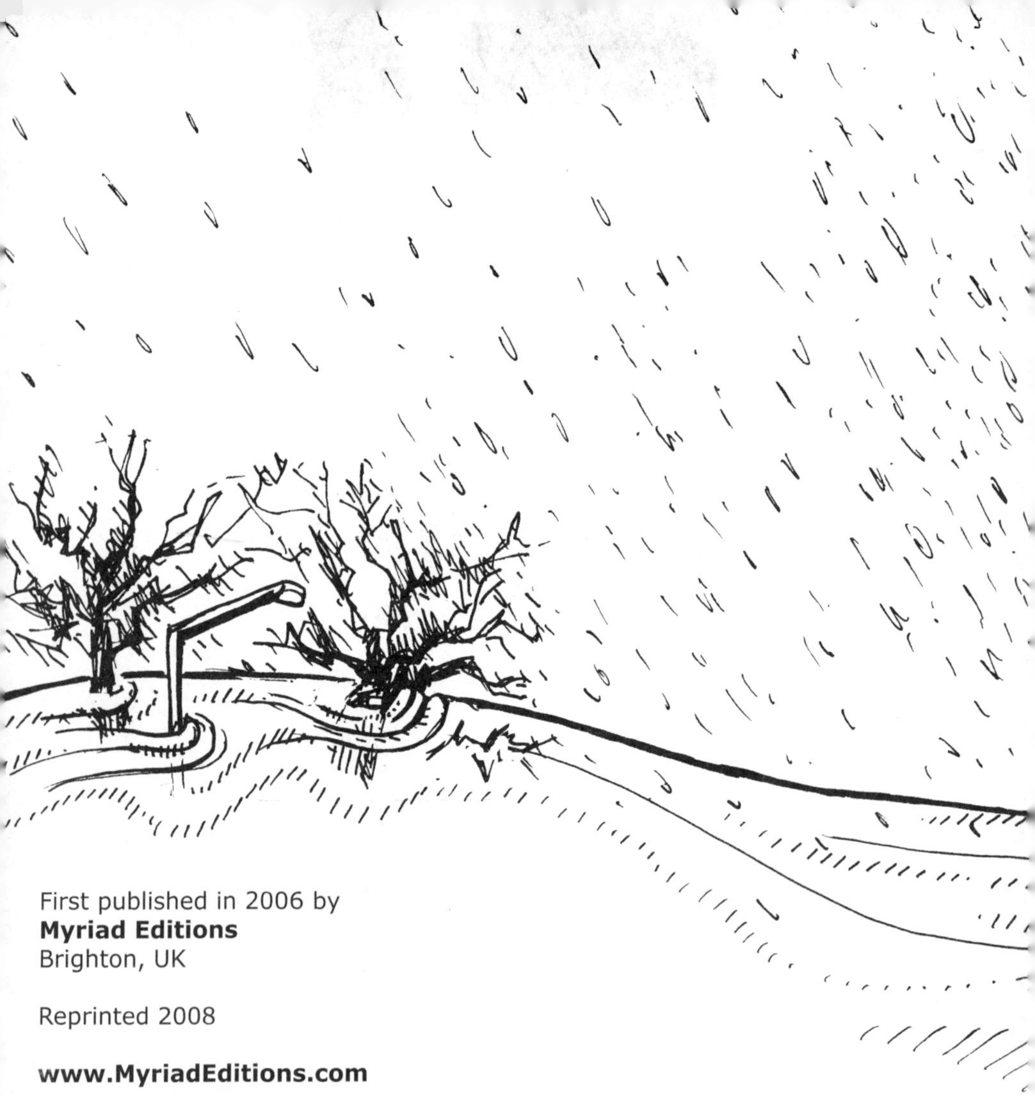

First published in 2006 by
Myriad Editions
Brighton, UK

Reprinted 2008

www.MyriadEditions.com

3 5 7 9 10 8 6 4 2

A CIP catalogue record for this book is available
from the British Library

ISBN: 978-0-9549309-3-6

Printed in Italy on paper produced from
sustainable plantations and well-managed forests
by Lito Terrazzi S.r.l. under the supervision of
Bob Cassels, The Hanway Press, London

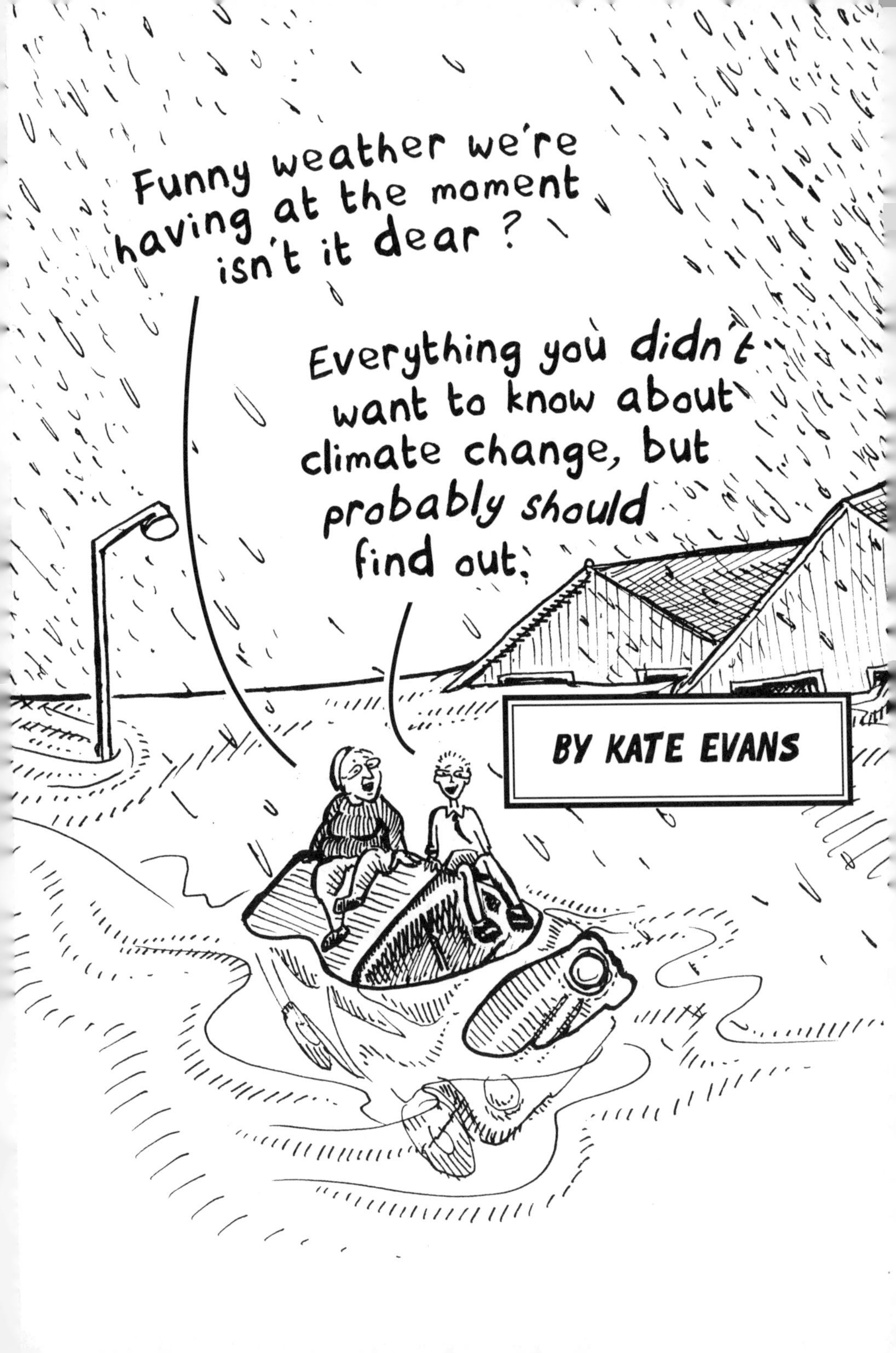
Funny weather we're having at the moment isn't it dear?
Everything you didn't want to know about climate change, but probably should find out.
BY KATE EVANS

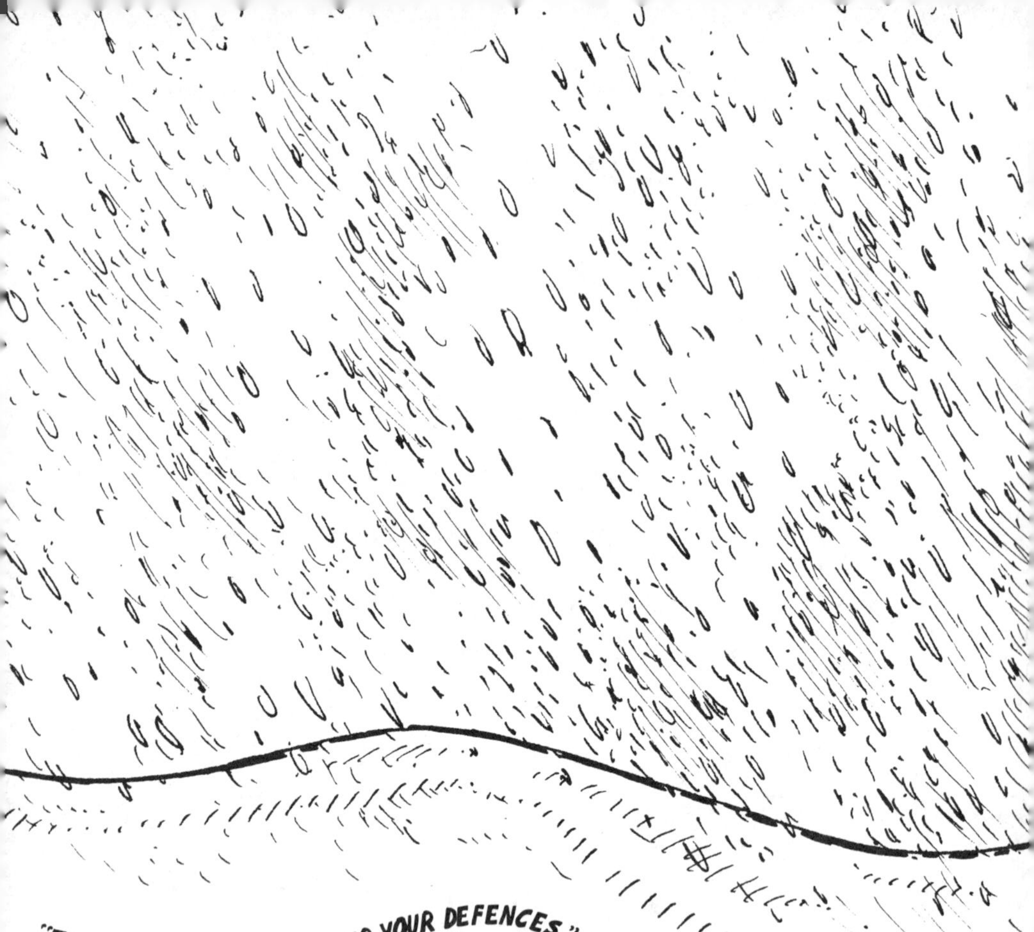

"THIS CARTOON WLL GET UNDER YOUR DEFENCES." MAYER HILLMAN
AUTHOR OF *HOW WE CAN SAVE THE PLANET*

"ITS REALLY FUNNY." MARK MASLIN, AUTHOR OF *GLOBAL WARMING, A VERY SHORT INTRODUCTION*

"IT GETS THE POINT ACROSS LIKE A SIX INCH NAIL HIT WITH A SLEDGEHAMMER."
COLIN FORREST, CLIMATE SCIENTIST

"A BRILLIANT RESOURCE!" DR. CLARE SAUNDERS, UNIVERSITY OF KENT

CONTENTS

THERE ARE ALSO **SCIENTIFIC REFERENCES** AT THE END OF EACH CHAPTER, ON PAGES 39, 58, 70 AND 89 RESPECTIVELY. SOME OF THESE PROVIDE A CONTEXT TO THE CARTOON, SO CHECK THEM OUT.

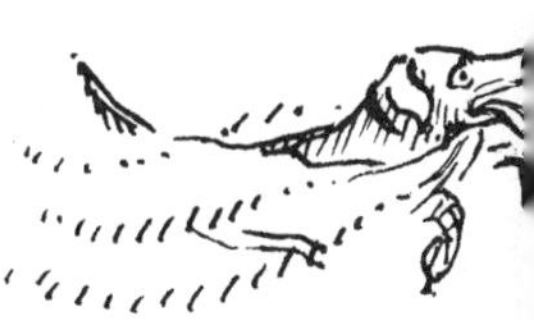

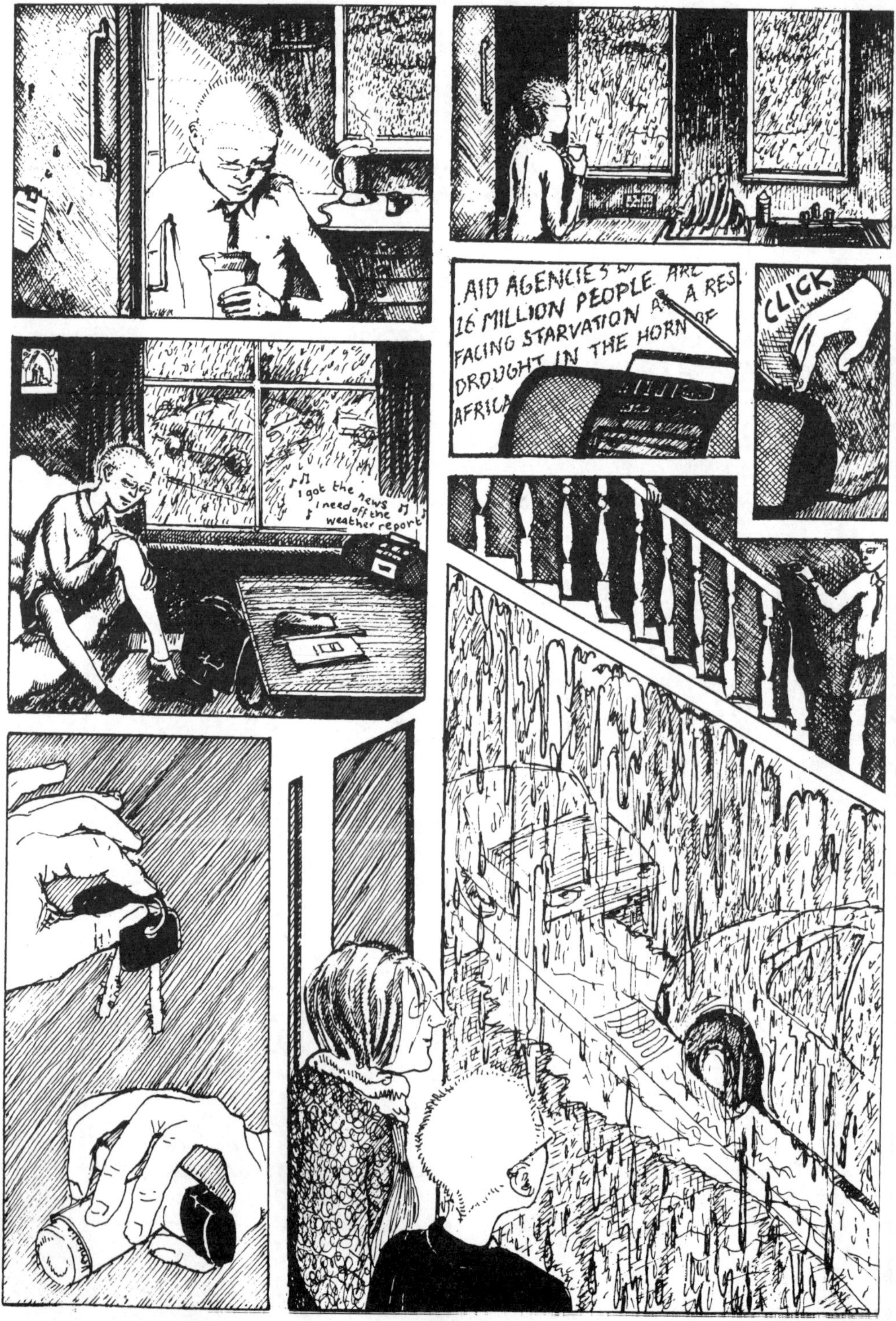
I got the news
I need off the
weather report
.AID AGENCIES
16 MILLION PEOPLE ARE
FACING STARVATION
A RES
DROUGHT IN THE HORN OF
AFRICA
CLICK

INTRODUCTION BY GEORGE MONBIOT

I think there are two reasons why climate change isn't yet the world's biggest political issue. The first is that unlike wars, crime, terrorism or economic crises, it can't be blamed entirely on other people. All of us are responsible for it, and no one more so than those well-educated, cosmopolitan, well-travelled people who might be expected to care the most.

The second is that, while we know that its total global effects are disastrous, we are also aware that climate change, in most rich, temperate countries, has so far been kind to us. Never again – unless the Gulf Stream stops - will the United Kingdom suffer a freeze of the kind we experienced in 1947, 1963 or 1982. Never again need we worry that our summers will be rained off. Yes, we'd like a bit more rain in the summer for growing our vegetables, and a bit less rain in the winter, if we were stupid enough to have bought a house on the floodplain. But for most of us, most of the time, our pollution looks like a blessing. We caused this problem, but it's going to hurt us far less than some of the poorest people on the planet.

So we claim to worry about climate change, and we claim to wish that someone would do something. But in reality, we hope they don't. Otherwise we might have to change the way we live.

Looking at the crazy decisions people are still making, it seems to me that we are almost challenging the climate to prove us wrong. Cars are becoming bigger and flights more frequent. Just as the effects of climate change are becoming universally acknowledged, we have started buying air conditioners and patio heaters. The most celebrated architect on earth, Frank Gehry, now builds open-air auditoriums with *outdoor* air conditioning. It is beginning to look like the last days of the Roman empire.

So what the hell do we do about it? How do we turn the world's biggest problem into the world's biggest issue? I've been droning on about it for years and getting nowhere. The people who can be bothered to read my books and articles are, on the whole, the people who are interested already. Television could make climate change sexy, but it's controlled by people who see the death of the planet as a far less urgent problem than finding a parking place for their second Porsche.

In other words, we need a new Messiah. Or failing that, Kate Evans. She has brought something to this subject that none of the rest of us have managed: she has told the story of climate change in a way that's accessible, funny and moving. For a long time I've been telling her she's one of the best cartoonists alive today and she ought to pull her finger out and draw a daily strip for some august publication. But now I'm quite glad she hasn't, as she has spent her time producing something much more worthwhile. I loved her last book – *Copse* – and I love this one even more. If anyone can reach the people who don't give a damn about the biosphere, it's her – and you, if you buy this book and give it to someone who needs to read it.

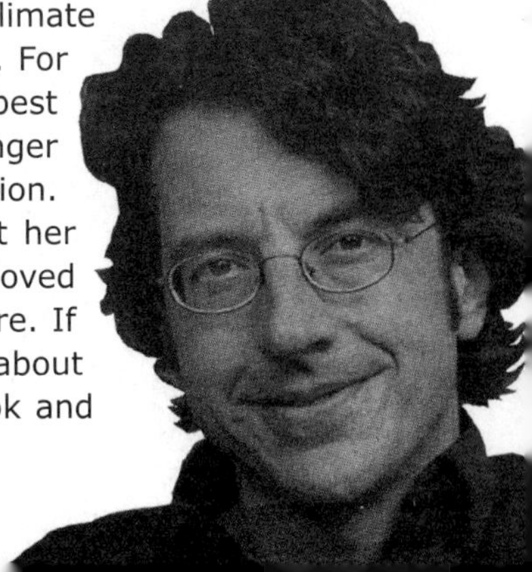

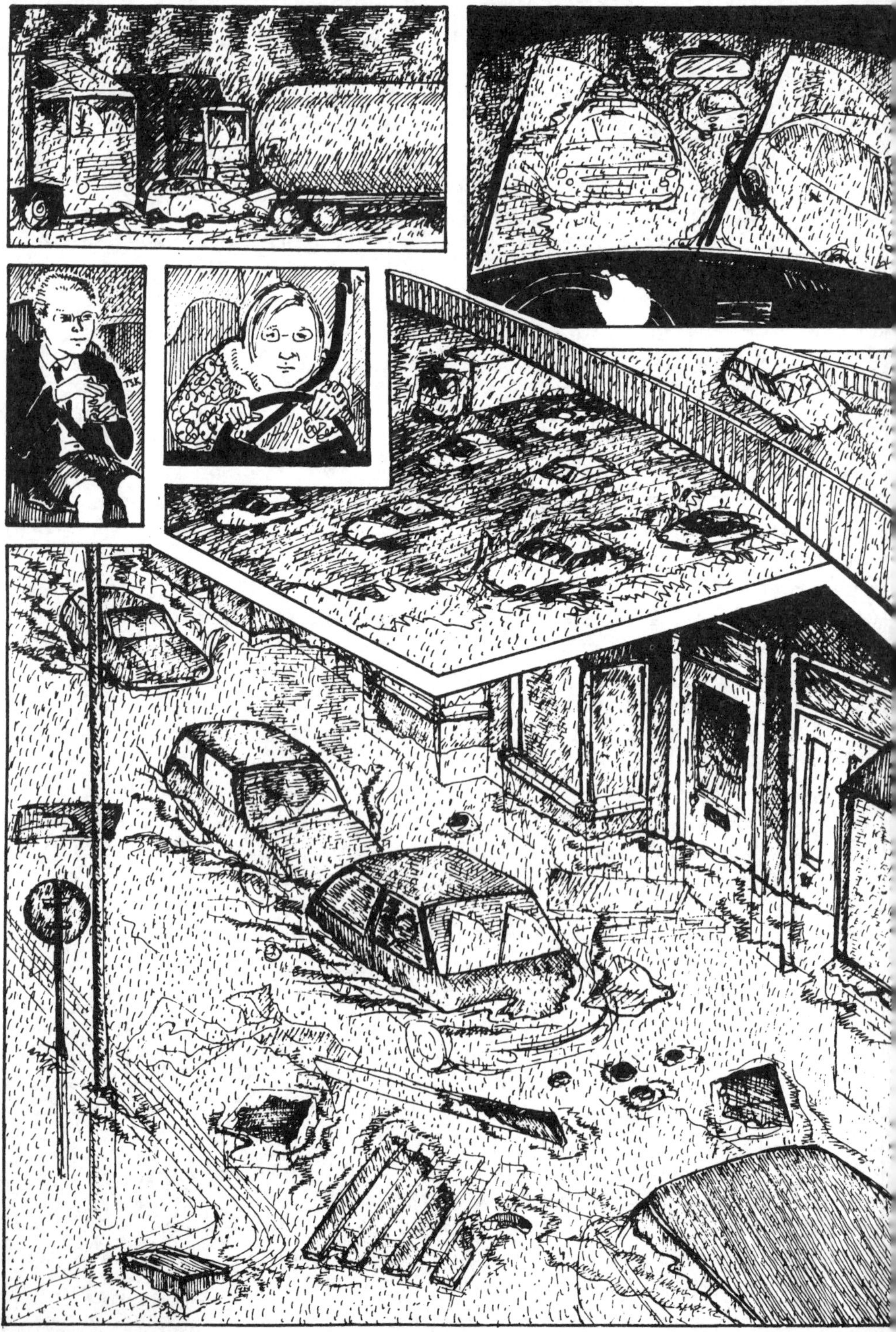

Chapter 1

SO, WHAT IS THIS GREENHOUSE EFFECT THEN?

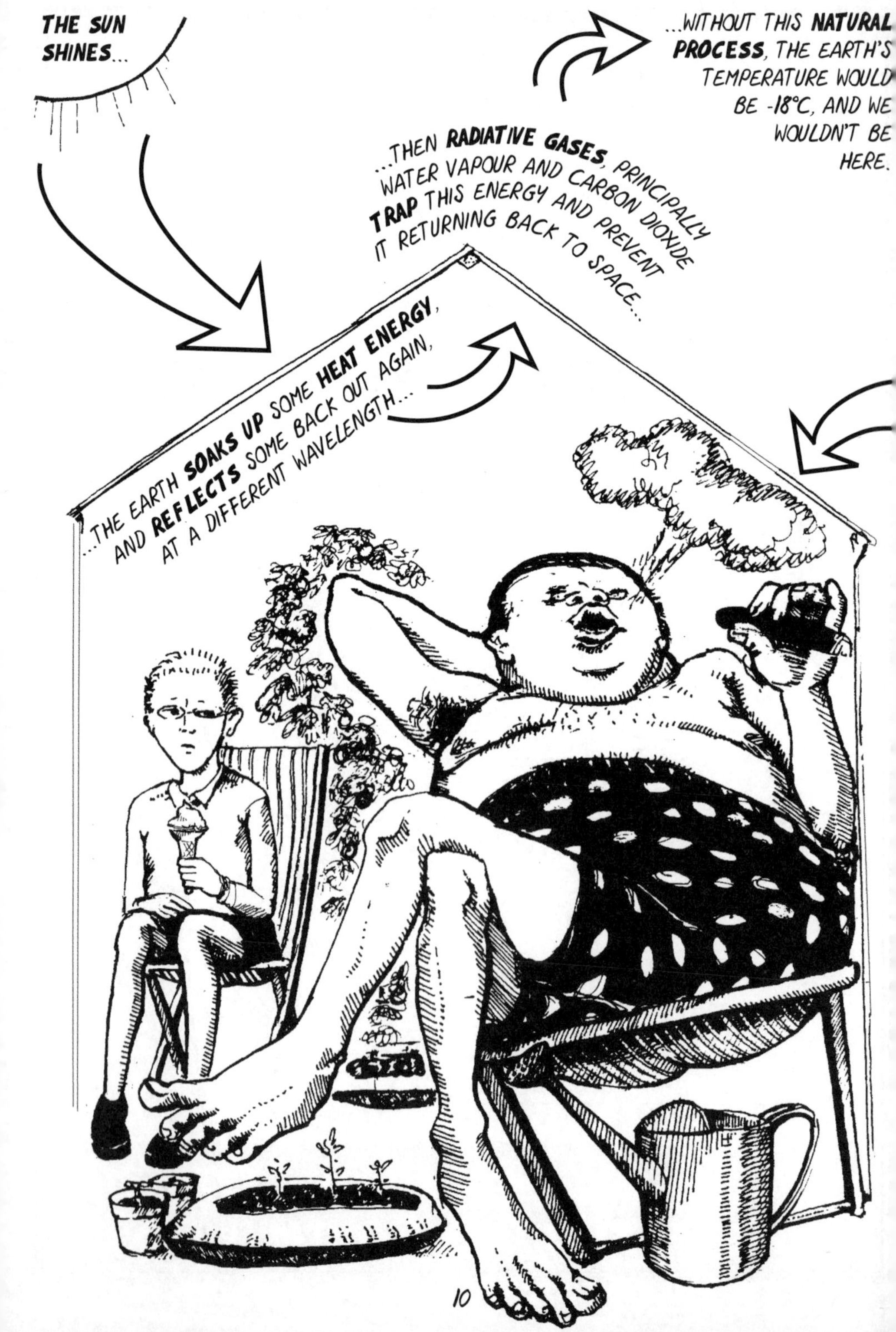
THE SUN SHINES...
...THE EARTH **SOAKS UP** SOME **HEAT ENERGY**, AND **REFLECTS** SOME BACK OUT AGAIN, AT A DIFFERENT WAVELENGTH...
...THEN **RADIATIVE GASES**, PRINCIPALLY WATER VAPOUR AND CARBON DIOXIDE **TRAP** THIS ENERGY AND PREVENT IT RETURNING BACK TO SPACE...
...WITHOUT THIS **NATURAL PROCESS**, THE EARTH'S TEMPERATURE WOULD BE -18°C, AND WE WOULDN'T BE HERE.

IN 1896, SWEDISH SCIENTIST SVANTE ARRHENIUS WORKED OUT HOW PUMPING **EXTRA CARBON DIOXIDE** INTO THE AIR, WITH THE LARGE-SCALE BURNING OF FOSSIL FUELS, IS **ADDING** TO THE NATURAL INSULATING PROPERTY OF THE ATMOSPHERE...

...IT'S NOW 2006 AND NO-ONE SEEMS TO HAVE LISTENED VERY MUCH. HUMANS ARE DUMPING **7 BILLION TONNES** OF CARBON DIOXIDE INTO THE ATMOSPHERE EACH YEAR. WE HAVE ARTIFICIALLY INCREASED THE AMOUNT OF CO_2 IN THE AIR BY A **THIRD**. ①

AT THE SAME TIME AS CO_2 (FROM FOSSIL FUEL BURNING) IS HOTTING THINGS UP, **SO_2**, THAT'S **SULPHUR DIOXIDE** (ALSO FROM FOSSIL FUEL BURNING) FORMS SULPHATE PARTICLES WHICH **COOL THE PLANET DOWN** BY REFLECTING INCOMING LIGHT BACK INTO SPACE. THESE TWO PROCESSES HAVE TO BE CONSIDERED TOGETHER TO GET AN ACCURATE PICTURE OF GLOBAL TEMPERATURE, BUT WHEN THEY ARE, IT'S CLEAR THAT **THINGS ARE GETTING WARMER**.

OTHER GASES CONTRIBUTE TO THE GREENHOUSE EFFECT. **METHANE** LEVELS HAVE RISEN 150%, **NITROUS OXIDE** HAS RISEN BY 15% AND MANMADE CHEMICALS **SULPHUR HEXAFLUORIDE** AND **CFC**S HAVE BEEN FOUND TO HAVE A POWERFUL WARMING ACTION ON THE PLANET. ②

THE GREENHOUSE EFFECT ISN'T THE ONLY FACTOR THAT DETERMINES GLOBAL CLIMATE. **VOLCANIC ACTIVITY** AND **SUNSPOT CYCLES** ALSO PLAY A PART, BUT THESE NATURAL PHENOMENA **SHOULD** HAVE ACTED TO COOL THE PLANET DOWN OVER THE PAST 100 YEARS. NOT HEAT IT UP...

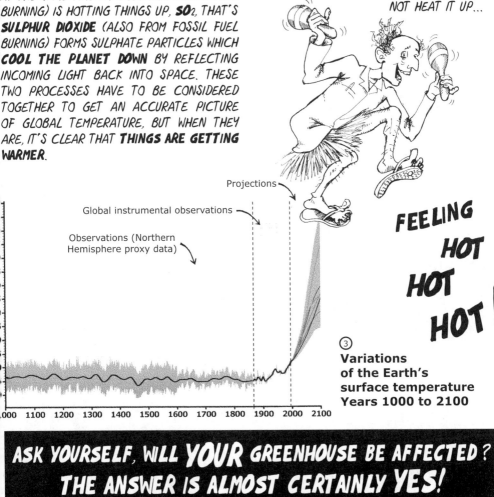

Projections

Global instrumental observations

Observations (Northern Hemisphere proxy data)

FEELING HOT HOT HOT HOT!

③ **Variations of the Earth's surface temperature Years 1000 to 2100**

.000 1100 1200 1300 1400 1500 1600 1700 1800 1900 2000 2100

ASK YOURSELF, WILL *YOUR* GREENHOUSE BE AFFECTED? THE ANSWER IS ALMOST CERTAINLY *YES!*

WHERE DO GREENHOUSE GASES COME FROM?

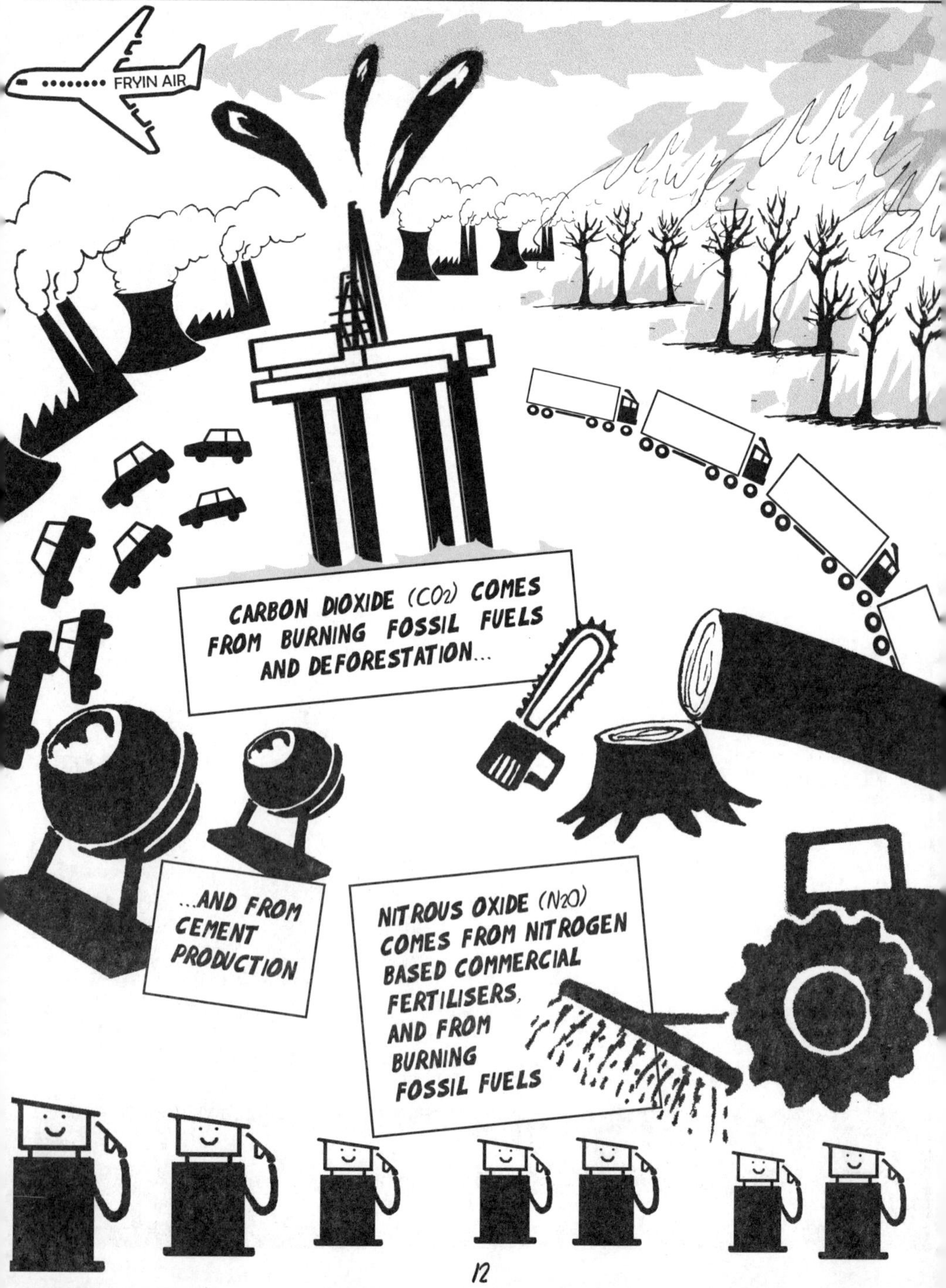
FRYIN AIR
CARBON DIOXIDE (CO_2) COMES FROM BURNING FOSSIL FUELS AND DEFORESTATION...
...AND FROM CEMENT PRODUCTION
NITROUS OXIDE (N_2O) COMES FROM NITROGEN BASED COMMERCIAL FERTILISERS, AND FROM BURNING FOSSIL FUELS

METHANE COMES FROM FLOODING LAND FOR RICE PRODUCTION, AND FROM COW FARTS...

BBRRRP

METHANE LASTS FOR 12 YEARS IN THE ATMOSPHERE, NITROUS OXIDE LASTS FOR 120 YEARS, AND CO_2 FOR UP TO 200 YEARS.

...ALSO FROM LANDFILL SITES AND FROM LEAKS OF NATURAL GAS, WHILE CFCS ARE EMITTED BY VITAL, SOCIALLY NECESSARY, LIFE ENRICHING SOFT DRINKS DISPENSERS

DRINK

Global Warming

④

Hey, we can sort that. We could switch to renewable electricity production, introduce energy conservation measures, and cheap, efficient public transport, start running vehicles on biodiesel, build things with local materials, plant trees, go organic, eat curry and chips instead of rice and drink warm lemonade.

WHO SAYS CLIMATE CHANGE IS EVEN HAPPENING ANYWAY? I'M NOT CONVINCED! WE NEED MORE PROOF!!!

WHAT?!! ARE YOU SOME KIND OF DANGEROUS ENVIRONMENTAL EXTREMIST?!!!

WHO SAYS CLIMATE CHANGE IS REALLY HAPPENING?

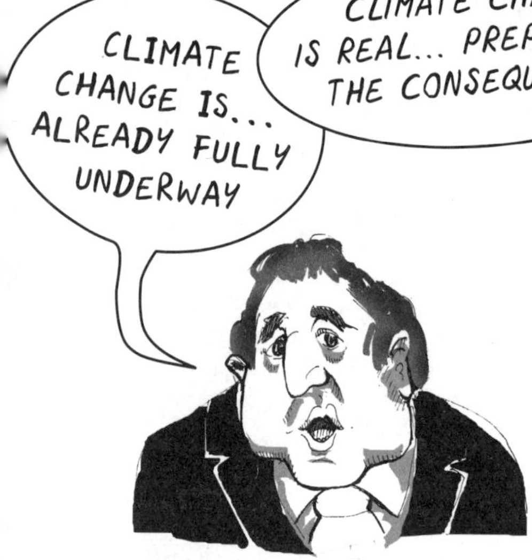
CLIMATE CHANGE IS... ALREADY FULLY UNDERWAY

Thomas Loster, Chief Executive of Insurance corporation Munich Re Foundation.

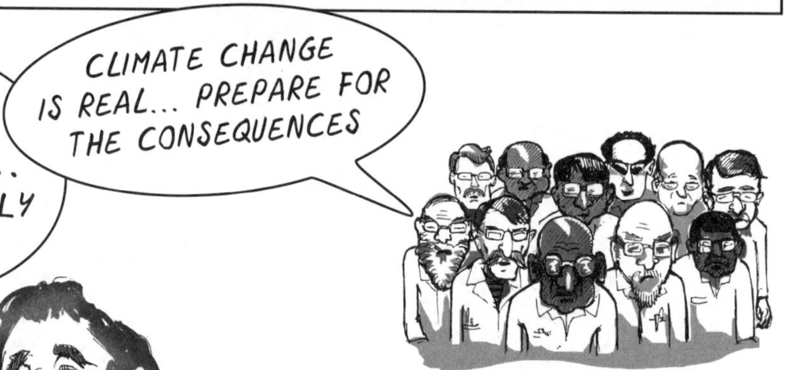
CLIMATE CHANGE IS REAL... PREPARE FOR THE CONSEQUENCES

Joint statement by the Science Academies of Brazil, Canada, China, France, Germany, India, Italy, Japan, Russia, the UK and the US.

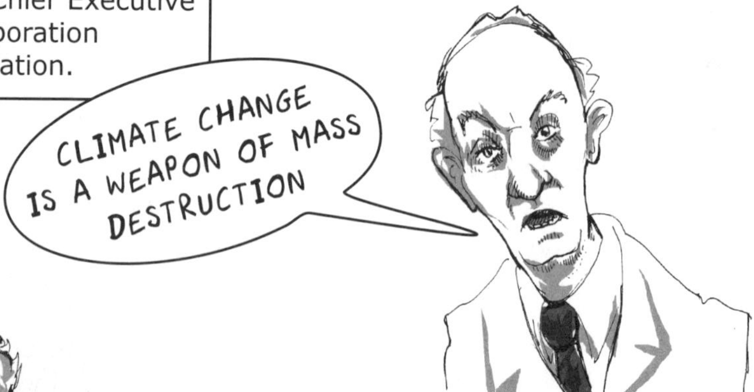
CLIMATE CHANGE IS A WEAPON OF MASS DESTRUCTION

Sir John Houghton, co-chair of the UN Intergovernmental Panel on Climate Change

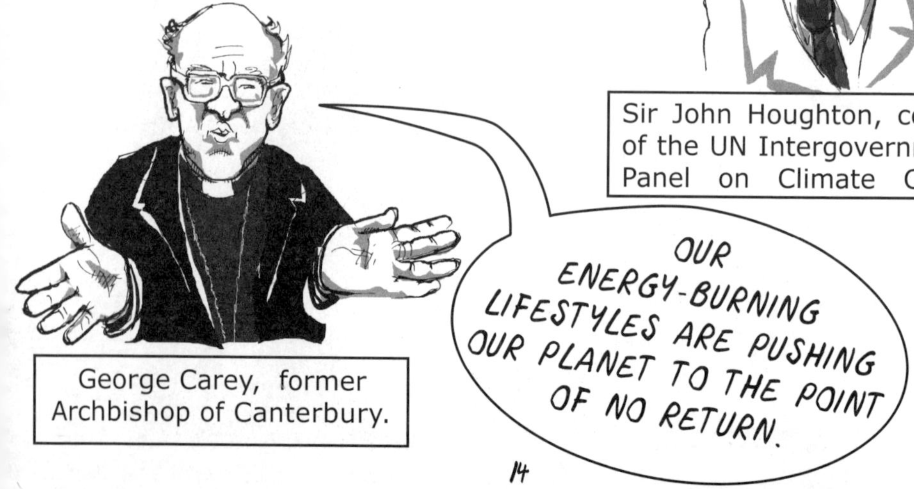
OUR ENERGY-BURNING LIFESTYLES ARE PUSHING OUR PLANET TO THE POINT OF NO RETURN.

George Carey, former Archbishop of Canterbury.

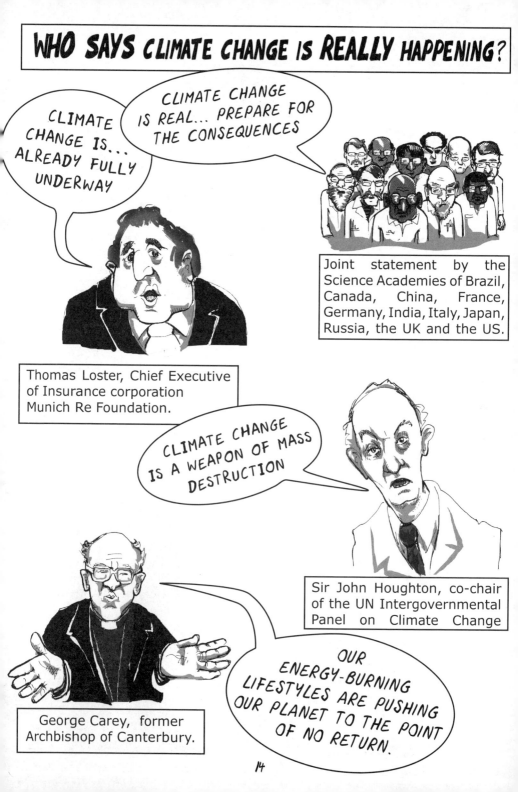

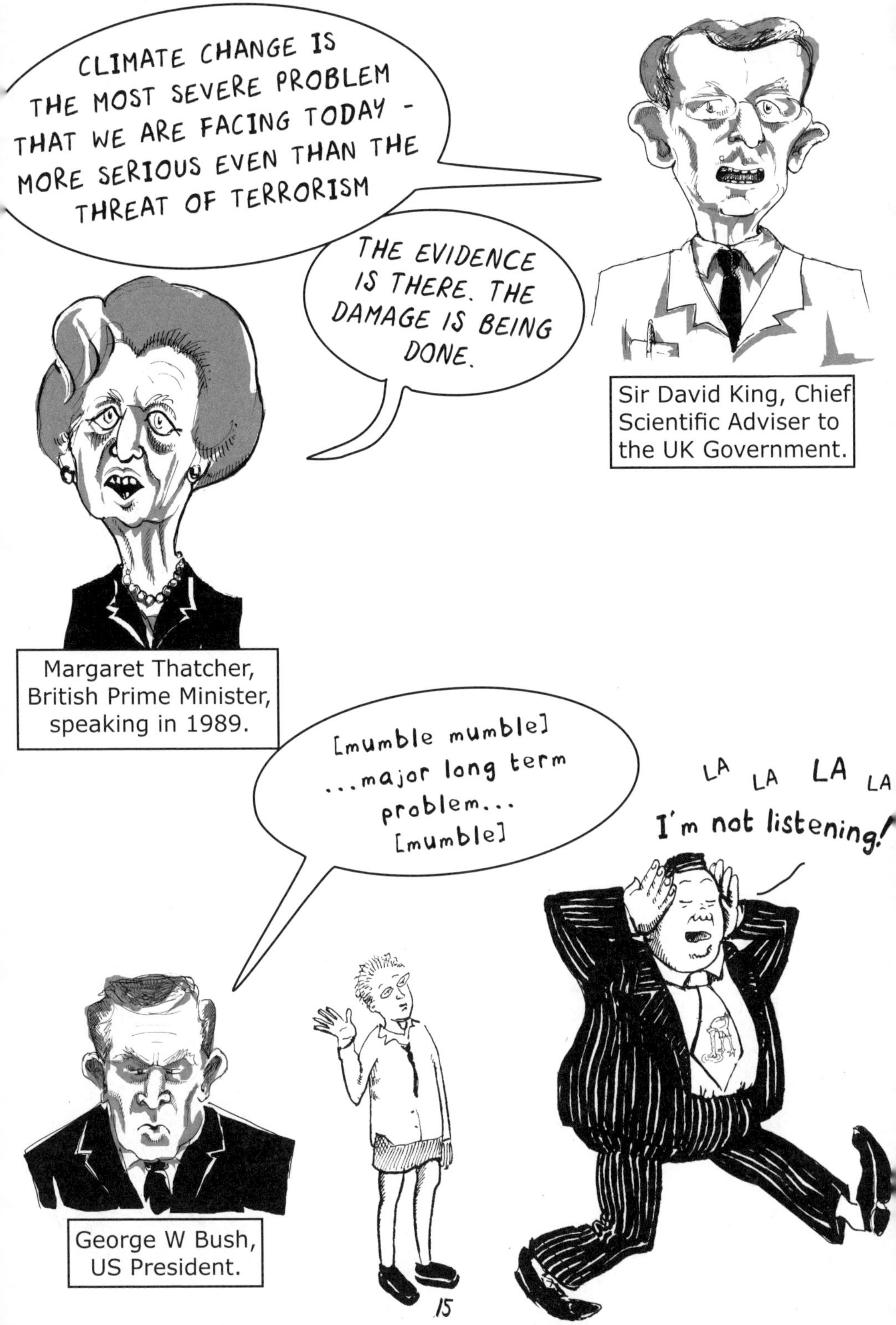
CLIMATE CHANGE IS THE MOST SEVERE PROBLEM THAT WE ARE FACING TODAY - MORE SERIOUS EVEN THAN THE THREAT OF TERRORISM
Sir David King, Chief Scientific Adviser to the UK Government.
THE EVIDENCE IS THERE. THE DAMAGE IS BEING DONE.
Margaret Thatcher, British Prime Minister, speaking in 1989.
[mumble mumble] ...major long term problem... [mumble]
George W Bush, US President.
LA LA LA LA
I'm not listening!

PROOF?

IN 1988, THE UNITED NATIONS SET UP THE **INTERGOVERNMENTAL PANEL ON CLIMATE CHANGE** (IPCC); AN INTERNATIONAL TEAM OF 2000 TOP SCIENTISTS AND **CLIMATE MODELLERS** WHO TRACK AND PREDICT TRENDS IN CLIMATE CHANGE.

HOT WIND

Let's just put a bit of desert in here.

SAND

BLUE

Amazon

PLAY DOUGH

BALSA WOOD

COLD WIND

Africa

IN 2001, THEY DECIDED THAT GLOBAL WARMING IS attributable to human activities. [5]

THE WORLD IS NOW 0.8°C WARMER THAN IN PRE-INDUSTRIAL TIMES. [6]

0.8°C ? THAT'S NOTHING! TINY! TINY! TINY!!!

Well, it isn't much, but since most of the planet is covered in deep water it takes a long time to heat up. At least 40 years. [7]

So what we're seeing now is the effect of CO_2 emissions in the 1960s.

TOP SECRET HISTORY

Raising the temperature of the world by just 1°C means pumping an incredible extra amount of energy into the weather system. Recent studies say we could be in line for a 10°C rise and during the last **ICE AGE** the planet was only 5°C colder than today.

www.climate prediction.net [8]

What are you reading?

Oh

That's not on the National Curriculum.

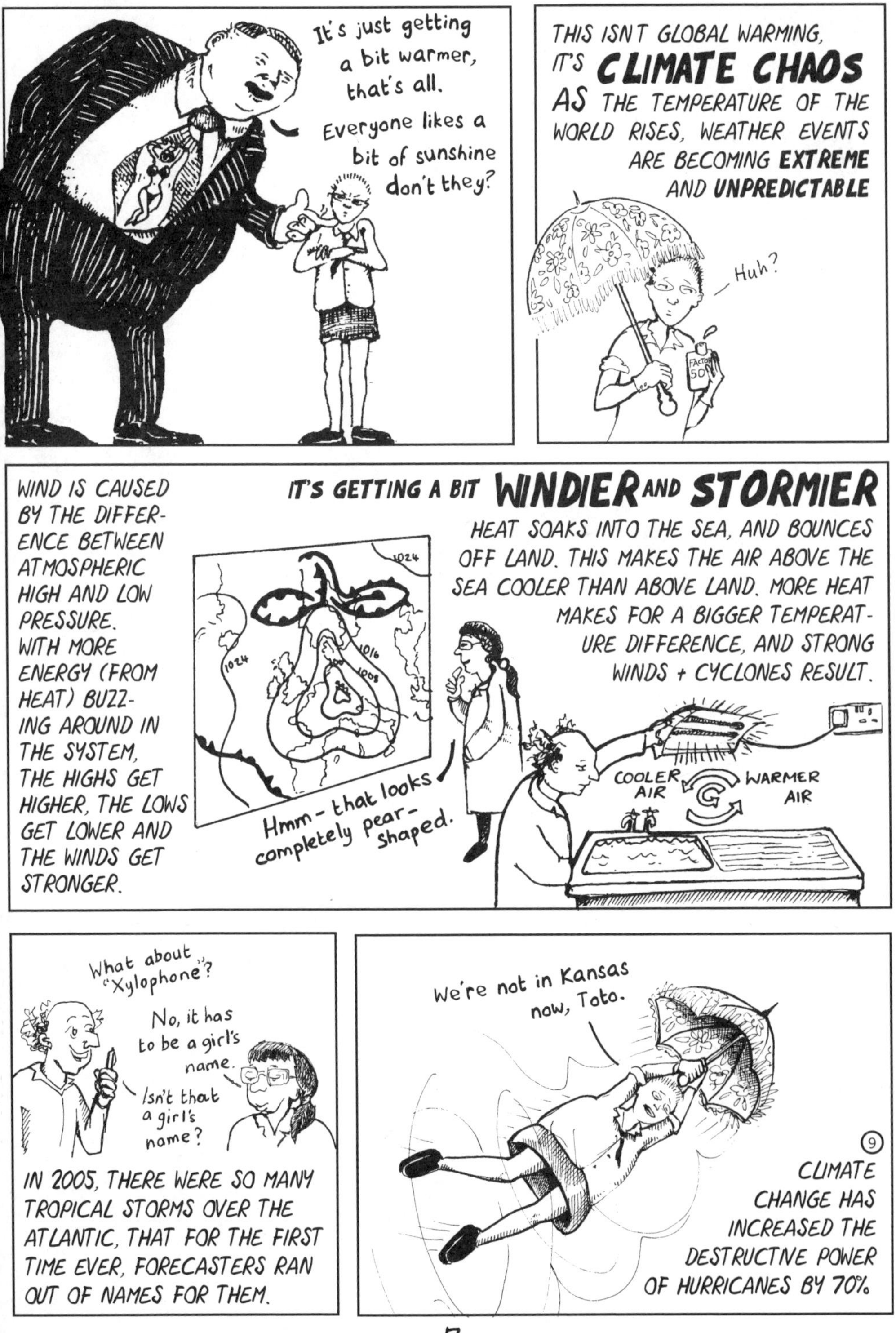
It's just getting a bit warmer, that's all.
Everyone likes a bit of sunshine don't they?
THIS ISN'T GLOBAL WARMING, IT'S CLIMATE CHAOS
AS THE TEMPERATURE OF THE WORLD RISES, WEATHER EVENTS ARE BECOMING EXTREME AND UNPREDICTABLE
Huh?
FACTOR 50
IT'S GETTING A BIT WINDIER AND STORMIER
WIND IS CAUSED BY THE DIFFERENCE BETWEEN ATMOSPHERIC HIGH AND LOW PRESSURE. WITH MORE ENERGY (FROM HEAT) BUZZING AROUND IN THE SYSTEM, THE HIGHS GET HIGHER, THE LOWS GET LOWER AND THE WINDS GET STRONGER.
1024
1024
1016
1008
Hmm - that looks completely pear-shaped.
HEAT SOAKS INTO THE SEA, AND BOUNCES OFF LAND. THIS MAKES THE AIR ABOVE THE SEA COOLER THAN ABOVE LAND. MORE HEAT MAKES FOR A BIGGER TEMPERATURE DIFFERENCE, AND STRONG WINDS + CYCLONES RESULT.
COOLER AIR
WARMER AIR
What about "Xylophone"?
No, it has to be a girl's name.
Isn't that a girl's name?
IN 2005, THERE WERE SO MANY TROPICAL STORMS OVER THE ATLANTIC, THAT FOR THE FIRST TIME EVER, FORECASTERS RAN OUT OF NAMES FOR THEM.
We're not in Kansas now, Toto.
9
CLIMATE CHANGE HAS INCREASED THE DESTRUCTIVE POWER OF HURRICANES BY 70%

....in the words of Hurricane Katrina survivors...

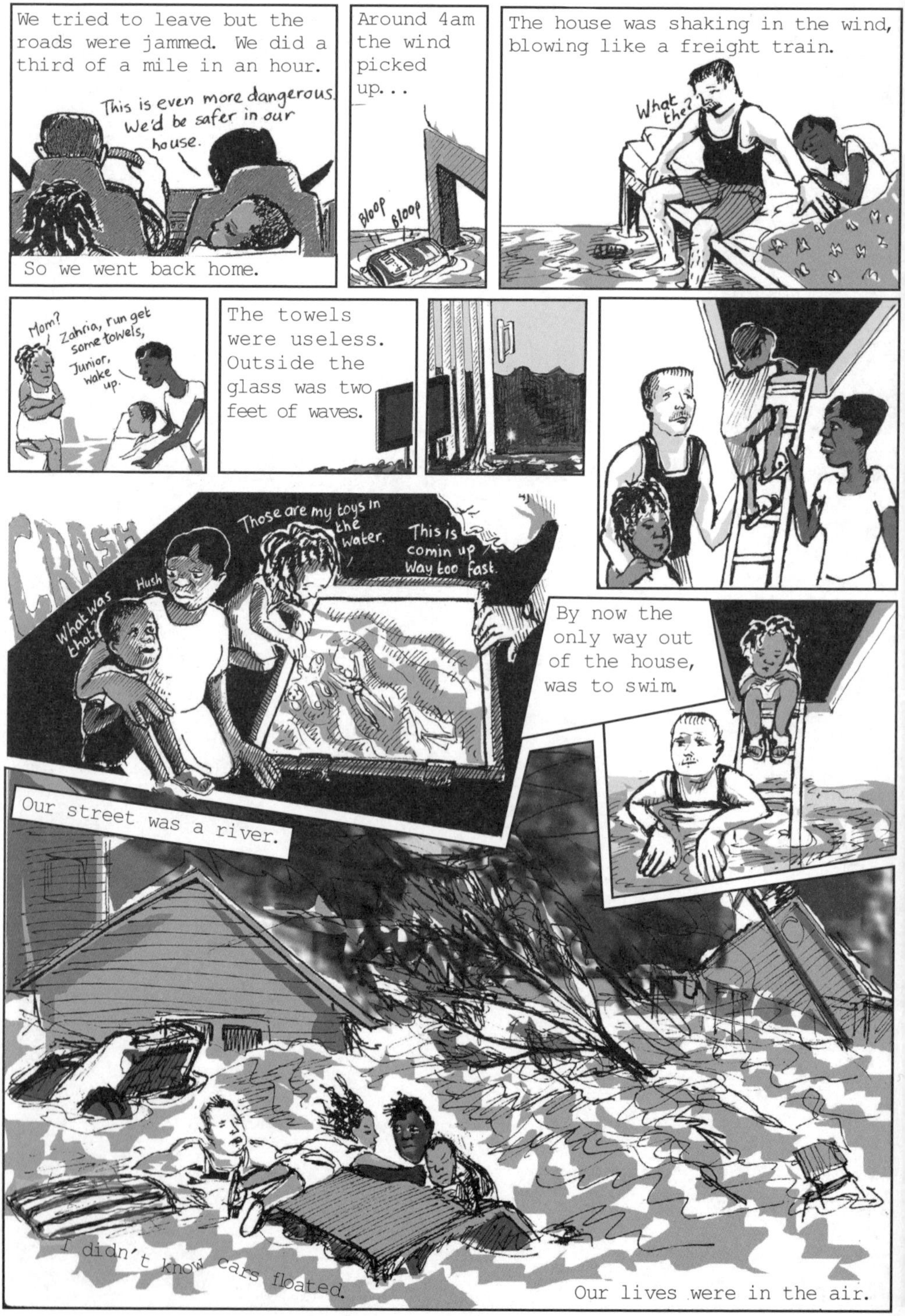

We tried to leave but the roads were jammed. We did a third of a mile in an hour.
This is even more dangerous. We'd be safer in our house.
So we went back home.
Around 4am the wind picked up...
Bloop
Bloop
The house was shaking in the wind, blowing like a freight train.
What the?
Mom?
Zahria, run get some towels,
Junior, wake up.
The towels were useless. Outside the glass was two feet of waves.
CRASH
Hush
What was that?
Those are my toys in the water.
This is comin up way too fast.
By now the only way out of the house, was to swim.
Our street was a river.
I didn't know cars floated.
Our lives were in the air.

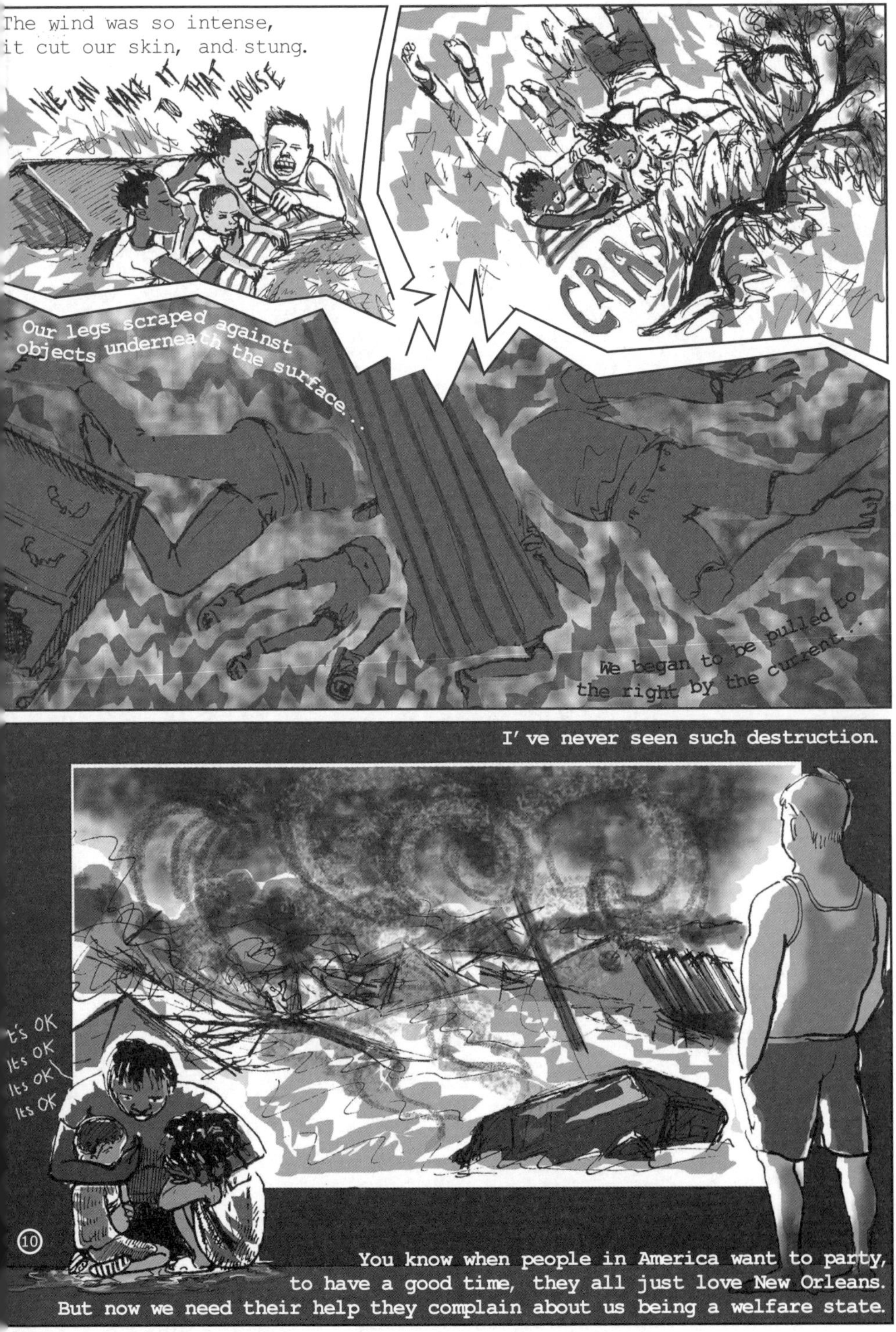
The wind was so intense,
it cut our skin, and stung.
WE CAN MAKE IT TO THAT HOUSE
CRAS
Our legs scraped against objects underneath the surface...
We began to be pulled to the right by the current...
I've never seen such destruction.
t's OK
Its OK
Its OK
Its OK
10
You know when people in America want to party,
to have a good time, they all just love New Orleans.
But now we need their help they complain about us being a welfare state.

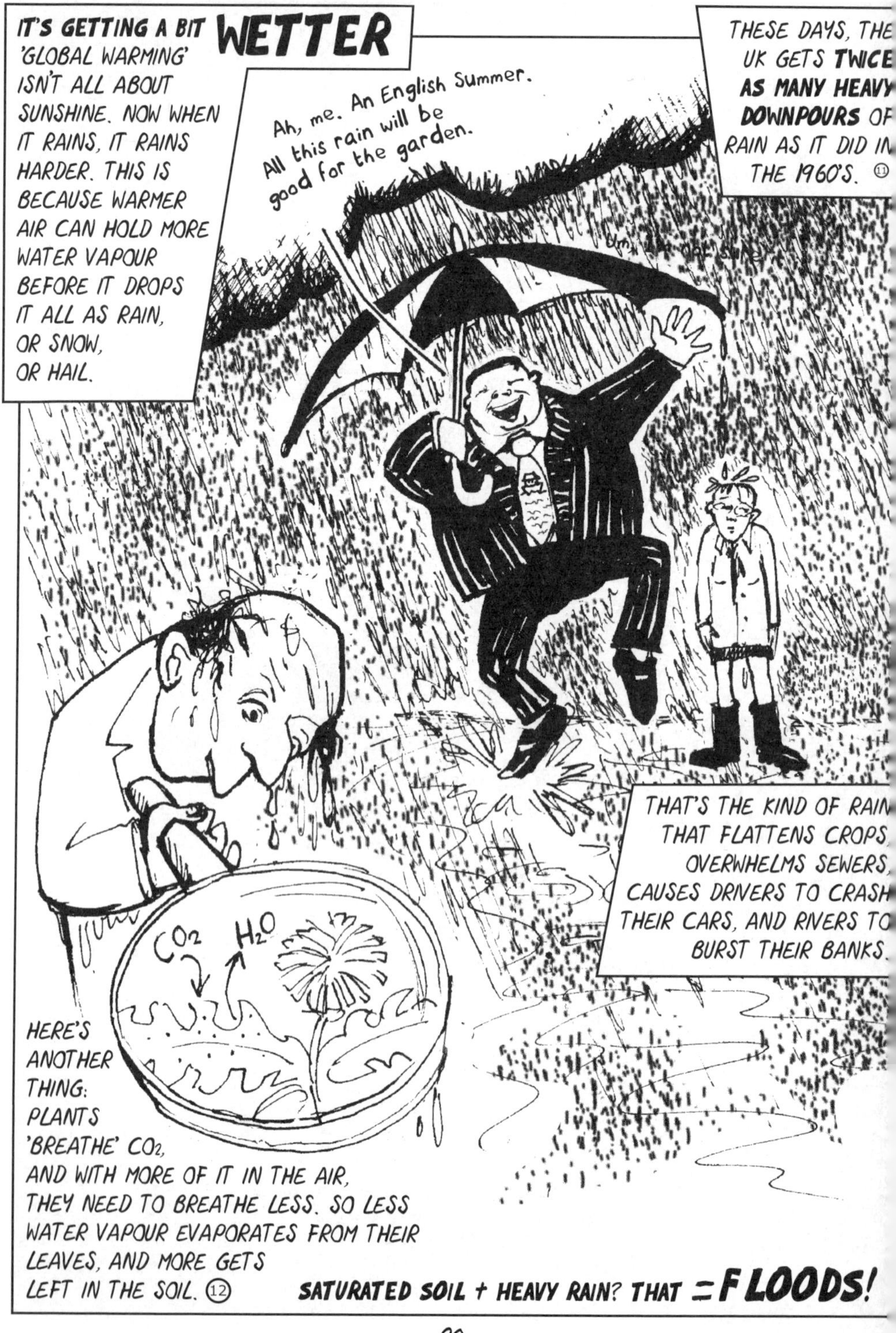

IT'S GETTING A BIT WETTER
'GLOBAL WARMING' ISN'T ALL ABOUT SUNSHINE. NOW WHEN IT RAINS, IT RAINS HARDER. THIS IS BECAUSE WARMER AIR CAN HOLD MORE WATER VAPOUR BEFORE IT DROPS IT ALL AS RAIN, OR SNOW, OR HAIL.
Ah, me. An English Summer. All this rain will be good for the garden.
THESE DAYS, THE UK GETS TWICE AS MANY HEAVY DOWNPOURS OF RAIN AS IT DID IN THE 1960'S. (11)
THAT'S THE KIND OF RAIN THAT FLATTENS CROPS, OVERWHELMS SEWERS, CAUSES DRIVERS TO CRASH THEIR CARS, AND RIVERS TO BURST THEIR BANKS.
CO_2
H_2O
HERE'S ANOTHER THING: PLANTS 'BREATHE' CO_2, AND WITH MORE OF IT IN THE AIR, THEY NEED TO BREATHE LESS. SO LESS WATER VAPOUR EVAPORATES FROM THEIR LEAVES, AND MORE GETS LEFT IN THE SOIL. (12)
SATURATED SOIL + HEAVY RAIN? THAT = FLOODS!

IN THE 1960s THERE WERE 16 WEATHER RELATED "NATURAL" DISASTERS

IN THE 1990s [13] THERE WERE 70

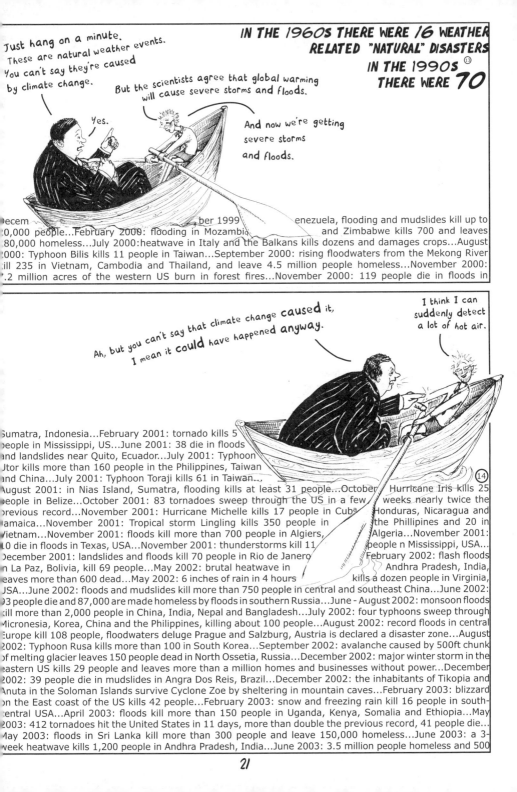

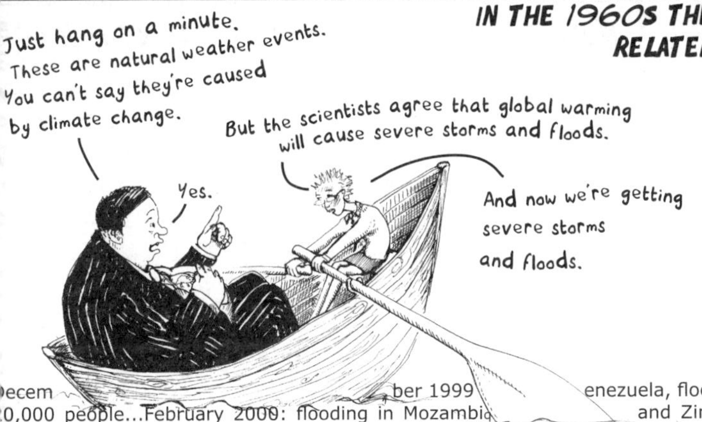
Just hang on a minute. These are natural weather events. You can't say they're caused by climate change.
But the scientists agree that global warming will cause severe storms and floods.
Yes.
And now we're getting severe storms and floods.

December 1999 enezuela, flooding and mudslides kill up to 0,000 people...February 2000: flooding in Mozambi and Zimbabwe kills 700 and leaves 80,000 homeless...July 2000: heatwave in Italy and the Balkans kills dozens and damages crops...August 2000: Typhoon Bilis kills 11 people in Taiwan...September 2000: rising floodwaters from the Mekong River kill 235 in Vietnam, Cambodia and Thailand, and leave 4.5 million people homeless...November 2000: .2 million acres of the western US burn in forest fires...November 2000: 119 people die in floods in

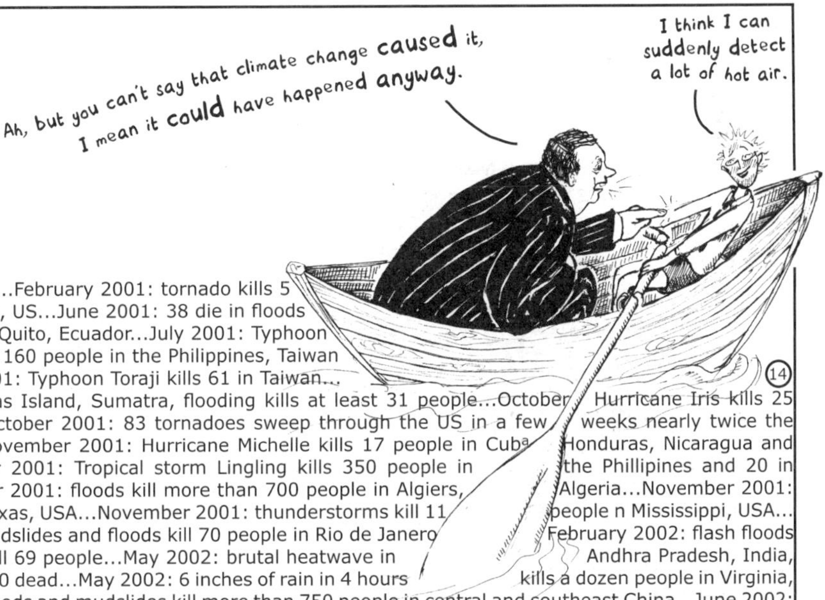
Ah, but you can't say that climate change caused it, I mean it could have happened anyway.
I think I can suddenly detect a lot of hot air.

Sumatra, Indonesia...February 2001: tornado kills 5 people in Mississippi, US...June 2001: 38 die in floods and landslides near Quito, Ecuador...July 2001: Typhoon Utor kills more than 160 people in the Philippines, Taiwan and China...July 2001: Typhoon Toraji kills 61 in Taiwan... [14] August 2001: in Nias Island, Sumatra, flooding kills at least 31 people...October Hurricane Iris kills 25 people in Belize...October 2001: 83 tornadoes sweep through the US in a few weeks nearly twice the previous record...November 2001: Hurricane Michelle kills 17 people in Cuba Honduras, Nicaragua and Jamaica...November 2001: Tropical storm Lingling kills 350 people in the Phillipines and 20 in Vietnam...November 2001: floods kill more than 700 people in Algiers, Algeria...November 2001: 10 die in floods in Texas, USA...November 2001: thunderstorms kill 11 people n Mississippi, USA...December 2001: landslides and floods kill 70 people in Rio de Janero February 2002: flash floods in La Paz, Bolivia, kill 69 people...May 2002: brutal heatwave in Andhra Pradesh, India, leaves more than 600 dead...May 2002: 6 inches of rain in 4 hours kills a dozen people in Virginia, USA...June 2002: floods and mudslides kill more than 750 people in central and southeast China...June 2002: 93 people die and 87,000 are made homeless by floods in southern Russia...June - August 2002: monsoon floods kill more than 2,000 people in China, India, Nepal and Bangladesh...July 2002: four typhoons sweep through Micronesia, Korea, China and the Philippines, killing about 100 people...August 2002: record floods in central Europe kill 108 people, floodwaters deluge Prague and Salzburg, Austria is declared a disaster zone...August 2002: Typhoon Rusa kills more than 100 in South Korea...September 2002: avalanche caused by 500ft chunk of melting glacier leaves 150 people dead in North Ossetia, Russia...December 2002: major winter storm in the eastern US kills 29 people and leaves more than a million homes and businesses without power...December 2002: 39 people die in mudslides in Angra Dos Reis, Brazil...December 2002: the inhabitants of Tikopia and Anuta in the Soloman Islands survive Cyclone Zoe by sheltering in mountain caves...February 2003: blizzard on the East coast of the US kills 42 people...February 2003: snow and freezing rain kill 16 people in south-central USA...April 2003: floods kill more than 150 people in Uganda, Kenya, Somalia and Ethiopia...May 2003: 412 tornadoes hit the United States in 11 days, more than double the previous record, 41 people die... May 2003: floods in Sri Lanka kill more than 300 people and leave 150,000 homeless...June 2003: a 3-week heatwave kills 1,200 people in Andhra Pradesh, India...June 2003: 3.5 million people homeless and 500

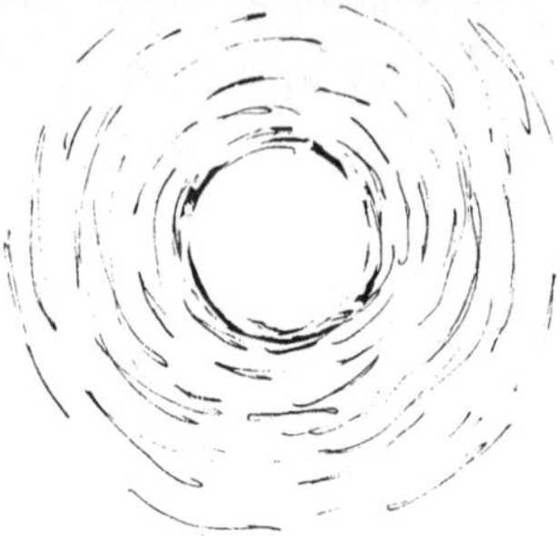

IT'S GETTING A BIT HOTTER (OF COURSE)

THIS BOOK WAS WRITTEN IN 2006. **2005 WAS THE HOTTEST YEAR** ON RECORD. **EIGHT** OUT OF THE PAST **TEN** YEARS HAVE TOPPED THE TEMPERATURE CHARTS.[15]

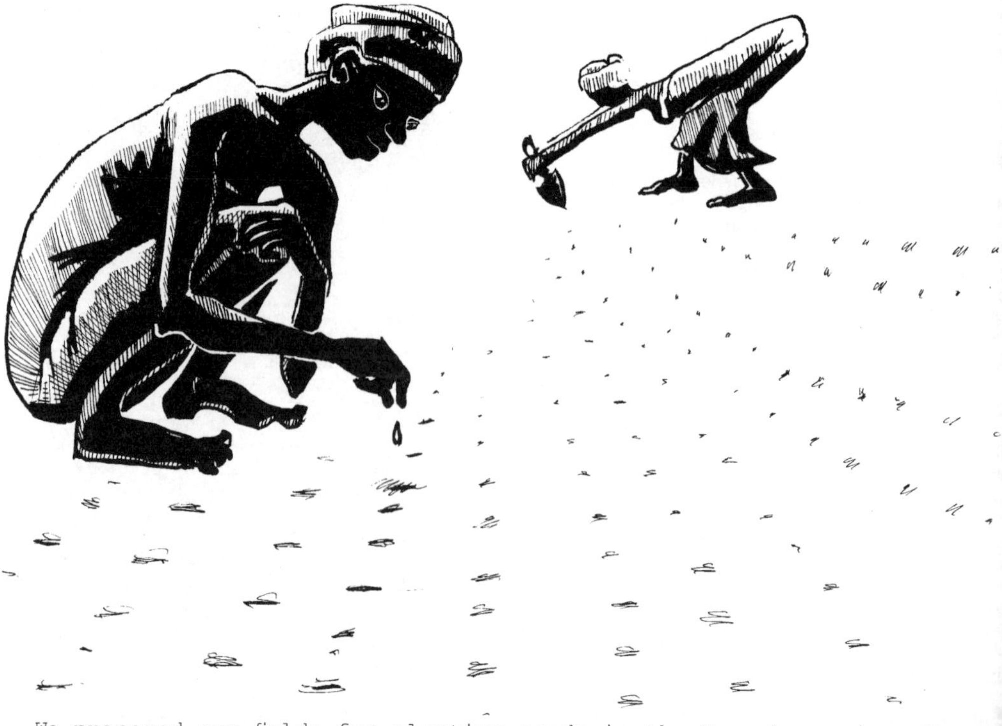

We prepared our fields for planting seeds in the November rains. We waited but the first drop didn't fall until December 20th. After a day, the rains stopped.

30% OF THE **WORLD** IS NOW AFFECTED BY DROUGHT. [16] THAT'S MORE THAN **TWICE** AS MUCH AS IN THE 1970S.

IT'S SIMPLE, **MORE WATER EVAPORATES FROM HOT SOIL**. EVENTUALLY IT DOES FALL BACK TO EARTH AS RAIN, BUT THE NEW CRAZY WIND PATTERNS MEAN THAT **IT'S NOW FALLING IN THE WRONG PLACE, AT THE WRONG TIME.**

IN 2005, THE UN WARNED THAT **ONE IN SIX COUNTRIES** WAS EXPERIENCING **DROUGHT-RELATED FOOD SHORTAGES**, AND THAT THIS IS PART OF **A NEW LONG TERM TREND**. [17]

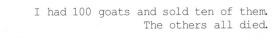

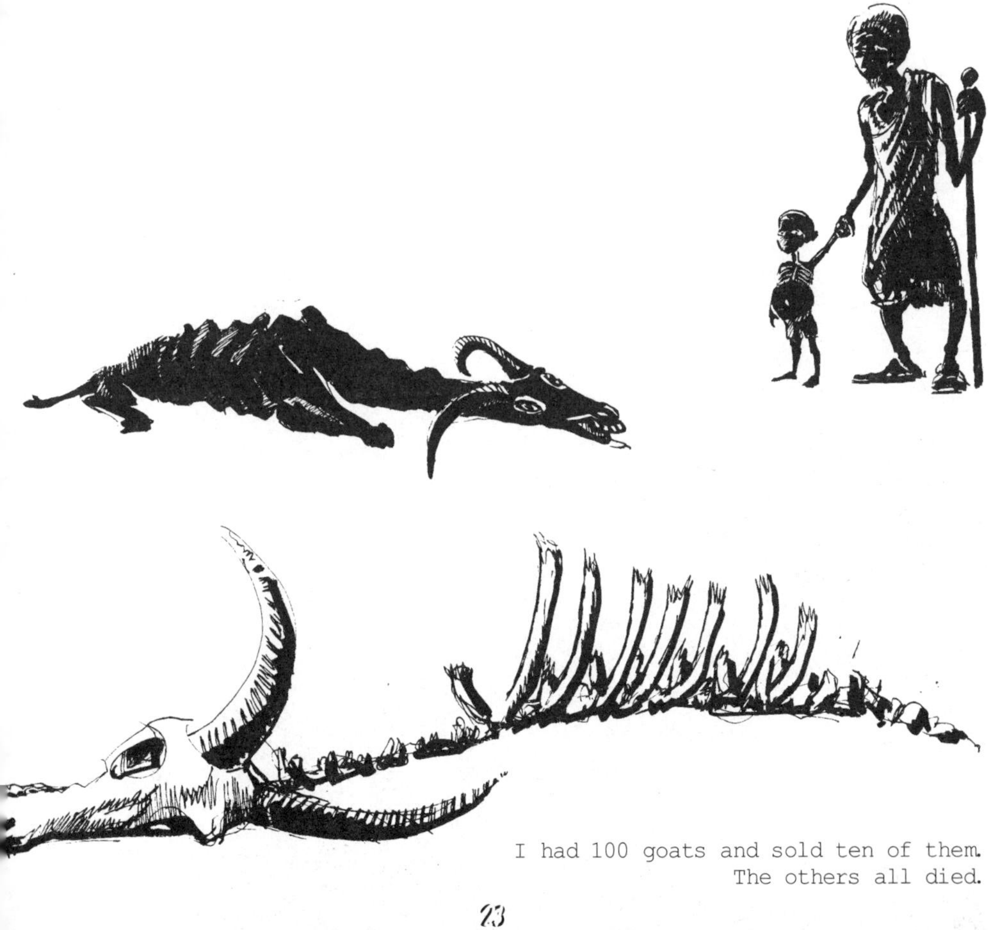

I had 100 goats and sold ten of them.
The others all died.

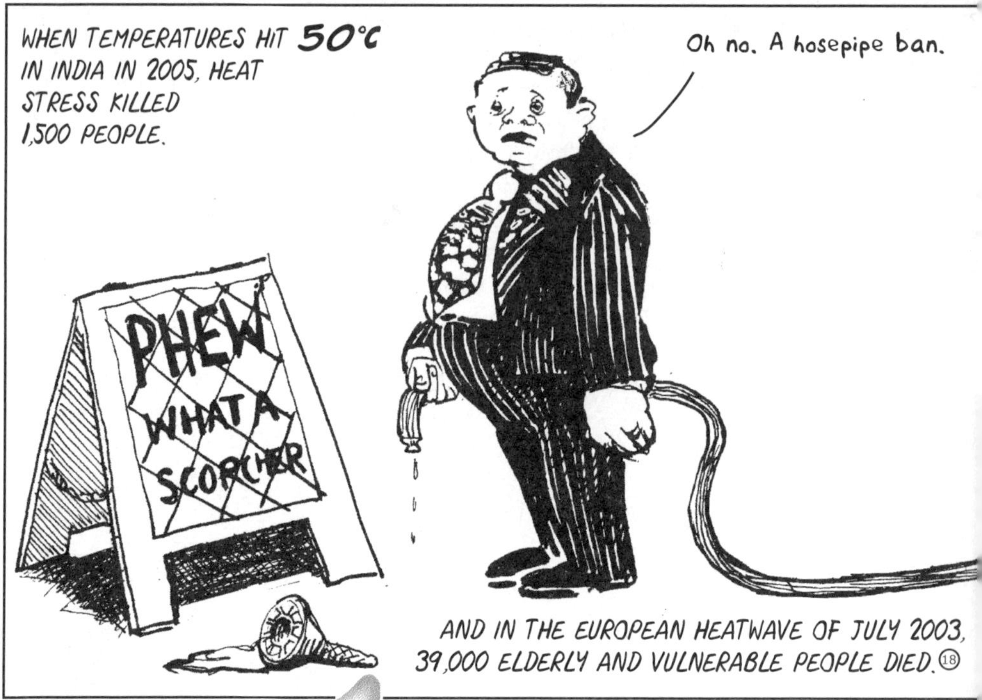
WHEN TEMPERATURES HIT 50°C IN INDIA IN 2005, HEAT STRESS KILLED 1,500 PEOPLE.
Oh no. A hosepipe ban.
PHEW WHAT A SCORCHER
AND IN THE EUROPEAN HEATWAVE OF JULY 2003, 39,000 ELDERLY AND VULNERABLE PEOPLE DIED.[18]

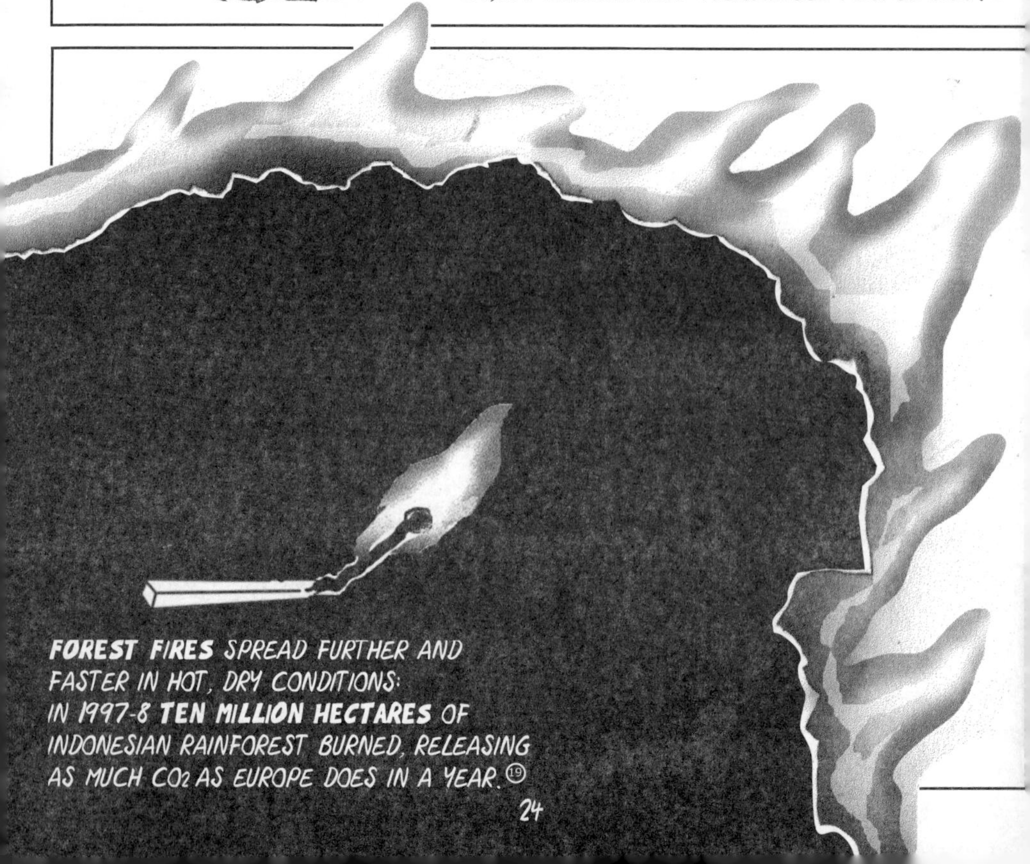
FOREST FIRES SPREAD FURTHER AND FASTER IN HOT, DRY CONDITIONS: IN 1997-8 TEN MILLION HECTARES OF INDONESIAN RAINFOREST BURNED, RELEASING AS MUCH CO2 AS EUROPE DOES IN A YEAR.[19]

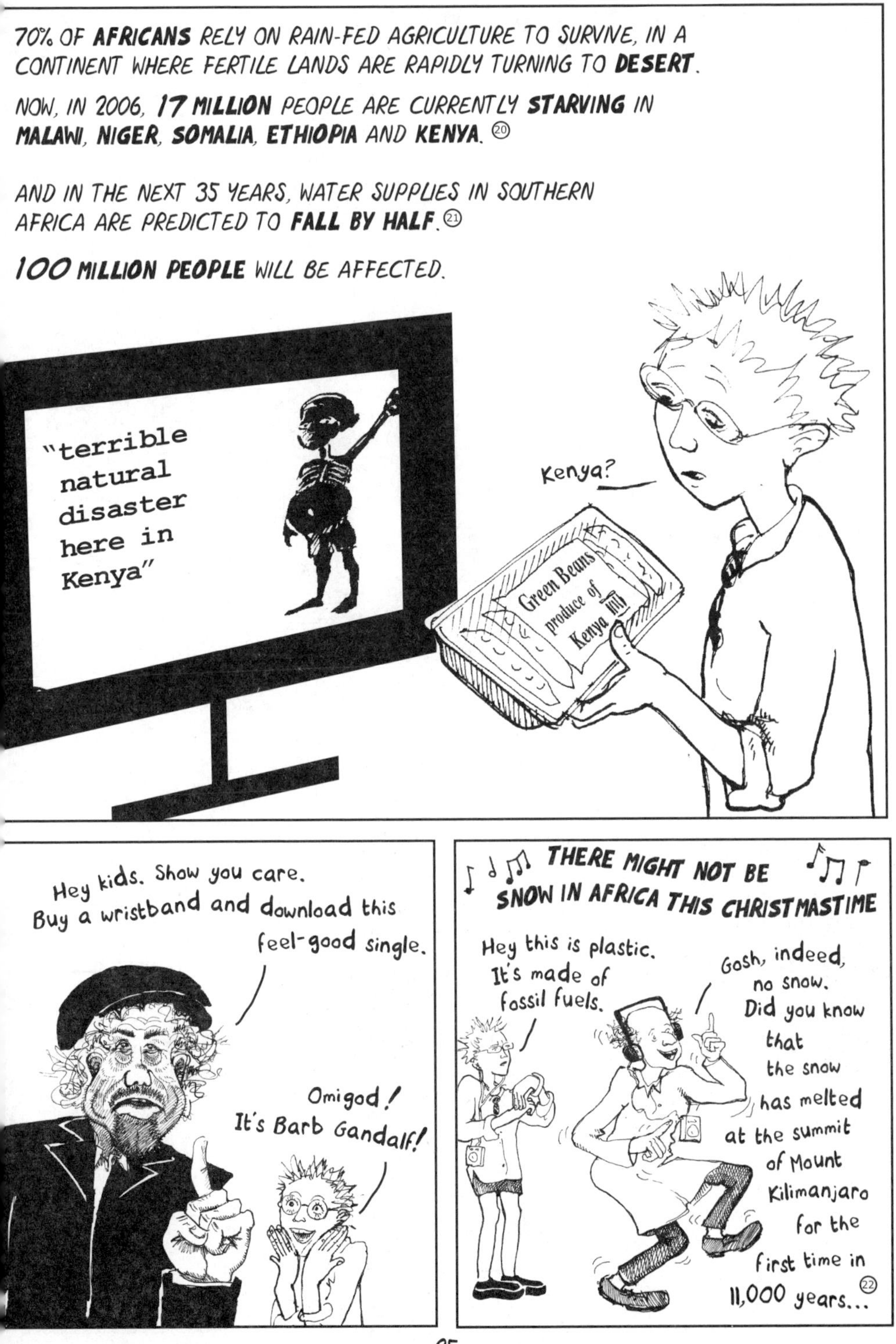
70% OF **AFRICANS** RELY ON RAIN-FED AGRICULTURE TO SURVIVE, IN A CONTINENT WHERE FERTILE LANDS ARE RAPIDLY TURNING TO **DESERT**.
NOW, IN 2006, **17 MILLION** PEOPLE ARE CURRENTLY **STARVING** IN **MALAWI**, **NIGER**, **SOMALIA**, **ETHIOPIA** AND **KENYA**. [20]
AND IN THE NEXT 35 YEARS, WATER SUPPLIES IN SOUTHERN AFRICA ARE PREDICTED TO **FALL BY HALF**. [21]
100 MILLION PEOPLE WILL BE AFFECTED.
"terrible natural disaster here in Kenya"
Green Beans produce of Kenya
Kenya?
Hey kids. Show you care. Buy a wristband and download this feel-good single.
Omigod! It's Barb Gandalf!
THERE MIGHT NOT BE SNOW IN AFRICA THIS CHRISTMASTIME
Hey this is plastic. It's made of fossil fuels.
Gosh, indeed, no snow. Did you know that the snow has melted at the summit of Mount Kilimanjaro for the first time in 11,000 years... [22]

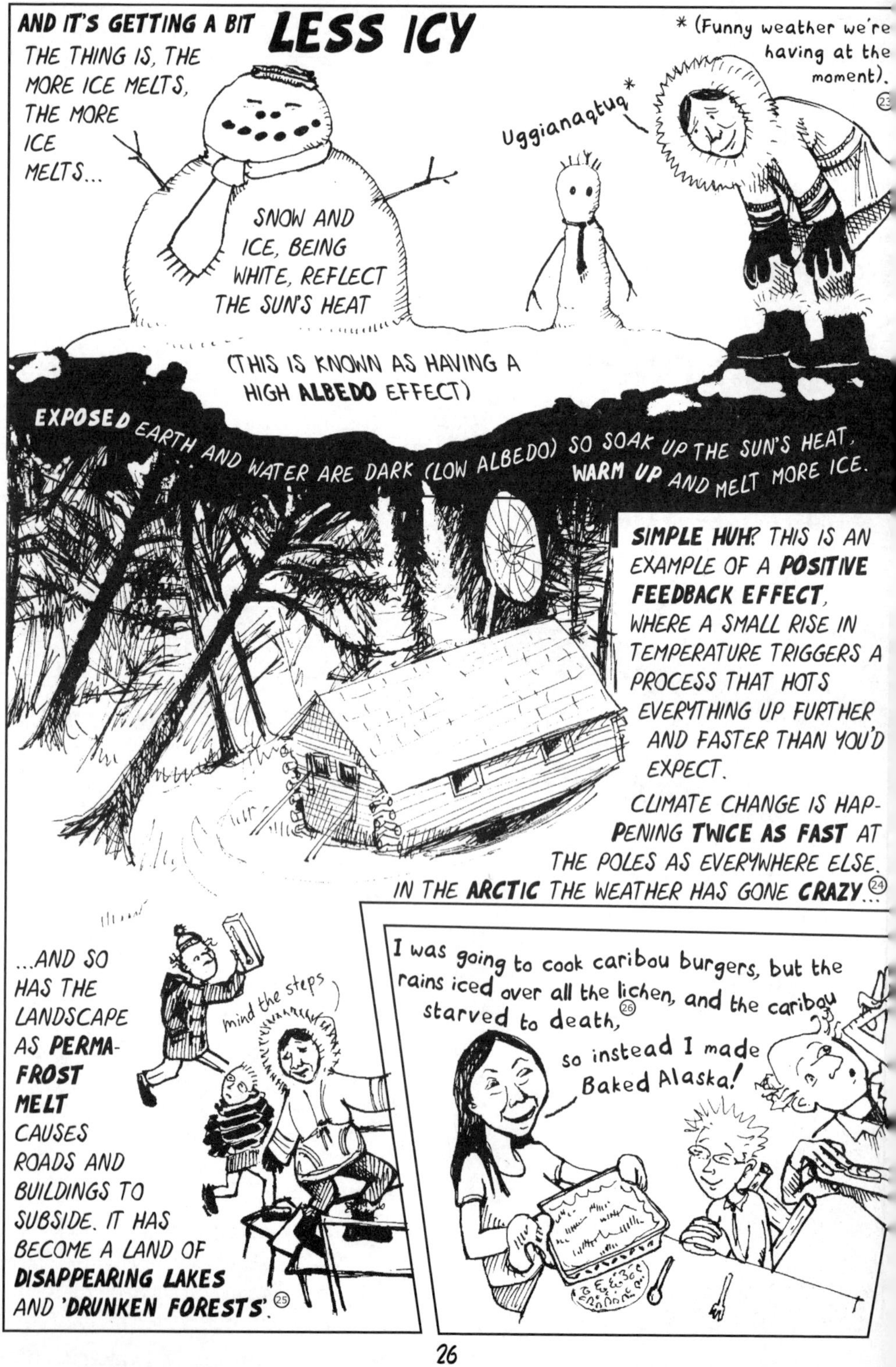

AND IT'S GETTING A BIT LESS ICY
THE THING IS, THE MORE ICE MELTS, THE MORE ICE MELTS...
SNOW AND ICE, BEING WHITE, REFLECT THE SUN'S HEAT
Uggianaqtuq*
* (Funny weather we're having at the moment).[23]
(THIS IS KNOWN AS HAVING A HIGH ALBEDO EFFECT)
EXPOSED EARTH AND WATER ARE DARK (LOW ALBEDO) SO SOAK UP THE SUN'S HEAT, WARM UP AND MELT MORE ICE.
SIMPLE HUH? THIS IS AN EXAMPLE OF A POSITIVE FEEDBACK EFFECT, WHERE A SMALL RISE IN TEMPERATURE TRIGGERS A PROCESS THAT HOTS EVERYTHING UP FURTHER AND FASTER THAN YOU'D EXPECT.
CLIMATE CHANGE IS HAPPENING TWICE AS FAST AT THE POLES AS EVERYWHERE ELSE. IN THE ARCTIC THE WEATHER HAS GONE CRAZY...[24]
...AND SO HAS THE LANDSCAPE AS PERMAFROST MELT CAUSES ROADS AND BUILDINGS TO SUBSIDE. IT HAS BECOME A LAND OF DISAPPEARING LAKES AND 'DRUNKEN FORESTS'.[25]
mind the steps
I was going to cook caribou burgers, but the rains iced over all the lichen, and the caribou starved to death,[26]
so instead I made Baked Alaska!

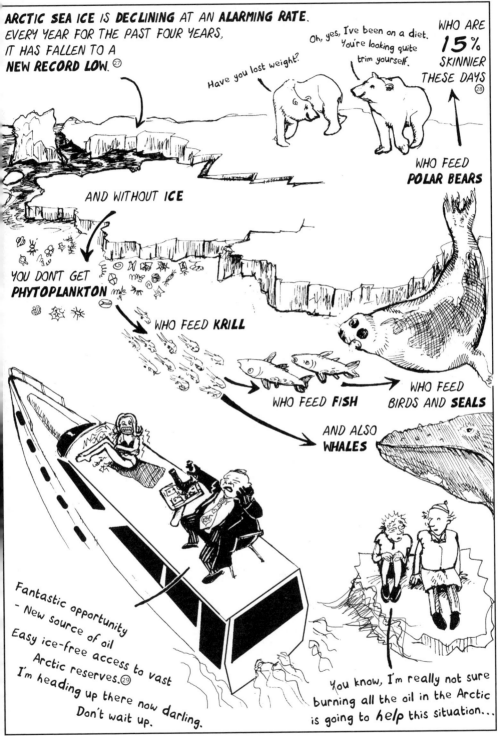

ARCTIC SEA ICE IS DECLINING AT AN ALARMING RATE. EVERY YEAR FOR THE PAST FOUR YEARS, IT HAS FALLEN TO A **NEW RECORD LOW.** (27)

Have you lost weight?

Oh, yes, I've been on a diet. You're looking quite trim yourself.

WHO ARE **15%** SKINNIER THESE DAYS (28)

WHO FEED **POLAR BEARS**

AND WITHOUT **ICE**

YOU DON'T GET **PHYTOPLANKTON**

WHO FEED **KRILL**

WHO FEED **FISH**

WHO FEED BIRDS AND **SEALS**

AND ALSO **WHALES**

Fantastic opportunity - New source of oil Easy ice-free access to vast Arctic reserves. (29) I'm heading up there now darling. Don't wait up.

You know, I'm really not sure burning all the oil in the Arctic is going to *help* this situation...

27

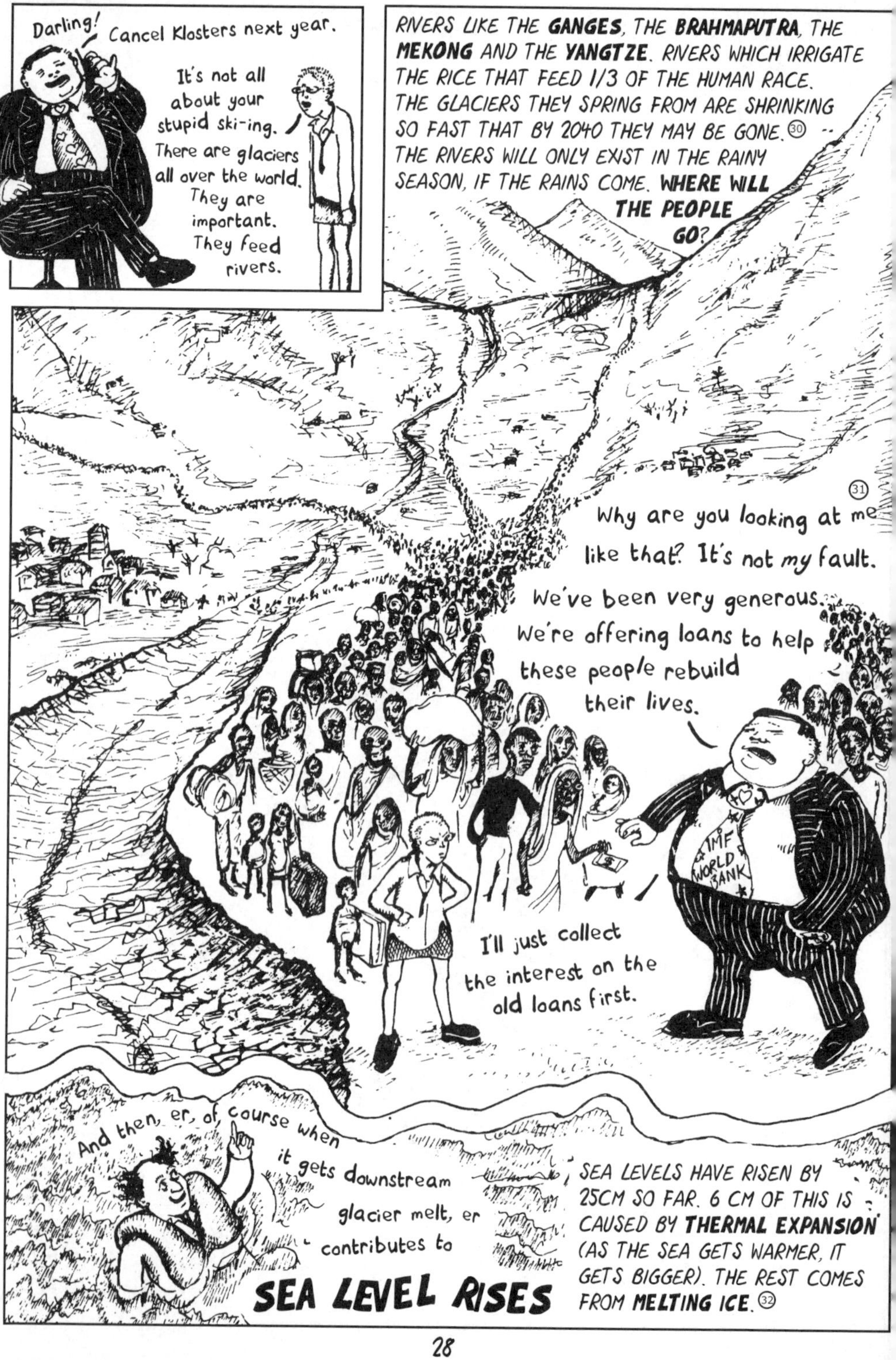
Darling! Cancel Klosters next year.
It's not all about your stupid ski-ing. There are glaciers all over the world. They are important. They feed rivers.
RIVERS LIKE THE **GANGES**, THE **BRAHMAPUTRA**, THE **MEKONG** AND THE **YANGTZE**. RIVERS WHICH IRRIGATE THE RICE THAT FEED 1/3 OF THE HUMAN RACE. THE GLACIERS THEY SPRING FROM ARE SHRINKING SO FAST THAT BY 2040 THEY MAY BE GONE. [30] THE RIVERS WILL ONLY EXIST IN THE RAINY SEASON, IF THE RAINS COME. **WHERE WILL THE PEOPLE GO?**
[31] Why are you looking at me like that? It's not *my* fault.
We've been very generous. We're offering loans to help these people rebuild their lives.
IMF WORLD BANK
I'll just collect the interest on the old loans first.
And then, er, of course when it gets downstream glacier melt, er contributes to
SEA LEVEL RISES
SEA LEVELS HAVE RISEN BY 25CM SO FAR. 6 CM OF THIS IS CAUSED BY **THERMAL EXPANSION** (AS THE SEA GETS WARMER, IT GETS BIGGER). THE REST COMES FROM **MELTING ICE**. [32]

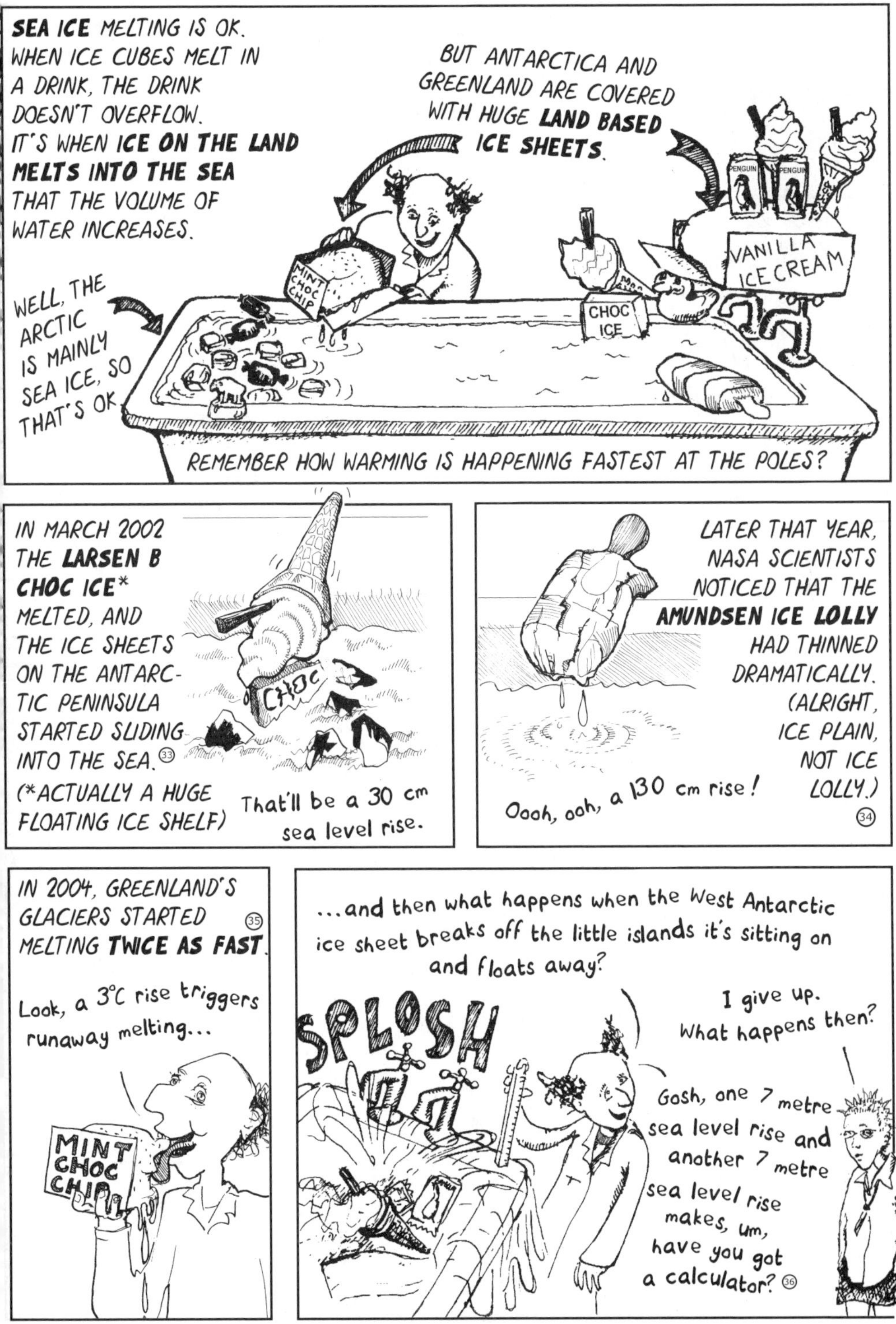

SEA ICE MELTING IS OK. WHEN ICE CUBES MELT IN A DRINK, THE DRINK DOESN'T OVERFLOW. IT'S WHEN ICE ON THE LAND MELTS INTO THE SEA THAT THE VOLUME OF WATER INCREASES.
BUT ANTARCTICA AND GREENLAND ARE COVERED WITH HUGE LAND BASED ICE SHEETS.
MINT CHOC CHIP
PENGUIN
PENGUIN
VANILLA ICE CREAM
WELL, THE ARCTIC IS MAINLY SEA ICE, SO THAT'S OK
CHOC ICE
REMEMBER HOW WARMING IS HAPPENING FASTEST AT THE POLES?
IN MARCH 2002 THE LARSEN B CHOC ICE* MELTED, AND THE ICE SHEETS ON THE ANTARCTIC PENINSULA STARTED SLIDING INTO THE SEA. [33]
(*ACTUALLY A HUGE FLOATING ICE SHELF)
CHOC
That'll be a 30 cm sea level rise.
LATER THAT YEAR, NASA SCIENTISTS NOTICED THAT THE AMUNDSEN ICE LOLLY HAD THINNED DRAMATICALLY. (ALRIGHT, ICE PLAIN, NOT ICE LOLLY.) [34]
Oooh, ooh, a 130 cm rise!
IN 2004, GREENLAND'S GLACIERS STARTED MELTING TWICE AS FAST. [35]
Look, a 3°C rise triggers runaway melting...
MINT CHOC CHIP
...and then what happens when the West Antarctic ice sheet breaks off the little islands it's sitting on and floats away?
SPLOSH
I give up. What happens then?
Gosh, one 7 metre sea level rise and another 7 metre sea level rise makes, um, have you got a calculator? [36]

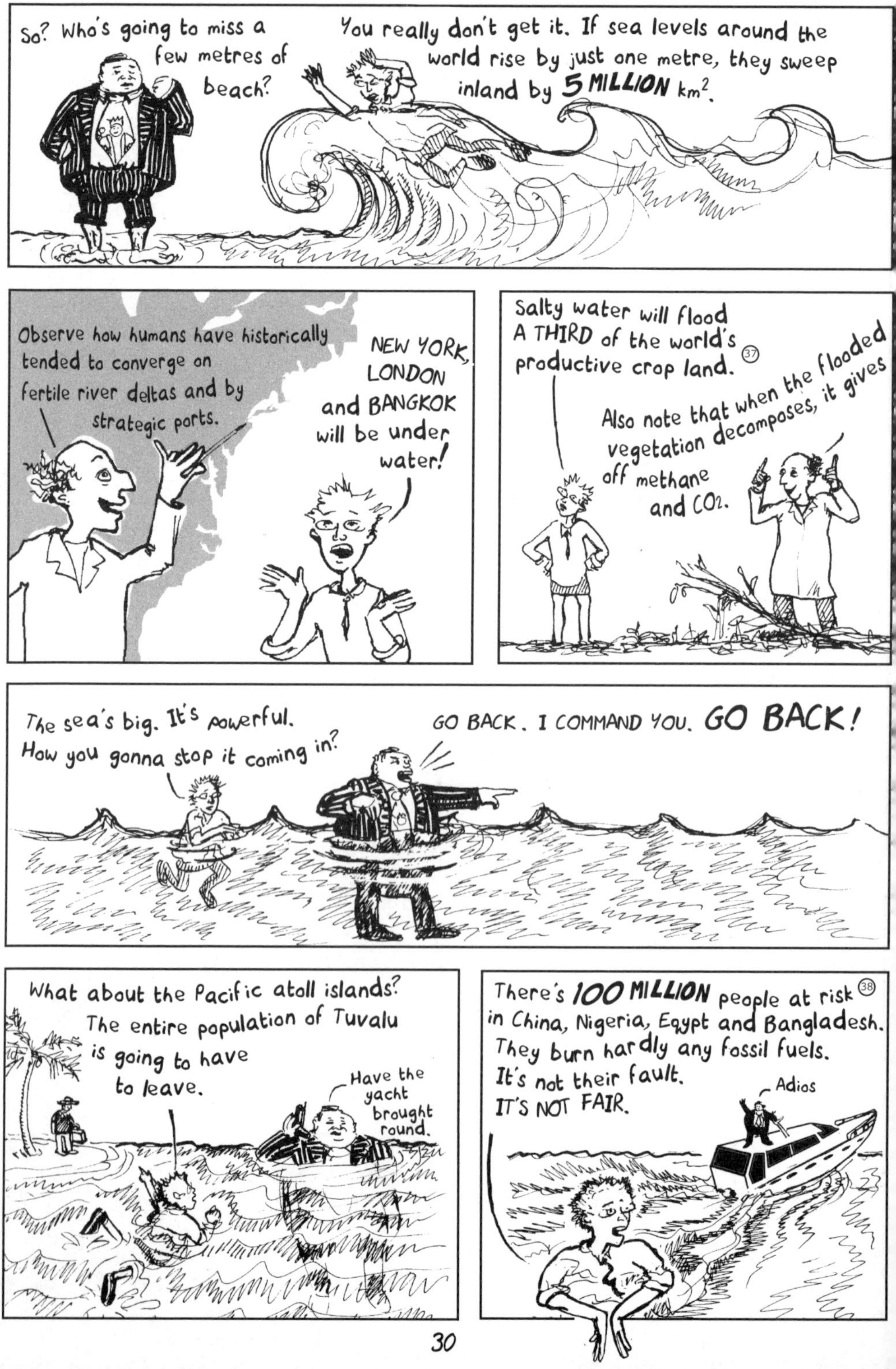
So? Who's going to miss a few metres of beach?
You really don't get it. If sea levels around the world rise by just one metre, they sweep inland by 5 MILLION km^2.
Observe how humans have historically tended to converge on fertile river deltas and by strategic ports.
NEW YORK, LONDON and BANGKOK will be under water!
Salty water will flood A THIRD of the world's productive crop land. [37]
Also note that when the flooded vegetation decomposes, it gives off methane and CO_2.
The sea's big. It's powerful. How you gonna stop it coming in?
GO BACK. I COMMAND YOU. GO BACK!
What about the Pacific atoll islands? The entire population of Tuvalu is going to have to leave.
Have the yacht brought round.
There's 100 MILLION people at risk [38] in China, Nigeria, Egypt and Bangladesh. They burn hardly any fossil fuels. It's not their fault. IT'S NOT FAIR.
Adios

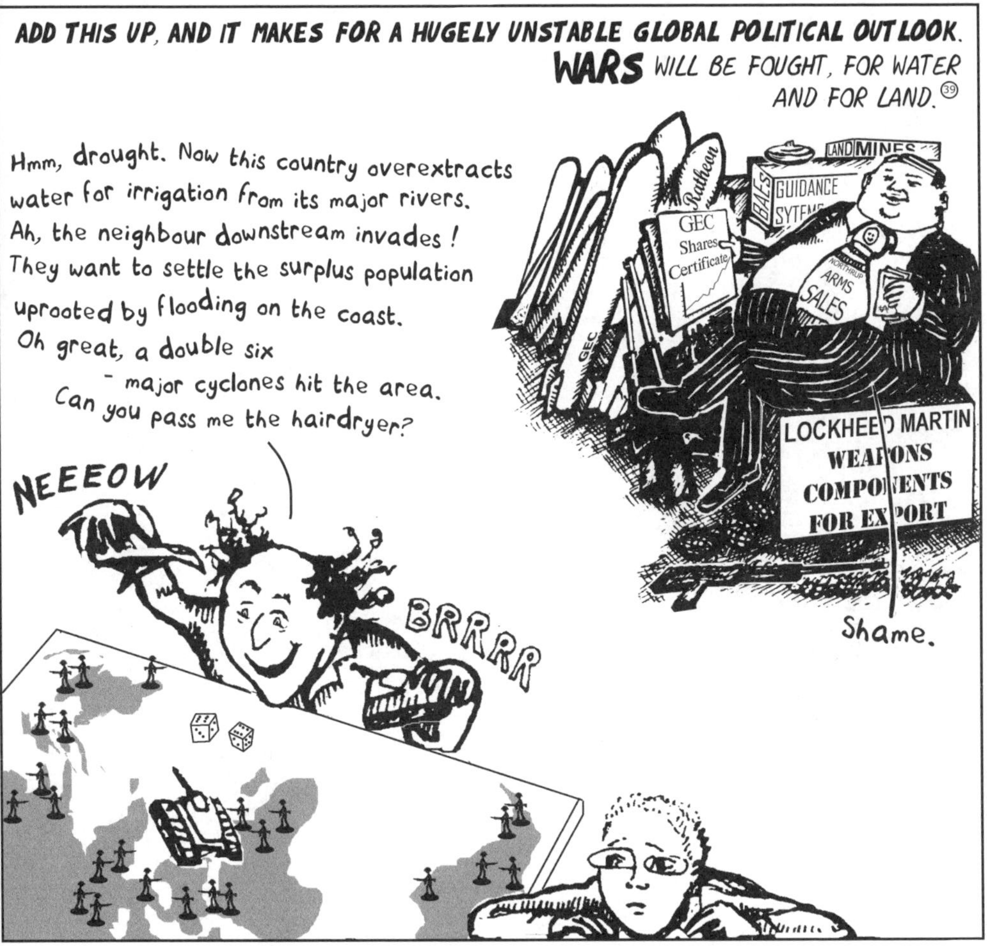
ADD THIS UP, AND IT MAKES FOR A HUGELY UNSTABLE GLOBAL POLITICAL OUTLOOK.
WARS WILL BE FOUGHT, FOR WATER AND FOR LAND.[39]
Hmm, drought. Now this country overextracts water for irrigation from its major rivers.
Ah, the neighbour downstream invades!
They want to settle the surplus population uprooted by flooding on the coast.
Oh great, a double six
- major cyclones hit the area.
Can you pass me the hairdryer?
NEEEOW
BRRRRR
Ratheon
GEC
Shares
Certificate
GEC
BAES
GUIDANCE
SYTEMS
LAND MINES
NORTHRUP
ARMS
SALES
LOCKHEED MARTIN
WEAPONS
COMPONENTS
FOR EXPORT
Shame.

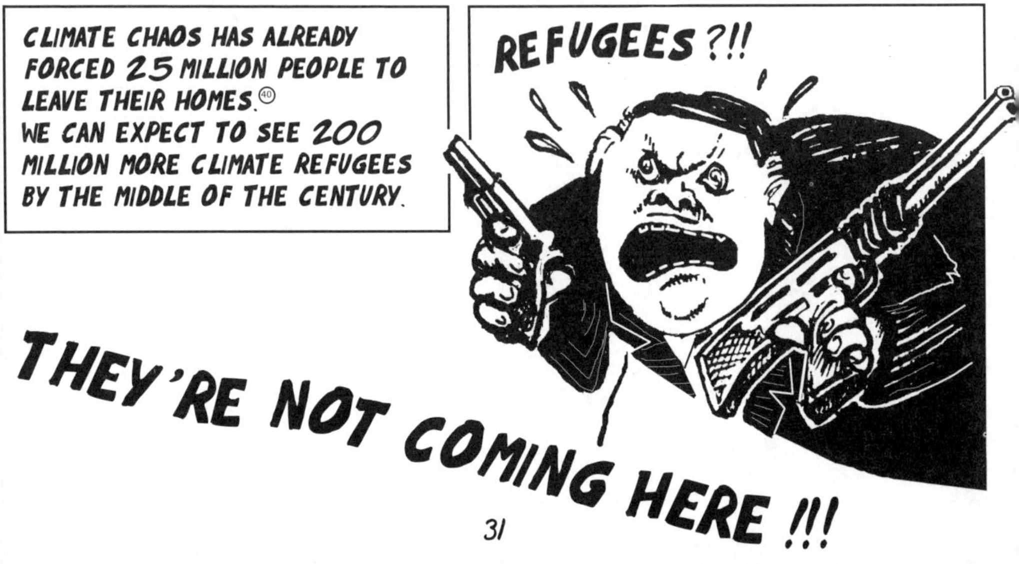
CLIMATE CHAOS HAS ALREADY FORCED 25 MILLION PEOPLE TO LEAVE THEIR HOMES.[40]
WE CAN EXPECT TO SEE 200 MILLION MORE CLIMATE REFUGEES BY THE MIDDLE OF THE CENTURY.
REFUGEES?!!
THEY'RE NOT COMING HERE !!!

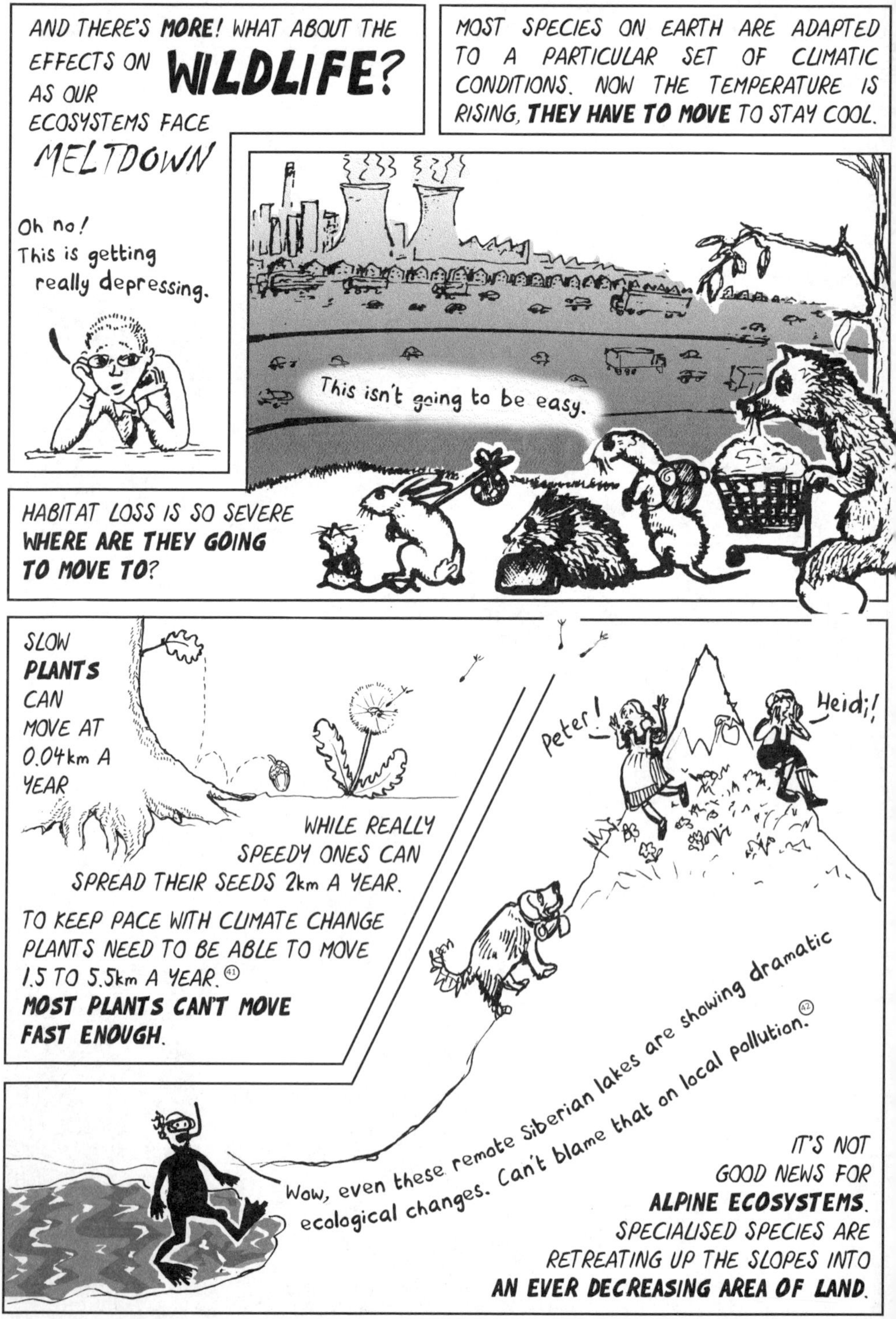
AND THERE'S MORE! WHAT ABOUT THE EFFECTS ON WILDLIFE? AS OUR ECOSYSTEMS FACE MELTDOWN
Oh no! This is getting really depressing.
MOST SPECIES ON EARTH ARE ADAPTED TO A PARTICULAR SET OF CLIMATIC CONDITIONS. NOW THE TEMPERATURE IS RISING, THEY HAVE TO MOVE TO STAY COOL.
This isn't going to be easy.
HABITAT LOSS IS SO SEVERE WHERE ARE THEY GOING TO MOVE TO?
SLOW PLANTS CAN MOVE AT 0.04km A YEAR
WHILE REALLY SPEEDY ONES CAN SPREAD THEIR SEEDS 2km A YEAR.
TO KEEP PACE WITH CLIMATE CHANGE PLANTS NEED TO BE ABLE TO MOVE 1.5 TO 5.5km A YEAR.[41]
MOST PLANTS CAN'T MOVE FAST ENOUGH.
Peter!
Heidi!
Wow, even these remote Siberian lakes are showing dramatic ecological changes. Can't blame that on local pollution.[42]
IT'S NOT GOOD NEWS FOR ALPINE ECOSYSTEMS. SPECIALISED SPECIES ARE RETREATING UP THE SLOPES INTO AN EVER DECREASING AREA OF LAND.

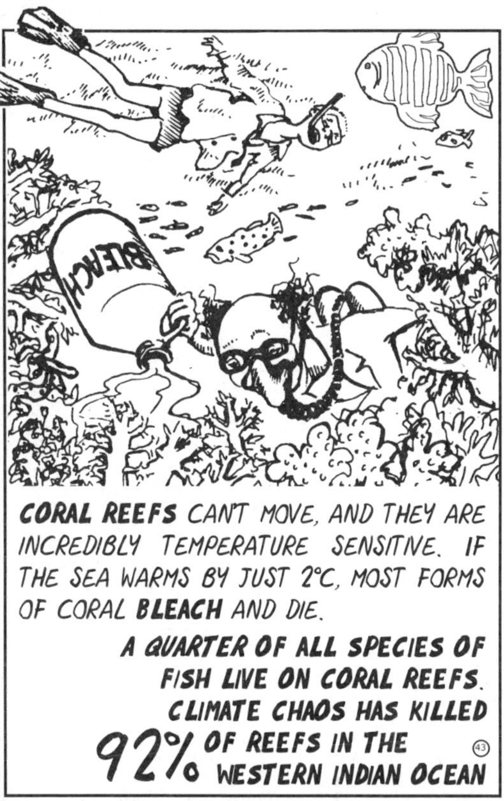
BLEACH
CORAL REEFS CAN'T MOVE, AND THEY ARE INCREDIBLY TEMPERATURE SENSITIVE. IF THE SEA WARMS BY JUST 2°C, MOST FORMS OF CORAL BLEACH AND DIE.
A QUARTER OF ALL SPECIES OF FISH LIVE ON CORAL REEFS. CLIMATE CHAOS HAS KILLED 92% OF REEFS IN THE WESTERN INDIAN OCEAN [43]

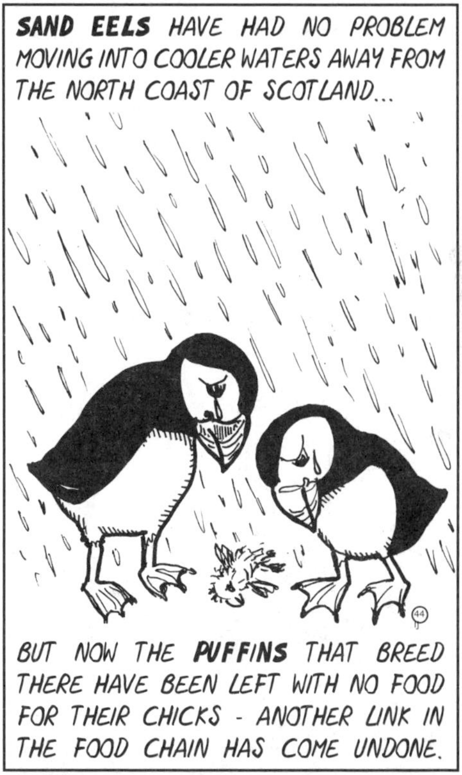
SAND EELS HAVE HAD NO PROBLEM MOVING INTO COOLER WATERS AWAY FROM THE NORTH COAST OF SCOTLAND...
[44]
BUT NOW THE PUFFINS THAT BREED THERE HAVE BEEN LEFT WITH NO FOOD FOR THEIR CHICKS - ANOTHER LINK IN THE FOOD CHAIN HAS COME UNDONE.

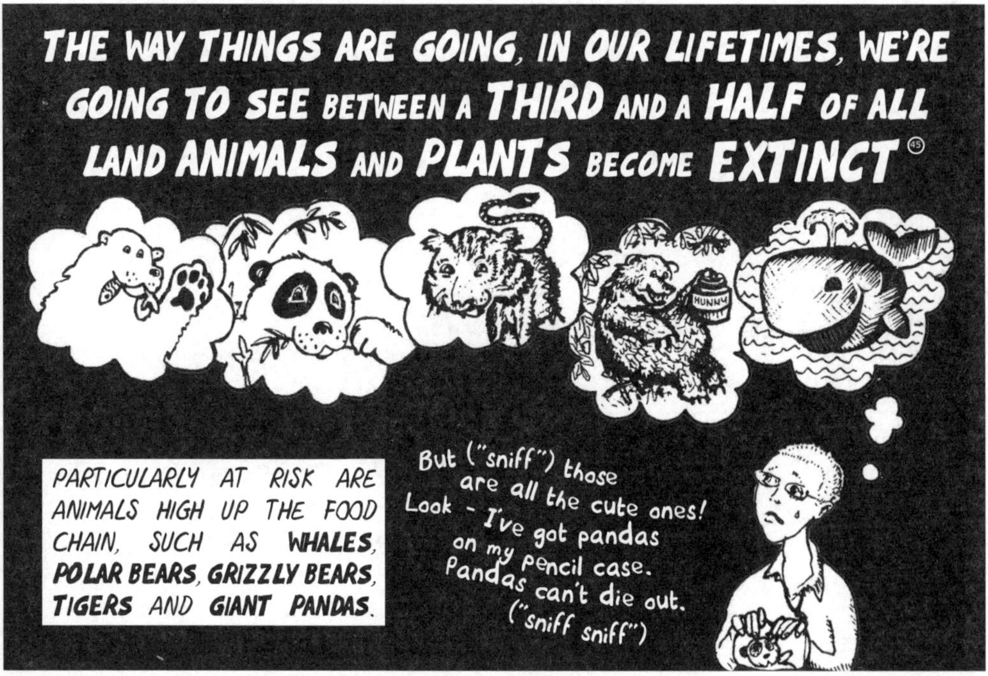
THE WAY THINGS ARE GOING, IN OUR LIFETIMES, WE'RE GOING TO SEE BETWEEN A THIRD AND A HALF OF ALL LAND ANIMALS AND PLANTS BECOME EXTINCT [45]
HUNNY
PARTICULARLY AT RISK ARE ANIMALS HIGH UP THE FOOD CHAIN, SUCH AS WHALES, POLAR BEARS, GRIZZLY BEARS, TIGERS AND GIANT PANDAS.
But ("sniff") those are all the cute ones! Look - I've got pandas on my pencil case. Pandas can't die out. ("sniff sniff")

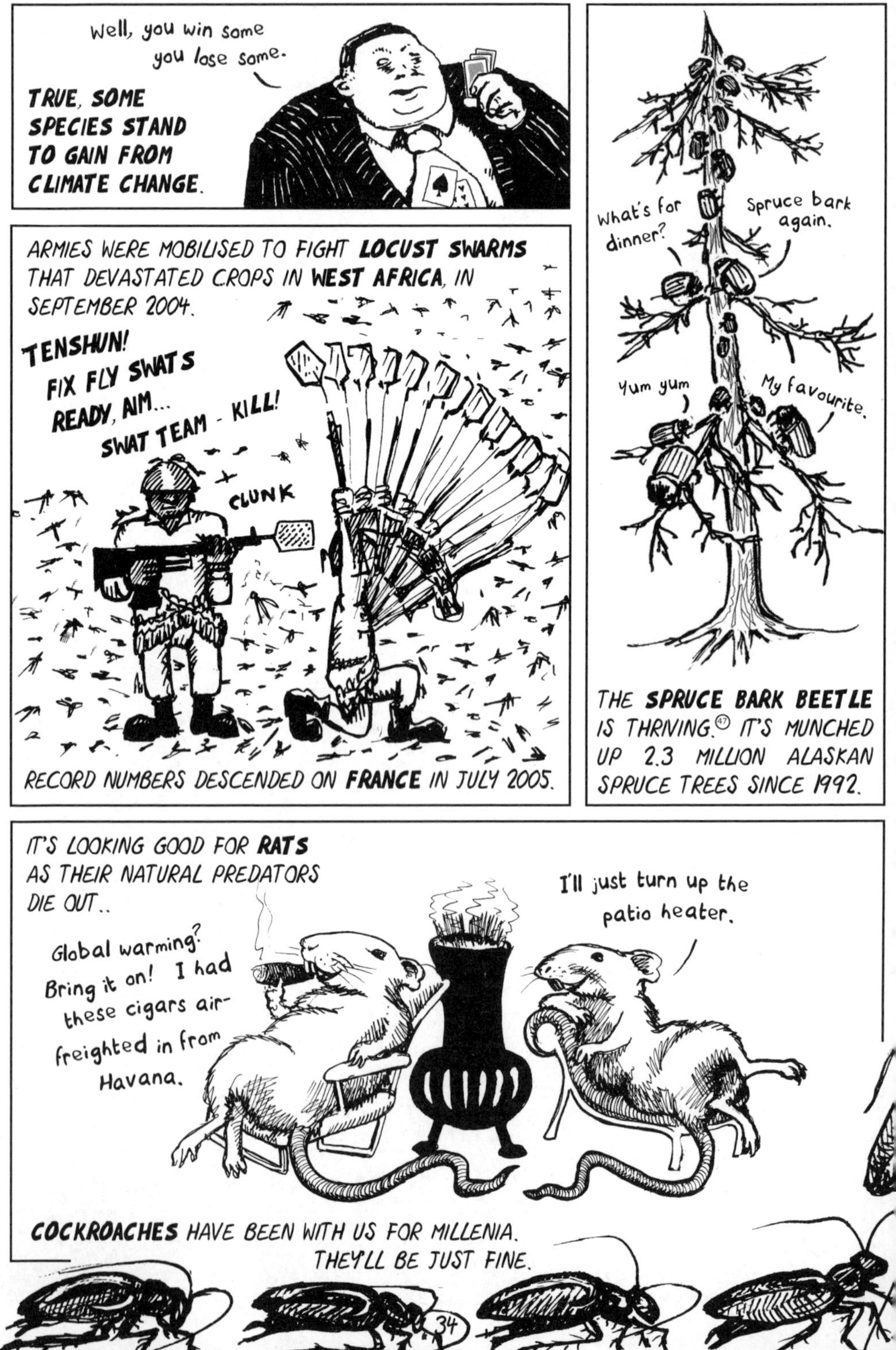
TRUE, SOME SPECIES STAND TO GAIN FROM CLIMATE CHANGE.
Well, you win some you lose some.
ARMIES WERE MOBILISED TO FIGHT LOCUST SWARMS THAT DEVASTATED CROPS IN WEST AFRICA, IN SEPTEMBER 2004.
TENSHUN!
FIX FLY SWATS
READY, AIM...
SWAT TEAM - KILL!
CLUNK
RECORD NUMBERS DESCENDED ON FRANCE IN JULY 2005.
What's for dinner?
Spruce bark again.
Yum yum
My favourite.
THE SPRUCE BARK BEETLE IS THRIVING.[47] IT'S MUNCHED UP 2.3 MILLION ALASKAN SPRUCE TREES SINCE 1992.
IT'S LOOKING GOOD FOR RATS AS THEIR NATURAL PREDATORS DIE OUT..
Global warming? Bring it on! I had these cigars air-freighted in from Havana.
I'll just turn up the patio heater.
COCKROACHES HAVE BEEN WITH US FOR MILLENIA.
THEY'LL BE JUST FINE.

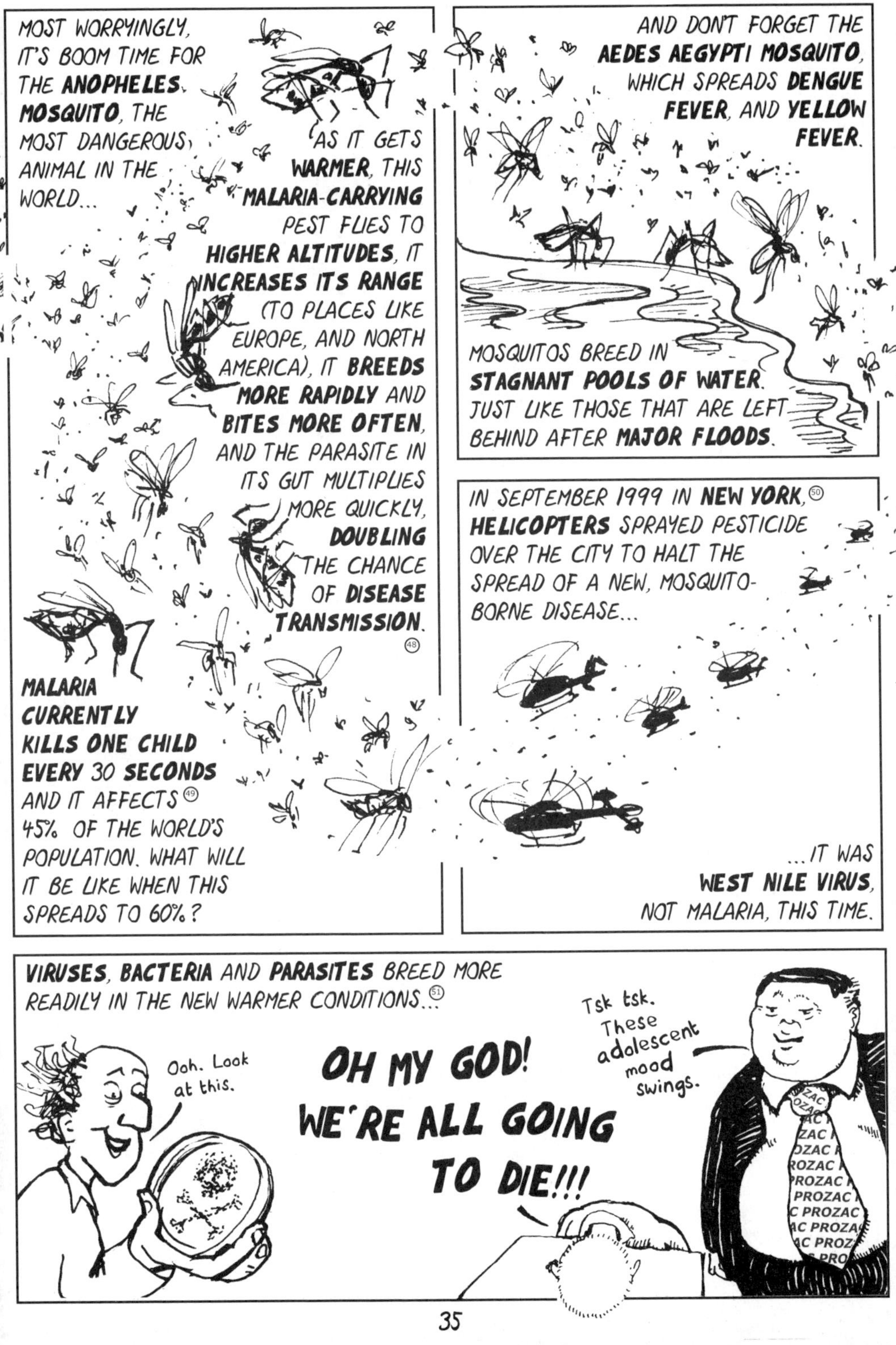
MOST WORRYINGLY, IT'S BOOM TIME FOR THE ANOPHELES MOSQUITO, THE MOST DANGEROUS ANIMAL IN THE WORLD...
AS IT GETS WARMER, THIS MALARIA-CARRYING PEST FLIES TO HIGHER ALTITUDES, IT INCREASES ITS RANGE (TO PLACES LIKE EUROPE, AND NORTH AMERICA), IT BREEDS MORE RAPIDLY AND BITES MORE OFTEN, AND THE PARASITE IN ITS GUT MULTIPLIES MORE QUICKLY, DOUBLING THE CHANCE OF DISEASE TRANSMISSION. [48]
MALARIA CURRENTLY KILLS ONE CHILD EVERY 30 SECONDS AND IT AFFECTS [49] 45% OF THE WORLD'S POPULATION. WHAT WILL IT BE LIKE WHEN THIS SPREADS TO 60%?
AND DON'T FORGET THE AEDES AEGYPTI MOSQUITO, WHICH SPREADS DENGUE FEVER, AND YELLOW FEVER.
MOSQUITOS BREED IN STAGNANT POOLS OF WATER. JUST LIKE THOSE THAT ARE LEFT BEHIND AFTER MAJOR FLOODS.
IN SEPTEMBER 1999 IN NEW YORK, [50] HELICOPTERS SPRAYED PESTICIDE OVER THE CITY TO HALT THE SPREAD OF A NEW, MOSQUITO-BORNE DISEASE...
...IT WAS WEST NILE VIRUS, NOT MALARIA, THIS TIME.
VIRUSES, BACTERIA AND PARASITES BREED MORE READILY IN THE NEW WARMER CONDITIONS... [51]
Ooh. Look at this.
OH MY GOD! WE'RE ALL GOING TO DIE!!!
Tsk tsk. These adolescent mood swings.
PROZAC PROZAC PROZAC

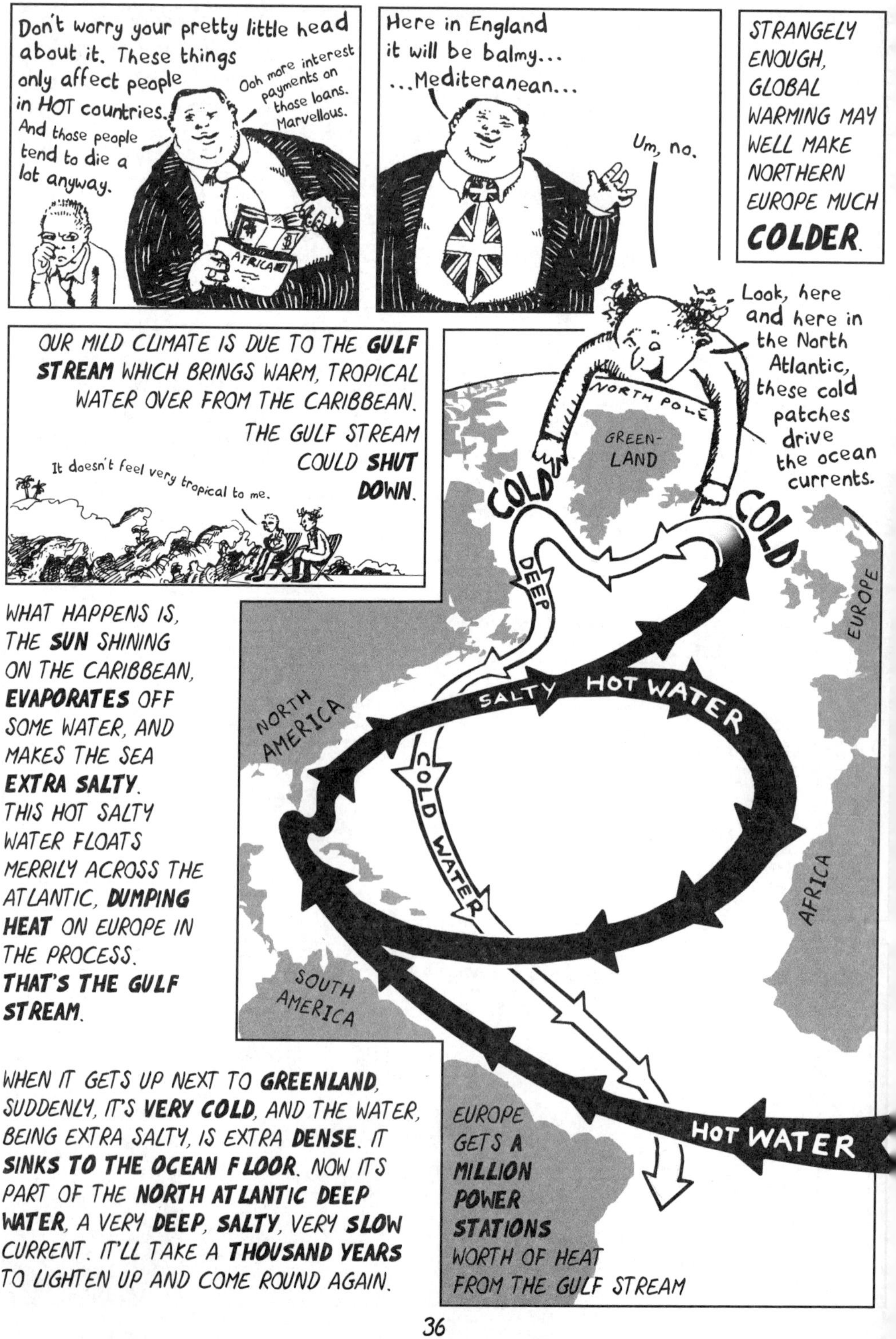

Don't worry your pretty little head about it. These things only affect people in HOT countries.
And those people tend to die a lot anyway.
Ooh more interest payments on those loans. Marvellous.
AFRICA
Here in England it will be balmy...
...Mediteranean...
Um, no.
STRANGELY ENOUGH, GLOBAL WARMING MAY WELL MAKE NORTHERN EUROPE MUCH **COLDER**.
OUR MILD CLIMATE IS DUE TO THE **GULF STREAM** WHICH BRINGS WARM, TROPICAL WATER OVER FROM THE CARIBBEAN. THE GULF STREAM COULD **SHUT DOWN**.
It doesn't feel very tropical to me.
Look, here and here in the North Atlantic, these cold patches drive the ocean currents.
NORTH POLE
GREEN-LAND
COLD
COLD
DEEP
EUROPE
NORTH AMERICA
SALTY
HOT WATER
COLD WATER
AFRICA
SOUTH AMERICA
HOT WATER
WHAT HAPPENS IS, THE **SUN** SHINING ON THE CARIBBEAN, **EVAPORATES** OFF SOME WATER, AND MAKES THE SEA **EXTRA SALTY**. THIS HOT SALTY WATER FLOATS MERRILY ACROSS THE ATLANTIC, **DUMPING HEAT** ON EUROPE IN THE PROCESS. **THAT'S THE GULF STREAM**.
WHEN IT GETS UP NEXT TO **GREENLAND**, SUDDENLY, IT'S **VERY COLD**, AND THE WATER, BEING EXTRA SALTY, IS EXTRA **DENSE**. IT **SINKS TO THE OCEAN FLOOR**. NOW ITS PART OF THE **NORTH ATLANTIC DEEP WATER**, A VERY **DEEP**, **SALTY**, VERY **SLOW** CURRENT. IT'LL TAKE A **THOUSAND YEARS** TO LIGHTEN UP AND COME ROUND AGAIN.
EUROPE GETS **A MILLION POWER STATIONS** WORTH OF HEAT FROM THE GULF STREAM

ALL YOU NEED TO DO TO HALT THIS MIGHTY OCEAN FLOW, IS TO **ADD** MORE **FRESH, UNSALTY WATER** TO THAT SALTY WATER IN THE NORTH ATLANTIC. SAY, BY **MELTING** SOME **GLACIERS** IN CANADA AND GREENLAND... IT'S HAPPENED BEFORE, AND IT COULD BE HAPPENING AGAIN. **IT LOOKS LIKE THE GULF STREAM HAS SLOWED BY 30% SINCE 1992!** [52]

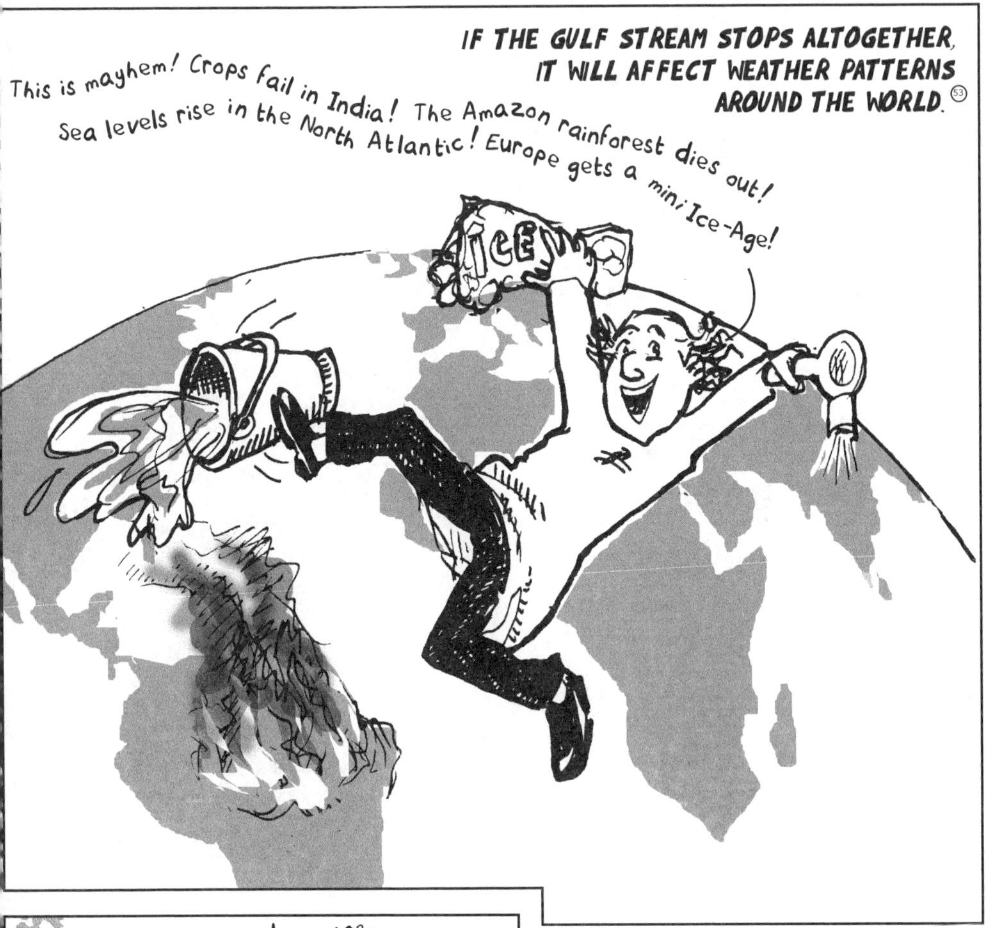
IF THE GULF STREAM STOPS ALTOGETHER, IT WILL AFFECT WEATHER PATTERNS AROUND THE WORLD. [53]
This is mayhem! Crops fail in India! The Amazon rainforest dies out! Sea levels rise in the North Atlantic! Europe gets a mini Ice-Age!
ICE

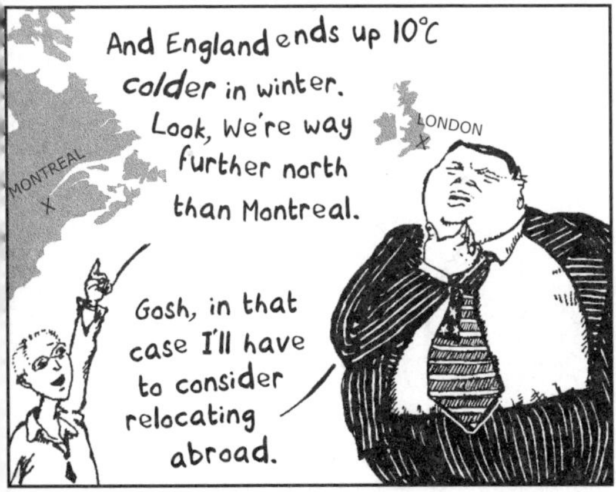
And England ends up 10°C colder in winter.
Look, We're way further north than Montreal.
MONTREAL
X
LONDON
X
Gosh, in that case I'll have to consider relocating abroad.

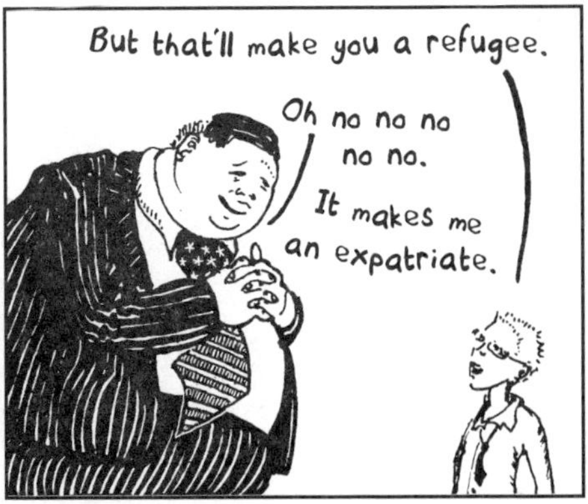
But that'll make you a refugee.
Oh no no no no no.
It makes me an expatriate.

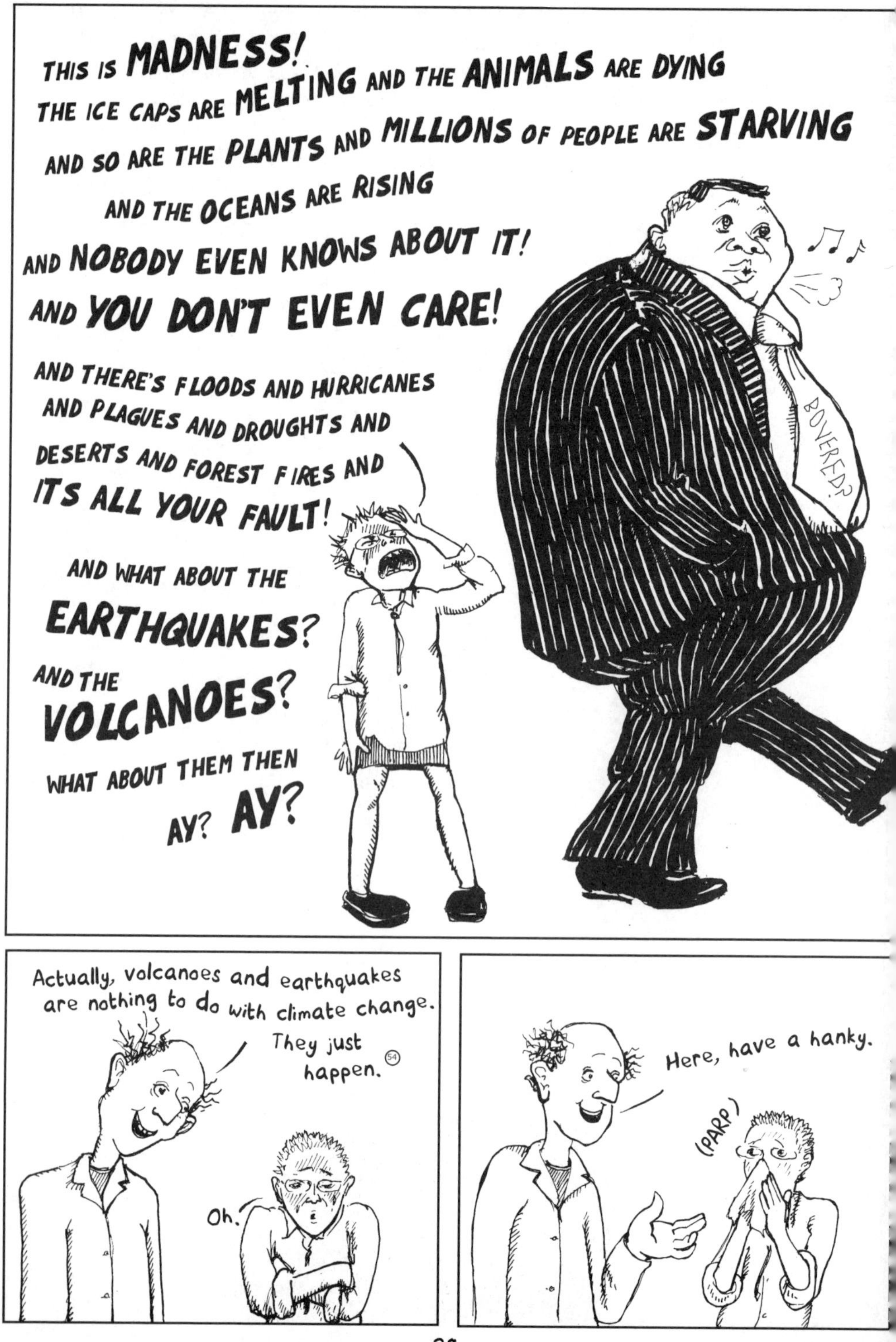
THIS IS MADNESS!
THE ICE CAPS ARE MELTING AND THE ANIMALS ARE DYING
AND SO ARE THE PLANTS AND MILLIONS OF PEOPLE ARE STARVING
AND THE OCEANS ARE RISING
AND NOBODY EVEN KNOWS ABOUT IT!
AND YOU DON'T EVEN CARE!
AND THERE'S FLOODS AND HURRICANES AND PLAGUES AND DROUGHTS AND DESERTS AND FOREST FIRES AND ITS ALL YOUR FAULT!
AND WHAT ABOUT THE EARTHQUAKES?
AND THE VOLCANOES?
WHAT ABOUT THEM THEN
AY? AY?
BOVERED?
Actually, volcanoes and earthquakes are nothing to do with climate change.
They just happen.[54]
Oh.
Here, have a hanky.
(PARP)

NOTES TO CHAPTER 1. PAGES 9 TO 38

1) *The Guardian* special report on Climate Change www.guardianunlimited.co.uk.

2) "We're Changing our Climate! Who Can Doubt It?" Simon Retallack and Peter Bunyard *The Ecologist* Vol 29 p 60.

3) This graph is taken from the IPCC Third Assessment Report 2001: Summary for Policymakers. It is popularly known as the hockey-stick graph. For an interesting investigation of the science behind it, please see "Climate: The great hockey stick debate" *New Scientist* 18/03/06.

4) Sources and rates of decomposition of greenhouse gases are taken from *Stormy Weather: 101 Solutions to Global Climate Change* by Guy Delancy and Patrick Mazza, also from *The Ecologist* Climate Crisis Issue, March/April 1999.

5) *IPCC Third Assessment Report 2001: Summary for Policymakers*.

6) Temperature rise from the late 19th century to 2003. "Uncertainty, risk and dangerous climate change" The Hadley Centre, The Met Office, Defra, UK Government.

7) This phenomenon is referred to as the "thermal inertia" of the planet. Ref: research by Tom Wigley at NCAR and Gerald Meehl, National Center for Atmospheric Research, (*New Scientist* 17/03/05), also from *The Ecologist* Climate Crisis Issue, March/April 1999.

8) A 10 degree rise in temperature is among the scenarios predicted by www.climateprediction. net, a distributed-computing project by Oxford University. The range of predicted scenarios ran from 1.9°C to 11.5°C. "There is no evidence that temperatures have ever been as high as in some of the climateprediction.net simulations." *New Scientist* 26/01/05. Also see Meinrat Andrae of the Max Planck Institute for Chemistry in Mainz, Germany, and Peter Cox and Chris Jones, of the UK's Hadley Centre who predict a temperature rise of between 6°C and 10°C, "Clearing smoke may trigger global warming rise" *New Scientist* 29/06/05.

9) Research by Kerry Emanuel of the Massachusetts Institute of Technology published in *Nature* vol 436 p 686, (*New Scientist* 03/12/05). In addition to this, P. Webster, and J. Curry, of the Georgia Institute of Technology in Atlanta, US, concluded in September 2005 that the number of intense hurricanes around the world have almost doubled in the past 35 years (*New Scientist* 16/03/06).

10) "In September, Sir John Houghton, chair of the Royal Commission on Environmental Pollution, said unequivocally that the super-powerful hurricanes battering the United States were the 'smoking gun' of global warming." *The Independent* 05/01/06. All text gleaned from Hurricane Katrina eyewitness testimony. Principally "zeta psi" at www.unsolvedmysteries.com, with additional words from www.survivedkatrina. org, CBBC newsround "One girl's escape story from Hurricane Katrina", BBC.co.uk articles "Policing the Venice from Hell" and "We Knew it was Going to Happen", and from Jim Edds ExtremeStorms.co.uk.

11) P. Frich et al 2002 "Observed coherent changes in climate extremes during the second half of the 20th century" *Climate Research*, 19, No.3, pp 193-212, and "Observed trends in the daily intensity of United Kingdom precipitation" 2000, T. Osborne, M. Hulme, P. Jones, and T. Basnett, *International Journal of Climatology*, 20, pp 347-364. Both quoted from *High Tide* by Mark Lynas.

12) Richard Betts of Britain's Hadley Centre for Climate Prediction and Research has calculated that the reduced uptake of groundwater by plants could increase groundwater by 10% over the next century. "Climatologists give waterworld warning for Earth" *New Scientist* 26/04/03.

13) *Unnatural Disasters: Climate Change and Developing Countries* Christian Aid, May 2000.

14) Statistics from infoplease.com.

15) NASA's Goddard Institute for Space Studies concluded that 2005 was the hottest year on record. The UK Meteorological Office and the US National Oceanic and Atmospheric Administration disagreed, and found that 1998 was marginally warmer. The temperature rise in 1998 was partly due to the El Niño phenomenon (a natural wobble in climatic conditions) while the 2005 high temperatures cannot be attributed to such an event. "2005 Continues the Warming Trend" *Washington Post* 16/12/05.

16) Research by Kevin Trenberth and others at National Center for Atmospheric Research in Boulder, Colorado, US. Their statement to the American Meteorological Society was reported in *New Scientist* 22/01/05. The research found very little difference in global drought conditions between 1870 and 1970, and a marked increase from 1970 onwards.

17) "Climate Change: One in Six Countries Facing Food Shortage" John Vidal and Tim Radford *The Guardian* 30/06/05. The words which accompany the illustrations

of African famine on pages 25 and 26 are those of African farmers and nomadic herders respectively. They are taken from "In the land where life is on hold" John Vidal The Guardian 30/06/05 and "Meagre food for babies first and elderly last, as villages empty of life" Jeevan Vasagar in Terbadeen, Niger, The Guardian 04/08/05.

18) Heat stress statistics from The Climate of Poverty: facts, fears and hope by Christian Aid May 2006, p 8.

19) Dr Kevin Tolhurst, a senior lecturer in fire ecology and management at the University of Melbourne has warned that climate change will bring "an increased number of larger, more devastating wildfires" University of Melbourne press release 9/12/03. Ten million hectares statistic is from The No-Nonsense Guide to Climate Change by Dinyar Godrej.

20) This figure is totalled from Wikipedia reports of drought-related food crises in Niger, Malawi and the Horn of Africa.

21) A 10% drop in rainfall translates into a 50% drop in available surface water due to increased aridity at higher temperatures; as calculated by Maarten de Wit of the University of Cape Town in South Africa (New Scientist 11/03/06).

22) Georg Kaser of the University of Innsbruck, Austria states that "there is a strong link between conditions on Kilimanjaro and global warming" in the face of some scientific debate on the subject , "Global Warming: the flaw in the thaw" New Scientist 27/08/05. Richard Taylor of The University College of London Department of Geography, published a study in Geophysical Research Letters (17/05/06) in which it is estimated that all the equatorial ice caps of the Rwenzori Mountains of East Africa will disappear in the next 20 years.

23) "Uggianaqtuq" is a Baffin Island Inuit word for unexpected and unpredictable. They get to use it a lot when talking about the weather these days.

24) P. Prestrud, "Arctic Climate Assessment Report" (New Scientist 2/11/04).

25) Based on account by Mark Lynas in his book High Tide. I nicked the joke about Baked Alaska from him too. There aren't that many laughs to be had about climate change.

26) Caribou starvation due to icing of lichen food plants on tundra, reported in "Arctic Climate Impact Assessment report 2004", quoted in The Weather Makers Tim Flannery, p 100.

27) Statement by the US National Snow and Ice Data Center, University of Colorado, Boulder, US (New Scientist 29/09/05).

28) Appenzeller, T. & Dimick, D.R. 2004 "The Heat is On", National Geographic 206, pp 72-5, quoted by Tim Flannery in The Weather Makers, p 102.

29) Pal Prestrud, researcher for the Arctic Climate Impact Assessment report 2004, has stated that about 25% of the Earth's remaining oil reserves are in the Arctic, and the "for the oil industry, it will be an advantage if the ice disappears, increasing access to oil and gas reserves" (New Scientist 02/11/05).

30) George Monbiot, The Guardian 10/08/04 See also "Ice-capped roof of world turns to desert" Geoffrey Lean, The Independent 07/05/06.

31) See The Little Earth Book by James Bruges for a critique of the World Bank and IMF, and an explanation of Third World versus First World debts and obligations.

32) The Ecologist Climate Crisis Issue, March/April 1999.

33) "If the ice on the [Antarctic] peninsula melts entirely it will raise global sea levels by 0.3 metres, and the west Antarctic ice sheet contains enough water to contribute metres more." "Antarctic ice sheet is an 'awakened giant'" J. Hogan, New Scientist 02/02/05.

34) Thomas, R et al. 2004 'Accelerated Sea-level Rise from West Antarctica' Science 306, pp 367-71. Reported in Tim Flannery's The Weather Makers, p 148, thus: "There is enough ice in the glaciers feeding into the Amundsen Sea to raise global sea levels by 1.3 metres. Their increasing rate of flow, and the incipient break-up of their ice-plain 'brake', are of concern to everyone."

35) Jonathan Gregory of the University of Reading and glaciologist Philippe Huybrechts of the Free University in Brussels, Belguim have concluded that a 3 C temperature rise will provide a trigger for runaway melting (New Scientist 07/04/04). See also "Greenland's glaciers are slip-sliding away", New Scientist 11/02/06, a report of research by Adrian Luckman of the University of Wales, Cardiff, which suggests a "sudden and synchronous" acceleration in the melting of Greenland's glaciers.

36) The Weather Makers, Tim Flannery, p 149. In addition to the above, Jim Hansen the director of NASA's Goddard Institute for Space Studies has stated that the collapse of the Greenland ice sheet could be "explosively rapid", with sea levels rising "a couple of metres this century, and several more next century" (New Scientist 04/02/06). Also see "Antarctic ice slipping faster into the sea" (New Scientist 22/10/05), a report of the findings of glaciologists at the Royal Society in London.

37) *The Ecologist* Climate Crisis Issue, March/April 1999.

38) *High Tide*, by Mark Lynas, p 114; also contains an amazing account of life on Tuvalu.

39) See *Resource Wars: the New Landscape of Global Conflict*, by Michael Klare.

40) Calculation on environmental refugees by Dr Norman Myers (source George Monbiot, *The Guardian*, 29/7/1999). The Red Cross uses the same estimate for the current number of environmental refugees in *World Disaster Reports* 2002. See also, a statement by the United Nations University's Institute for Environment and Human Security (03/05/06) where they estimate the number of environmental refugees as reaching 50 million by 2010, and call for the international community to define, recognise and extend support to this new category of refugee (Source OneWorld.net).

41) Plant movement needs to be between 1.5km and 5.5km a year, from *The No-Nonsense Guide to Climate Change* by Dinyar Godrej, pp 81-2.

42) J. Smol, Queen's University, Kingston, Ontario, Canada, researched sediment cores from 45 remote Arctic lakes, and found evidence of "regime shifts" in their ecologies which are synchronous with rising temperature *(New Scientist* 05/03/05).

43) N. Graham of the University of Newcastle Upon Tyne surveyed the health of coral reefs in the Seychelles, north of Madagascar and found that coral cover was at 7.5% of pre-1998 levels *Proceedings of the National Academy of Sciences*, 16/05/06. Reporting the study, National Geographic News quotes Nancy Knowlton, a marine biology professor at the Scripps Institution of Oceanography in La Jolla, California as saying that "by and large, reefs have collapsed catastrophically just in the three decades that I've been studying them." *National Geographic News* 16/05/06.

44) 2004 and 2005 saw record low numbers of breeding seabirds in the North of Scotland. Marine warden Sarah Money commented "This is a really worrying sign that something is badly wrong with the health of our seas" (*The Telegraph*, 28/07/05). See "Seabirds in the North Sea: victims of climate change?" *Birdlife International*, 01/05/05, for a description of the extent of the collapse.

45) Research by C. Thomas et al. University of Leeds, UK, Jan 2004. Projected extinctions by 2050 under the IPCC's "business as usual" scenario. Even with drastic, immediate cuts in CO2, an estimated nine percent of land species face extinction (*New Scientist* 07/01/04).

46) "Africa declares 'war' on locusts" bbc.co.uk 01/09/2004 and "Plague of locusts invades France" *The Observer* 17/07/05.

47) *High Tide*, Mark Lynas, p 60.

48) *The No-Nonsense Guide to Climate Change*, Dinyar Godrej, p 46-7 which also states that the Anopheles mosquito has increased the altitude at which it breeds by 500 feet in 30 years. This has led to new outbreaks of the disease in Kenya, Ethiopia, Rwanda, Tanzania, Uganda, Zimbabwe, Papua New Guinea and West Papua.

49) "Effective Medical Care in crisis situations" Medicins Sans Frontieres, April 2006.

50) *The No-Nonsense Guide to Climate Change*, Dinyar Godrej, p 46. The disease recurred in 2000.

51) *The Climate of Poverty: facts, fears and hope* by Christian Aid (May 2006, p 11) contains the calculation that, by the end of the century, 182 million people in Sub-saharan Africa could die of diseases directly attributed to climate change. In addition to mosquito-borne disease, diarrhoea, cholera, Rift Valley fever, leishmaniasis and meningitis are predicted to increase.

52) Research by Harry Bryden of the National Oceanography Centre in Southampton, UK, (*The Independent* 30/11/05). Bryden's team found that the flow remained steady between 1957 and 1992, then tailed off dramatically. Commenting on the findings, Tore Furevik of the University of Bergen in Norway said "There are certainly large changes going on beneath the surface of the North Atlantic, but we are still missing to many pieces of the puzzle to know what they are." (*New Scientist* 15/04/06). Permanent monitoring of the Gulf Stream flow is now in place to track further changes.

53) According to research by Richard Wood of the Hadley Centre for Climate Prediction and Research in Exeter, UK (*New Scientist* 15/04/06).

54) Research by NASA geophysicist Jeanne Sauber and geologist Bruce Molnia of the US Geological Survey, 2004, suggests that there may be a link between dramatic sea level rise and increased seismic activity (*New Scientist* 27/06/06). The theory is that as the weight of the water is redistributed around the globe, then the continental shelves may rebound, increasing the occurrence of volcanic eruptions and earthquakes. There is no firm evidence that sea level rises to date have triggered such a process at this stage. The 2005 Asian tsunami was not caused by climate change.

CHAPTER 2
FEEDBACKS

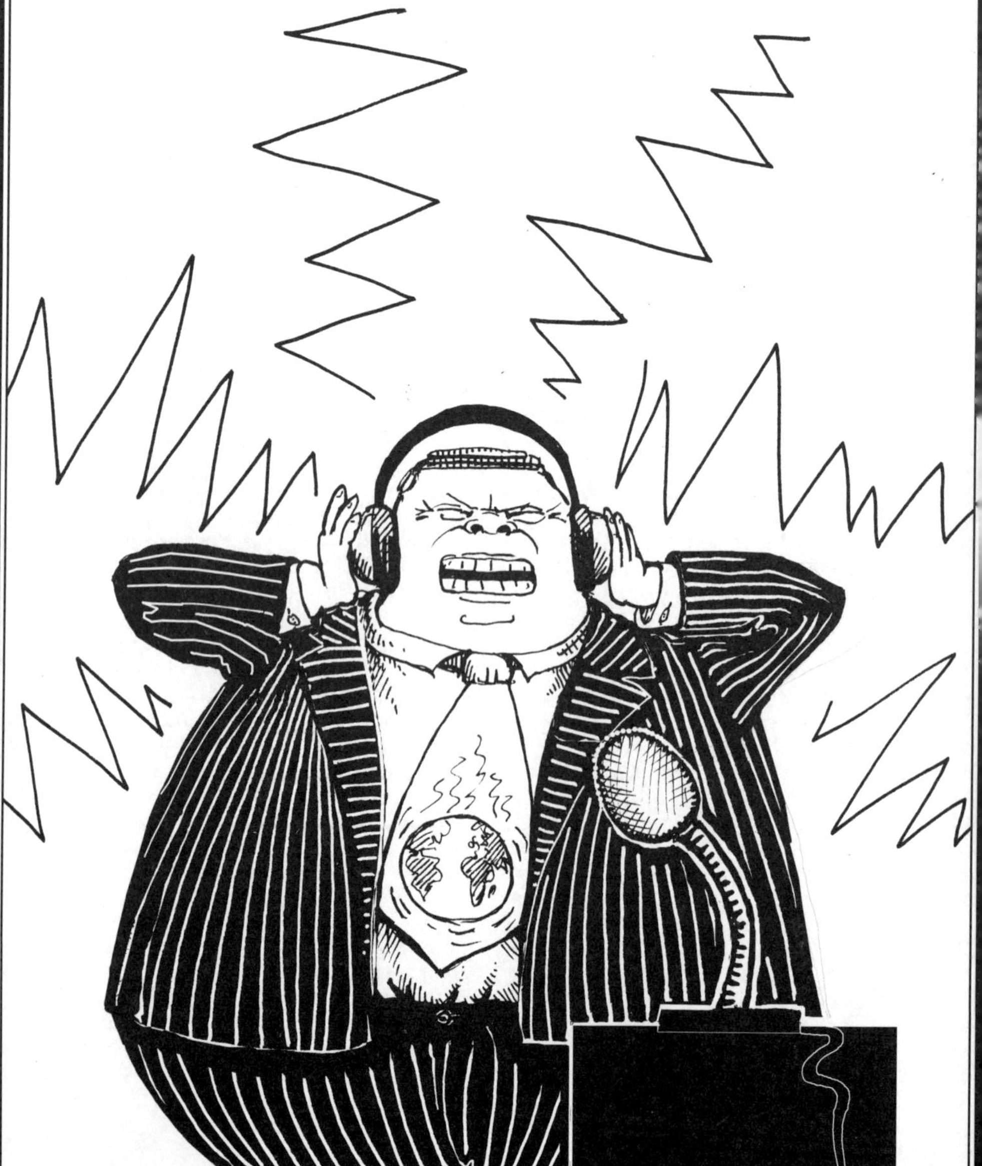

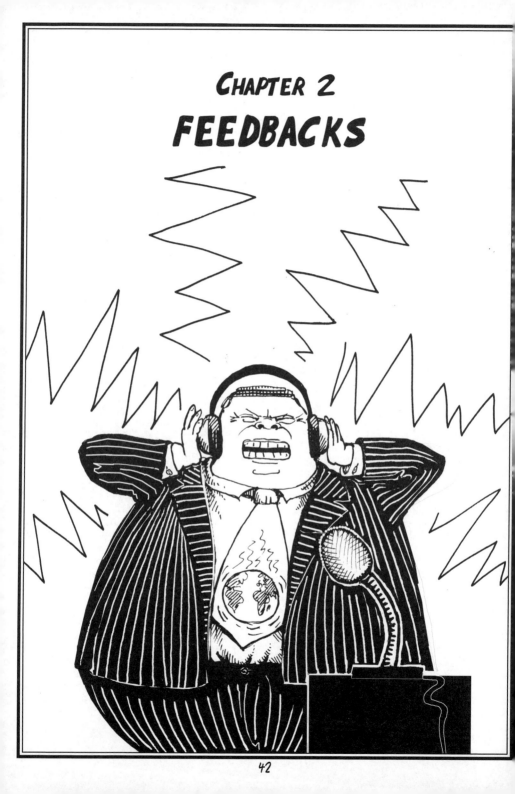

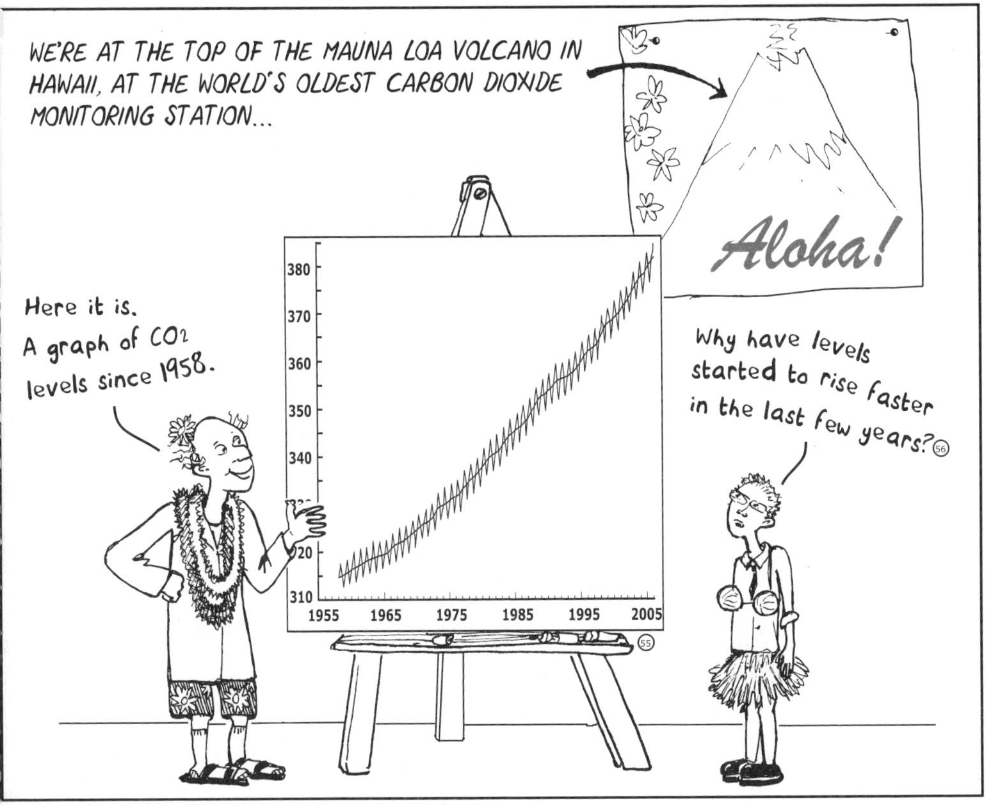
WE'RE AT THE TOP OF THE MAUNA LOA VOLCANO IN HAWAII, AT THE WORLD'S OLDEST CARBON DIOXIDE MONITORING STATION...
Aloha!
380
370
360
350
340
310
1955
1965
1975
1985
1995
2005
55
Here it is. A graph of CO2 levels since 1958.
Why have levels started to rise faster in the last few years? 56

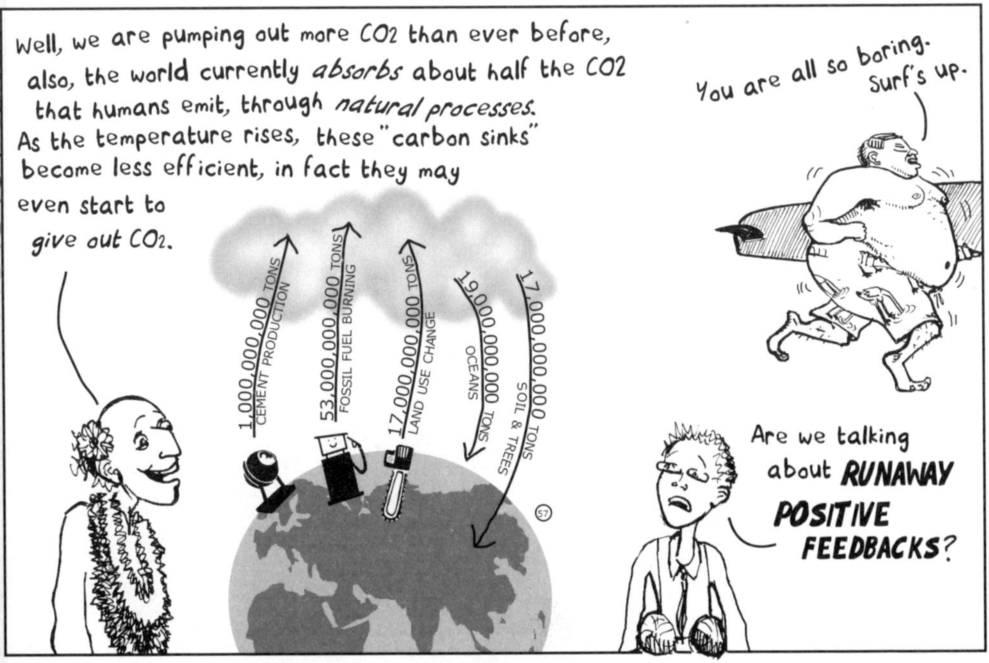
Well, we are pumping out more CO2 than ever before, also, the world currently *absorbs* about half the CO2 that humans emit, through *natural processes*. As the temperature rises, these "carbon sinks" become less efficient, in fact they may even start to *give out* CO2.
1,000,000,000 TONS
CEMENT PRODUCTION
53,000,000,000 TONS
FOSSIL FUEL BURNING
17,000,000,000 TONS
LAND USE CHANGE
19,000,000,000 TONS
OCEANS
17,000,000,000 TONS
SOIL & TREES
57
You are all so boring. Surf's up.
Are we talking about **RUNAWAY POSITIVE FEEDBACKS**?

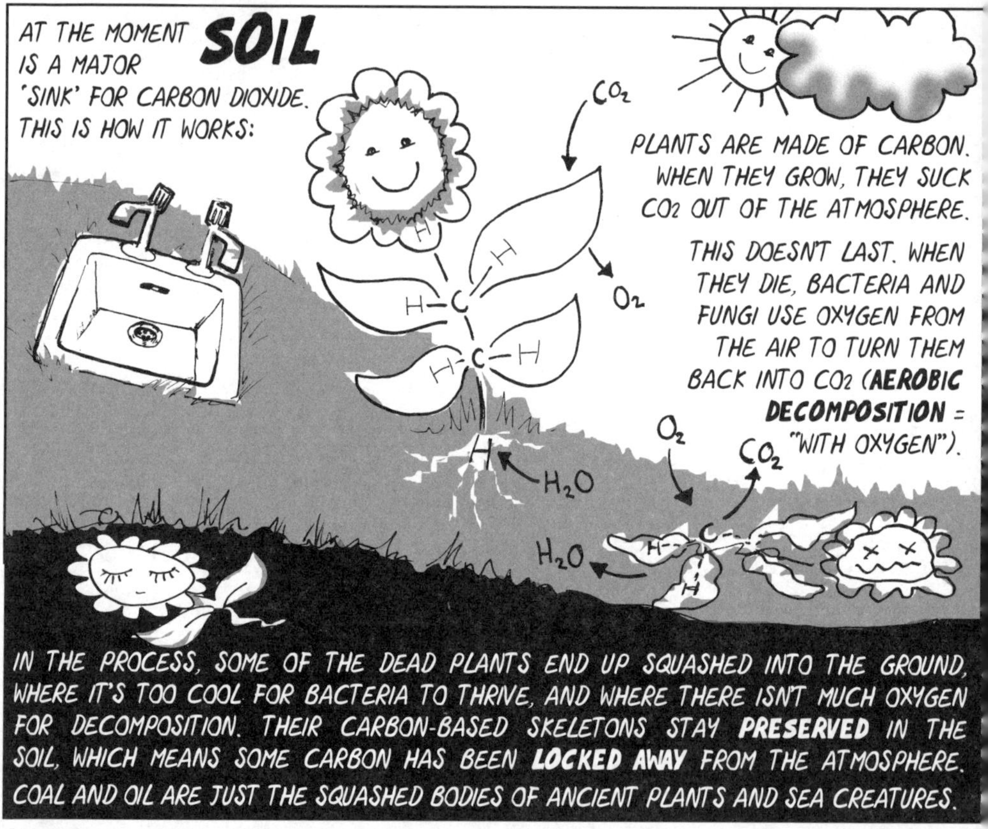
AT THE MOMENT **SOIL** IS A MAJOR 'SINK' FOR CARBON DIOXIDE. THIS IS HOW IT WORKS:
CO_2
PLANTS ARE MADE OF CARBON. WHEN THEY GROW, THEY SUCK CO_2 OUT OF THE ATMOSPHERE.
O_2
THIS DOESN'T LAST. WHEN THEY DIE, BACTERIA AND FUNGI USE OXYGEN FROM THE AIR TO TURN THEM BACK INTO CO_2 (**AEROBIC DECOMPOSITION** = "WITH OXYGEN").
H_2O
O_2
CO_2
H_2O
IN THE PROCESS, SOME OF THE DEAD PLANTS END UP SQUASHED INTO THE GROUND, WHERE IT'S TOO COOL FOR BACTERIA TO THRIVE, AND WHERE THERE ISN'T MUCH OXYGEN FOR DECOMPOSITION. THEIR CARBON-BASED SKELETONS STAY **PRESERVED** IN THE SOIL, WHICH MEANS SOME CARBON HAS BEEN **LOCKED AWAY** FROM THE ATMOSPHERE. COAL AND OIL ARE JUST THE SQUASHED BODIES OF ANCIENT PLANTS AND SEA CREATURES.

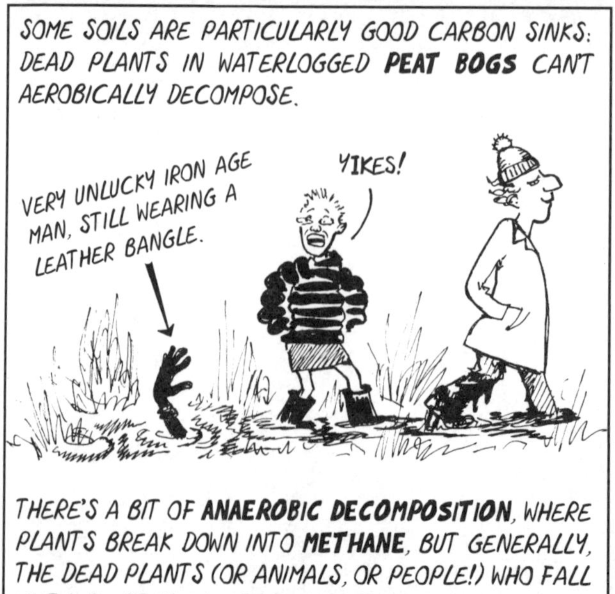
SOME SOILS ARE PARTICULARLY GOOD CARBON SINKS: DEAD PLANTS IN WATERLOGGED **PEAT BOGS** CAN'T AEROBICALLY DECOMPOSE.
VERY UNLUCKY IRON AGE MAN, STILL WEARING A LEATHER BANGLE.
YIKES!
THERE'S A BIT OF **ANAEROBIC DECOMPOSITION**, WHERE PLANTS BREAK DOWN INTO **METHANE**, BUT GENERALLY, THE DEAD PLANTS (OR ANIMALS, OR PEOPLE!) WHO FALL IN THERE STAY ALMOST PERFECTLY PRESERVED.

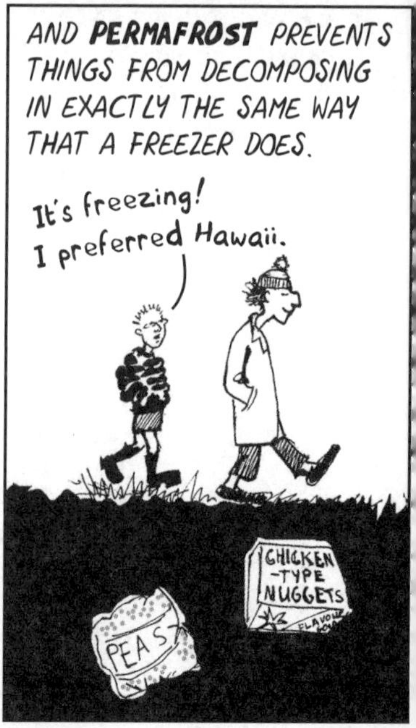
AND **PERMAFROST** PREVENTS THINGS FROM DECOMPOSING IN EXACTLY THE SAME WAY THAT A FREEZER DOES.
It's freezing! I preferred Hawaii.
CHICKEN -TYPE NUGGETS
PEAS

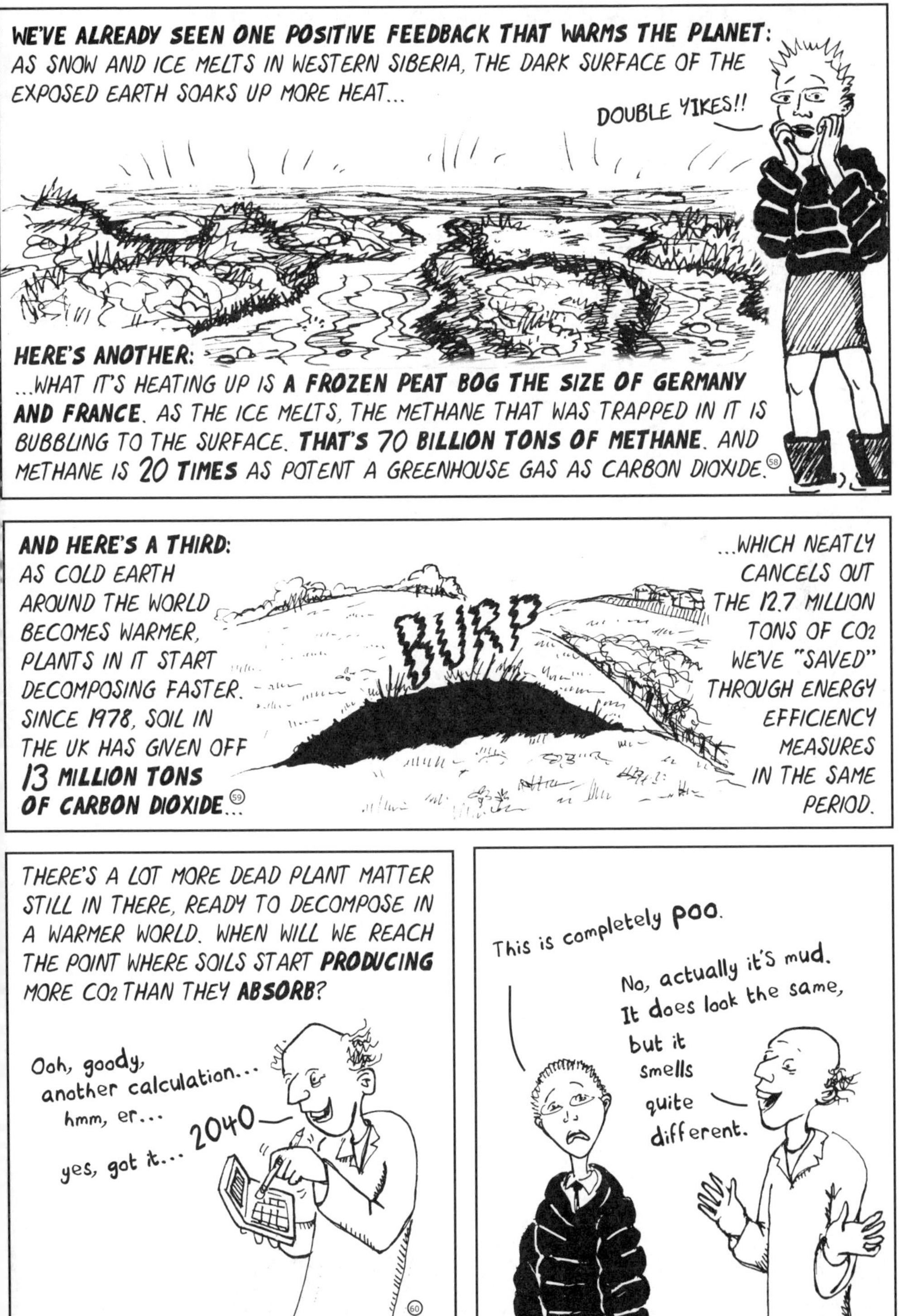
WE'VE ALREADY SEEN ONE POSITIVE FEEDBACK THAT WARMS THE PLANET: AS SNOW AND ICE MELTS IN WESTERN SIBERIA, THE DARK SURFACE OF THE EXPOSED EARTH SOAKS UP MORE HEAT...
DOUBLE YIKES!!
HERE'S ANOTHER: ...WHAT IT'S HEATING UP IS A FROZEN PEAT BOG THE SIZE OF GERMANY AND FRANCE. AS THE ICE MELTS, THE METHANE THAT WAS TRAPPED IN IT IS BUBBLING TO THE SURFACE. THAT'S 70 BILLION TONS OF METHANE. AND METHANE IS 20 TIMES AS POTENT A GREENHOUSE GAS AS CARBON DIOXIDE.[58]
AND HERE'S A THIRD: AS COLD EARTH AROUND THE WORLD BECOMES WARMER, PLANTS IN IT START DECOMPOSING FASTER. SINCE 1978, SOIL IN THE UK HAS GIVEN OFF 13 MILLION TONS OF CARBON DIOXIDE[59]...
BURP
...WHICH NEATLY CANCELS OUT THE 12.7 MILLION TONS OF CO2 WE'VE "SAVED" THROUGH ENERGY EFFICIENCY MEASURES IN THE SAME PERIOD.
THERE'S A LOT MORE DEAD PLANT MATTER STILL IN THERE, READY TO DECOMPOSE IN A WARMER WORLD. WHEN WILL WE REACH THE POINT WHERE SOILS START PRODUCING MORE CO2 THAN THEY ABSORB?
Ooh, goody, another calculation... hmm, er... yes, got it... 2040
[60]
This is completely poo.
No, actually it's mud. It does look the same, but it smells quite different.

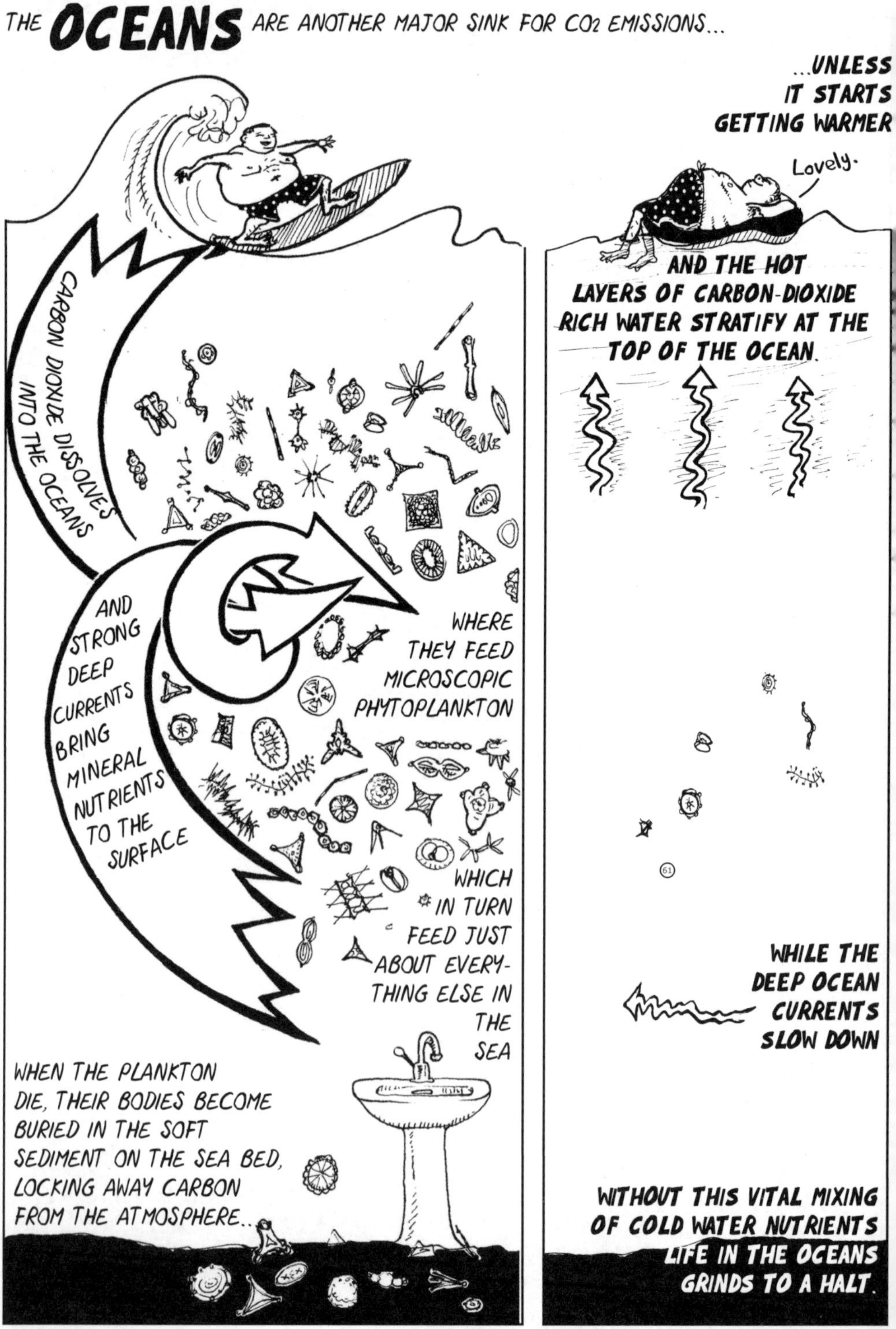
THE OCEANS ARE ANOTHER MAJOR SINK FOR CO2 EMISSIONS...
CARBON DIOXIDE DISSOLVES INTO THE OCEANS
AND STRONG DEEP CURRENTS BRING MINERAL NUTRIENTS TO THE SURFACE
WHERE THEY FEED MICROSCOPIC PHYTOPLANKTON
WHICH IN TURN FEED JUST ABOUT EVERY-THING ELSE IN THE SEA
WHEN THE PLANKTON DIE, THEIR BODIES BECOME BURIED IN THE SOFT SEDIMENT ON THE SEA BED, LOCKING AWAY CARBON FROM THE ATMOSPHERE...
...UNLESS IT STARTS GETTING WARMER
Lovely.
AND THE HOT LAYERS OF CARBON-DIOXIDE RICH WATER STRATIFY AT THE TOP OF THE OCEAN.
WHILE THE DEEP OCEAN CURRENTS SLOW DOWN
WITHOUT THIS VITAL MIXING OF COLD WATER NUTRIENTS LIFE IN THE OCEANS GRINDS TO A HALT.

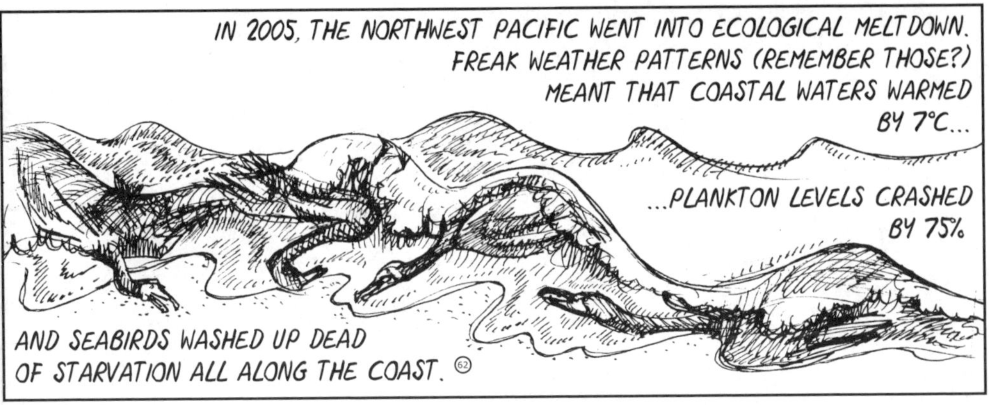
IN 2005, THE NORTHWEST PACIFIC WENT INTO ECOLOGICAL MELTDOWN. FREAK WEATHER PATTERNS (REMEMBER THOSE?) MEANT THAT COASTAL WATERS WARMED BY 7°C...
...PLANKTON LEVELS CRASHED BY 75%
AND SEABIRDS WASHED UP DEAD OF STARVATION ALL ALONG THE COAST. (62)

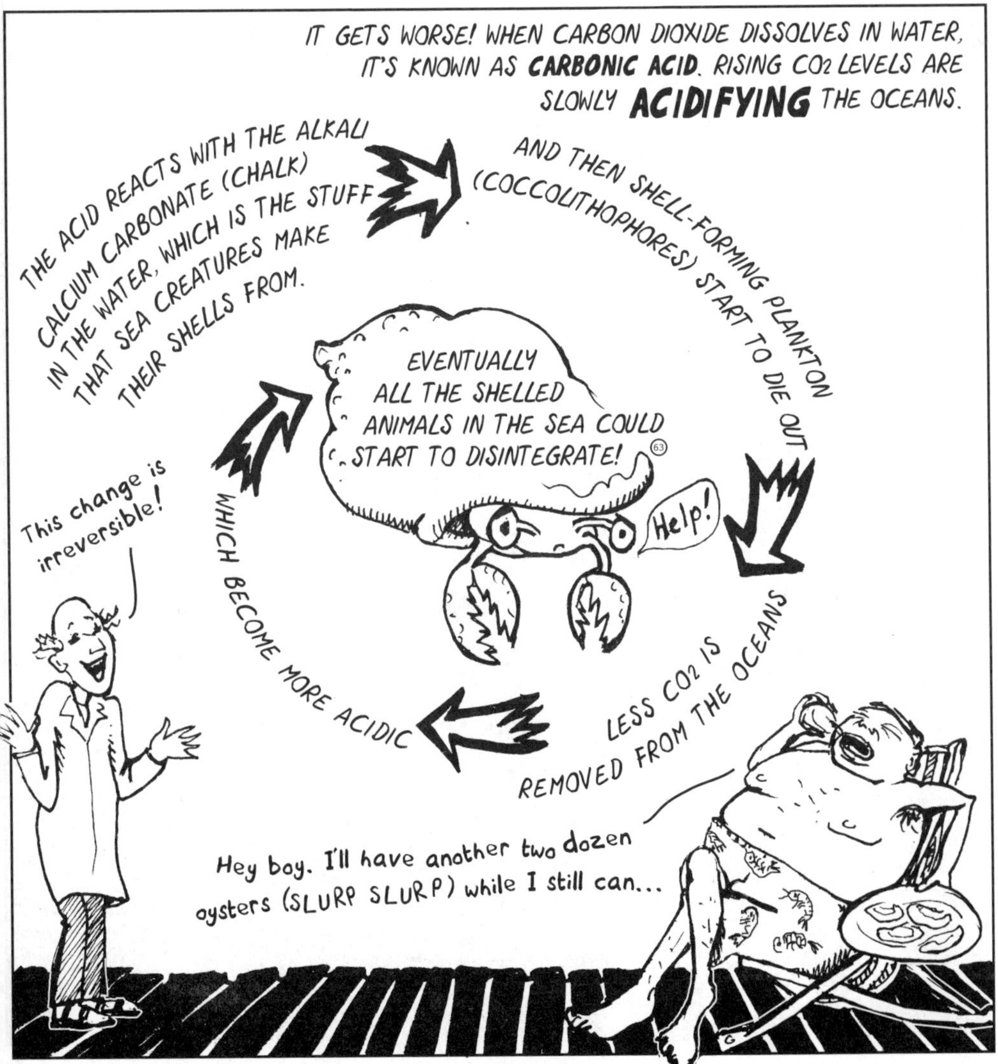
IT GETS WORSE! WHEN CARBON DIOXIDE DISSOLVES IN WATER, IT'S KNOWN AS **CARBONIC ACID**. RISING CO_2 LEVELS ARE SLOWLY **ACIDIFYING** THE OCEANS.
THE ACID REACTS WITH THE ALKALI CALCIUM CARBONATE (CHALK) IN THE WATER, WHICH IS THE STUFF THAT SEA CREATURES MAKE THEIR SHELLS FROM.
AND THEN SHELL-FORMING PLANKTON (COCCOLITHOPHORES) START TO DIE OUT
LESS CO_2 IS REMOVED FROM THE OCEANS
WHICH BECOME MORE ACIDIC
EVENTUALLY ALL THE SHELLED ANIMALS IN THE SEA COULD START TO DISINTEGRATE! (63)
Help!
This change is irreversible!
Hey boy. I'll have another two dozen oysters (SLURP SLURP) while I still can...

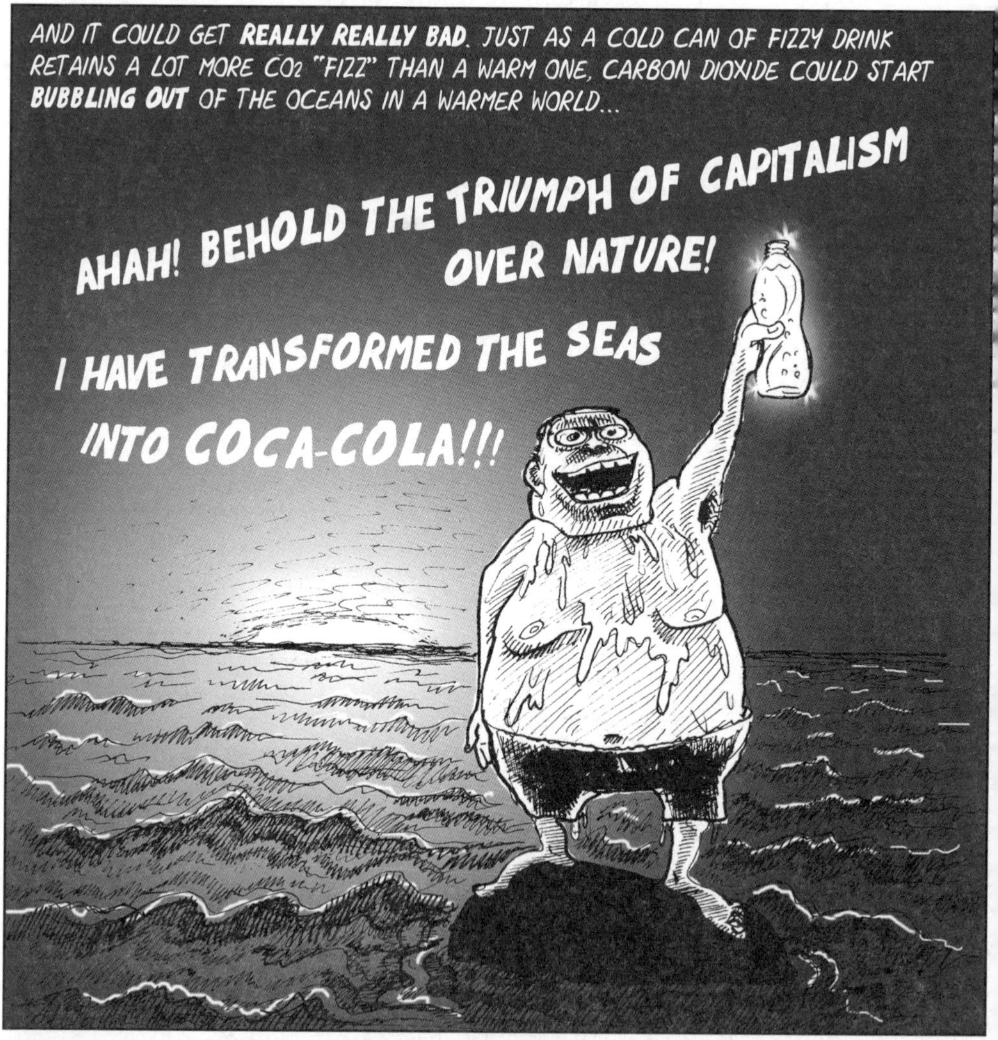
AND IT COULD GET **REALLY REALLY BAD**. JUST AS A COLD CAN OF FIZZY DRINK RETAINS A LOT MORE CO_2 "FIZZ" THAN A WARM ONE, CARBON DIOXIDE COULD START **BUBBLING OUT** OF THE OCEANS IN A WARMER WORLD...
AHAH! BEHOLD THE TRIUMPH OF CAPITALISM OVER NATURE!
I HAVE TRANSFORMED THE SEAS INTO COCA-COLA!!!

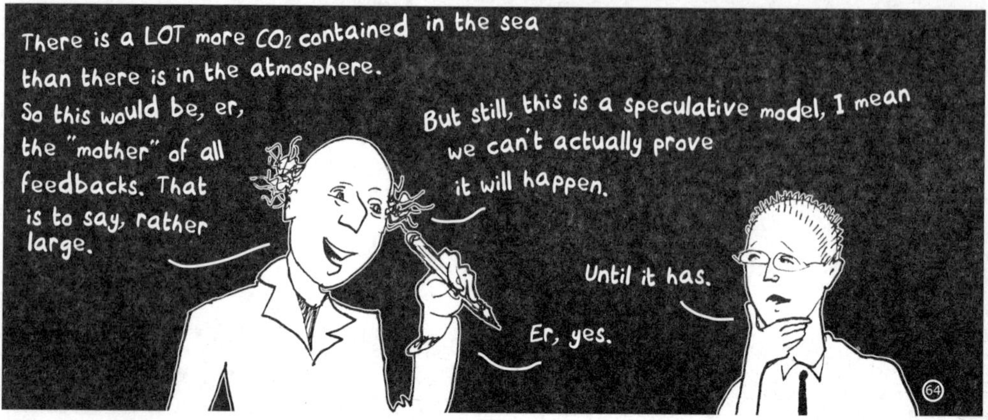
There is a LOT more CO_2 contained in the sea than there is in the atmosphere. So this would be, er, the "mother" of all feedbacks. That is to say, rather large.
But still, this is a speculative model, I mean we can't actually prove it will happen.
Until it has.
Er, yes.
64

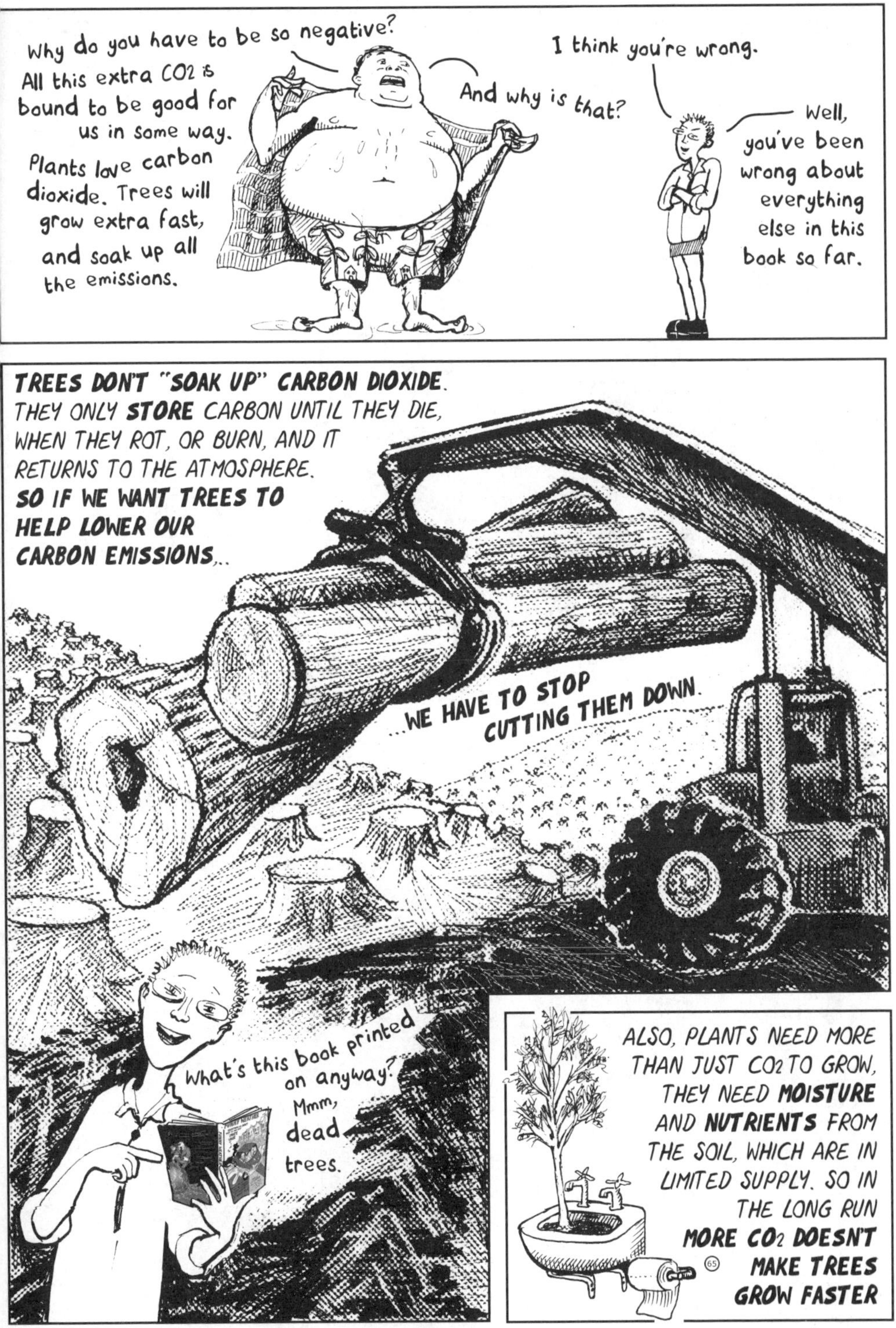
Why do you have to be so negative?
All this extra CO2 is bound to be good for us in some way. Plants love carbon dioxide. Trees will grow extra fast, and soak up all the emissions.
And why is that?
I think you're wrong.
Well, you've been wrong about everything else in this book so far.
TREES DON'T "SOAK UP" CARBON DIOXIDE. THEY ONLY STORE CARBON UNTIL THEY DIE, WHEN THEY ROT, OR BURN, AND IT RETURNS TO THE ATMOSPHERE. SO IF WE WANT TREES TO HELP LOWER OUR CARBON EMISSIONS...
...WE HAVE TO STOP CUTTING THEM DOWN.
What's this book printed on anyway? Mmm, dead trees.
ALSO, PLANTS NEED MORE THAN JUST CO2 TO GROW, THEY NEED MOISTURE AND NUTRIENTS FROM THE SOIL, WHICH ARE IN LIMITED SUPPLY. SO IN THE LONG RUN MORE CO2 DOESN'T MAKE TREES GROW FASTER
65

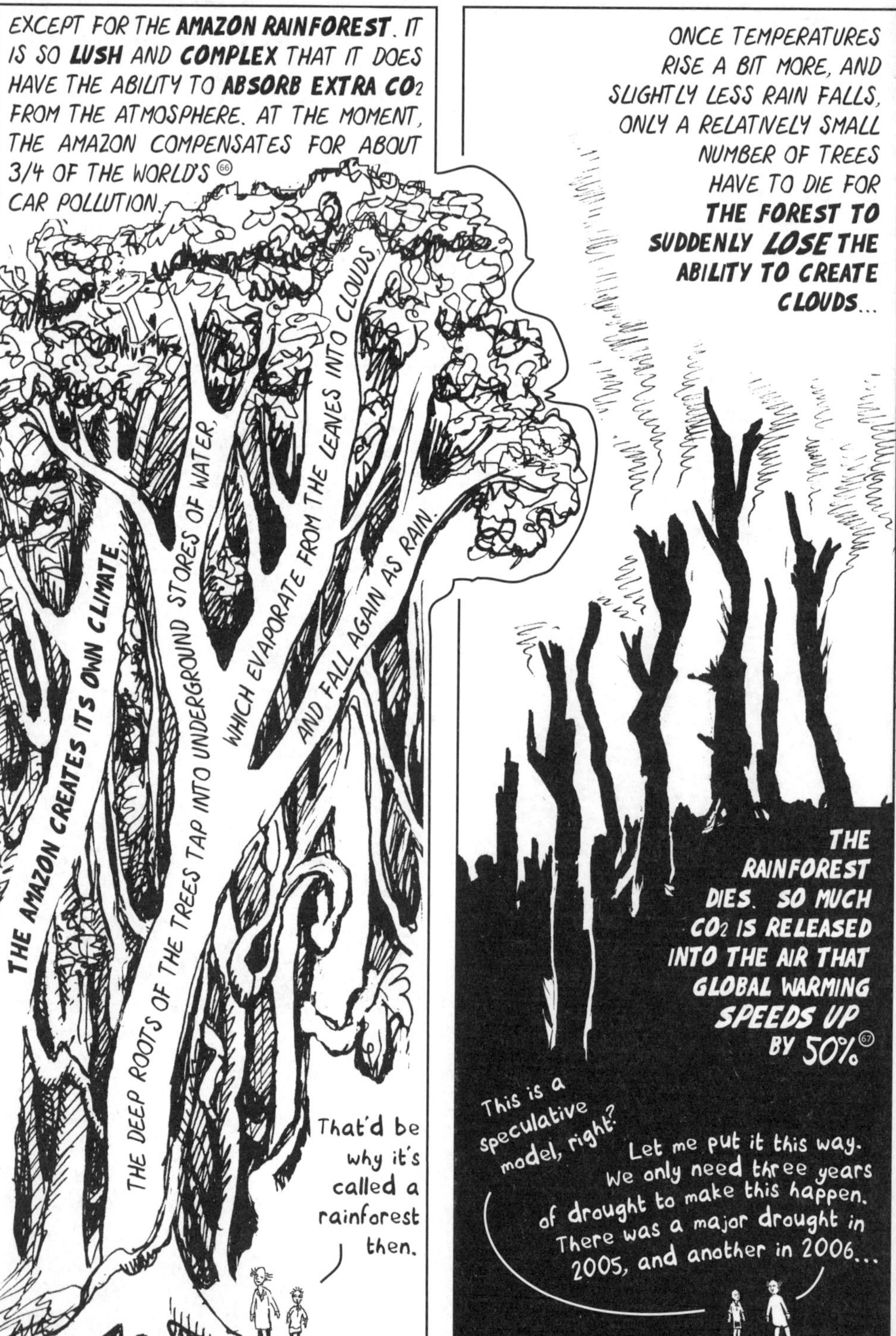
EXCEPT FOR THE AMAZON RAINFOREST. IT IS SO LUSH AND COMPLEX THAT IT DOES HAVE THE ABILITY TO ABSORB EXTRA CO_2 FROM THE ATMOSPHERE. AT THE MOMENT, THE AMAZON COMPENSATES FOR ABOUT 3/4 OF THE WORLD'S CAR POLLUTION.[66]
THE AMAZON CREATES ITS OWN CLIMATE.
THE DEEP ROOTS OF THE TREES TAP INTO UNDERGROUND STORES OF WATER,
WHICH EVAPORATE FROM THE LEAVES INTO CLOUDS,
AND FALL AGAIN AS RAIN.
That'd be why it's called a rainforest then.
ONCE TEMPERATURES RISE A BIT MORE, AND SLIGHTLY LESS RAIN FALLS, ONLY A RELATIVELY SMALL NUMBER OF TREES HAVE TO DIE FOR THE FOREST TO SUDDENLY LOSE THE ABILITY TO CREATE CLOUDS...
THE RAINFOREST DIES. SO MUCH CO_2 IS RELEASED INTO THE AIR THAT GLOBAL WARMING SPEEDS UP BY 50%[67]
This is a speculative model, right?
Let me put it this way. We only need three years of drought to make this happen. There was a major drought in 2005, and another in 2006...

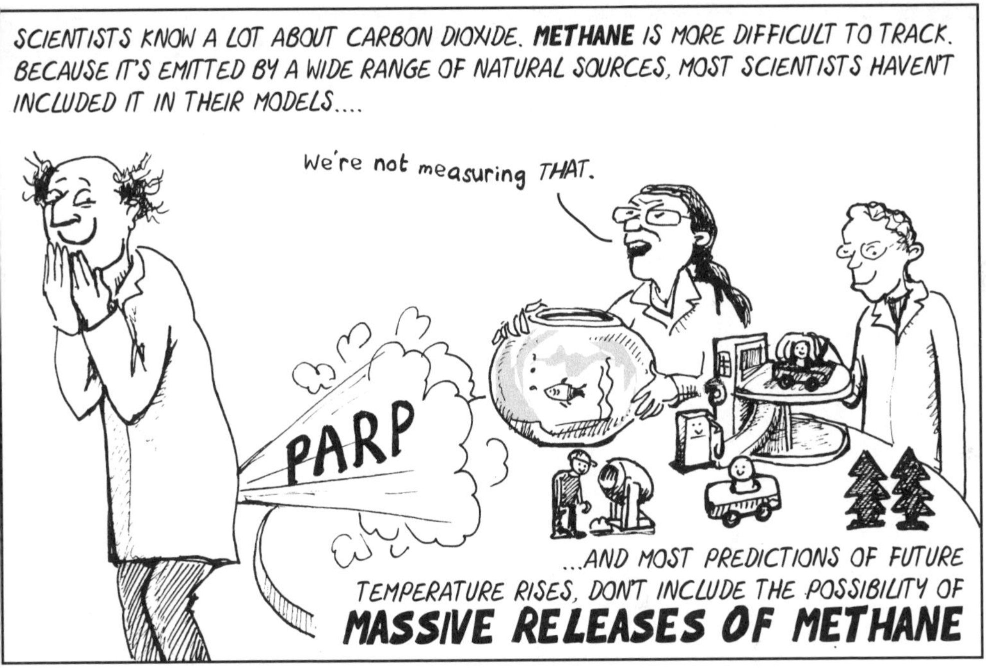
SCIENTISTS KNOW A LOT ABOUT CARBON DIOXIDE. **METHANE** IS MORE DIFFICULT TO TRACK. BECAUSE IT'S EMITTED BY A WIDE RANGE OF NATURAL SOURCES, MOST SCIENTISTS HAVEN'T INCLUDED IT IN THEIR MODELS....
We're not measuring THAT.
PARP
...AND MOST PREDICTIONS OF FUTURE TEMPERATURE RISES, DON'T INCLUDE THE POSSIBILITY OF
MASSIVE RELEASES OF METHANE

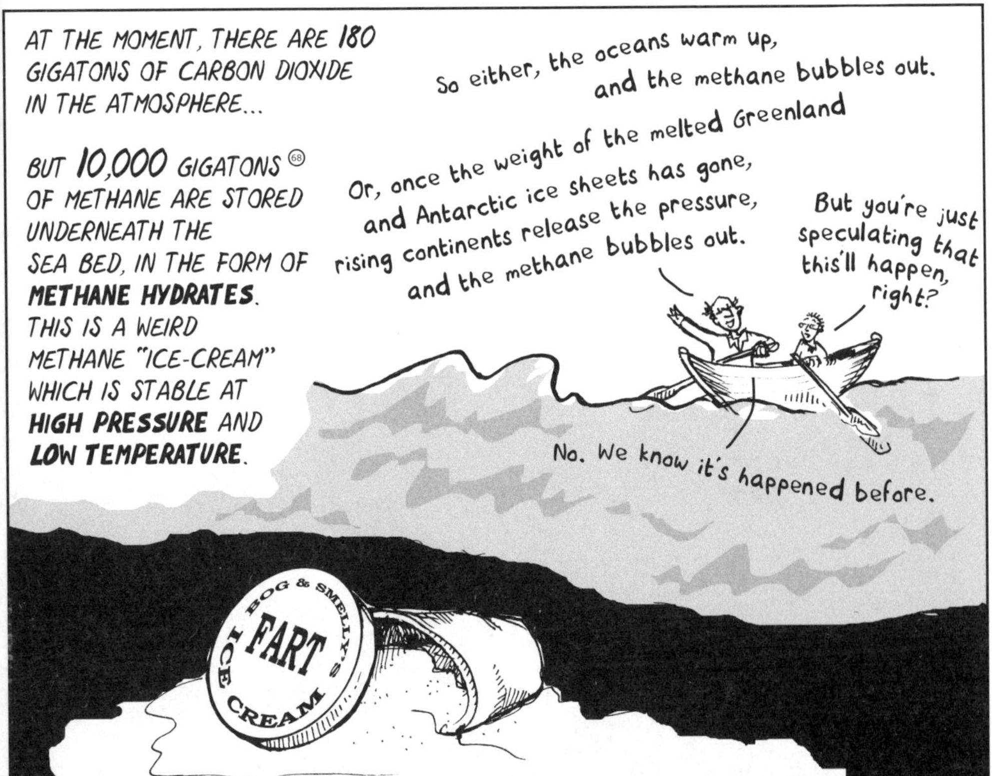
AT THE MOMENT, THERE ARE 180 GIGATONS OF CARBON DIOXIDE IN THE ATMOSPHERE...
BUT 10,000 GIGATONS [68] OF METHANE ARE STORED UNDERNEATH THE SEA BED, IN THE FORM OF **METHANE HYDRATES**. THIS IS A WEIRD METHANE "ICE-CREAM" WHICH IS STABLE AT **HIGH PRESSURE** AND **LOW TEMPERATURE**.
So either, the oceans warm up, and the methane bubbles out.
Or, once the weight of the melted Greenland and Antarctic ice sheets has gone, rising continents release the pressure, and the methane bubbles out.
But you're just speculating that this'll happen, right?
No. We know it's happened before.
BOG & SMELLY'S
FART
ICE CREAM

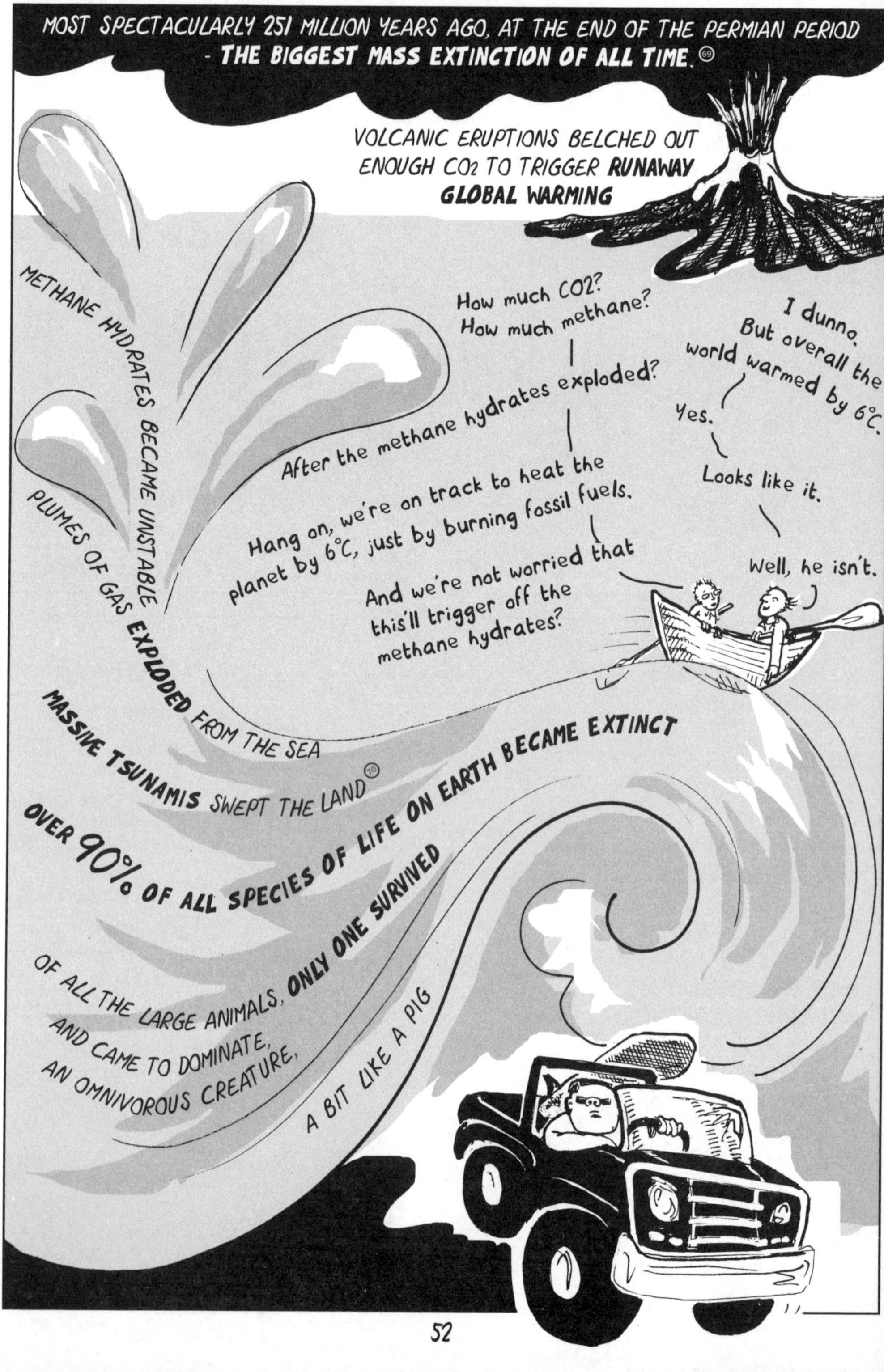

MOST SPECTACULARLY 251 MILLION YEARS AGO, AT THE END OF THE PERMIAN PERIOD - THE BIGGEST MASS EXTINCTION OF ALL TIME. (69)
VOLCANIC ERUPTIONS BELCHED OUT ENOUGH CO2 TO TRIGGER RUNAWAY GLOBAL WARMING
METHANE HYDRATES BECAME UNSTABLE
PLUMES OF GAS EXPLODED FROM THE SEA
MASSIVE TSUNAMIS SWEPT THE LAND (70)
OVER 90% OF ALL SPECIES OF LIFE ON EARTH BECAME EXTINCT
OF ALL THE LARGE ANIMALS, ONLY ONE SURVIVED
AND CAME TO DOMINATE,
AN OMNIVOROUS CREATURE,
A BIT LIKE A PIG
How much CO2? How much methane?
After the methane hydrates exploded?
I dunno. But overall the world warmed by 6°C.
Yes.
Hang on, we're on track to heat the planet by 6°C, just by burning fossil fuels.
Looks like it.
And we're not worried that this'll trigger off the methane hydrates?
Well, he isn't.

HANG ON A MINUTE. **THE EARTH TAKES A LONG TIME TO WARM UP**. WE'LL ONLY **START** TO SEE THE EFFECT OF TODAY'S EMISSIONS IN 40 YEARS TIME. AND IT TAKES **A THOUSAND YEARS** FOR THE OCEANS TO WARM UP FULLY. **IF WE WAIT** FOR IT TO GET 2°C WARMER, THEN **IT'LL BE TOO LATE**, WE'LL ALREADY BE **COMMITTED** TO MUCH MORE.

RIGHT NOW THERE'S ENOUGH GREENHOUSE GAS IN THE ATMOSPHERE TO CAUSE ANOTHER 0.8°C OF WARMING.[74]

IF WE ALL STOPPED EMITTING GREENHOUSE GASES TODAY, THEN THE WORLD WOULD STILL WARM UP AS MUCH AS IT ALREADY HAS, ALL OVER AGAIN.

SO WHAT TIMEFRAME ARE WE TALKING ABOUT FOR THIS 2°C RISE?

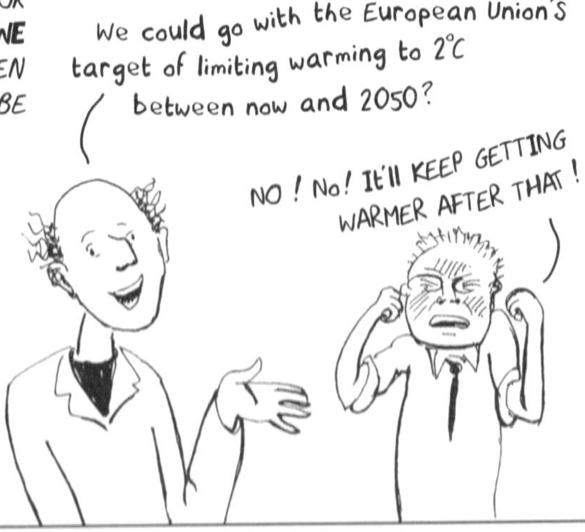
We could go with the European Union's target of limiting warming to 2°C between now and 2050?
NO! No! It'll KEEP GETTING WARMER AFTER THAT!

OK, 2°C IN 44 YEARS. NOW LET'S WORK OUT

WHAT LEVEL OF CARBON DIOXIDE WILL CAUSE THIS AMOUNT OF WARMING?[75]

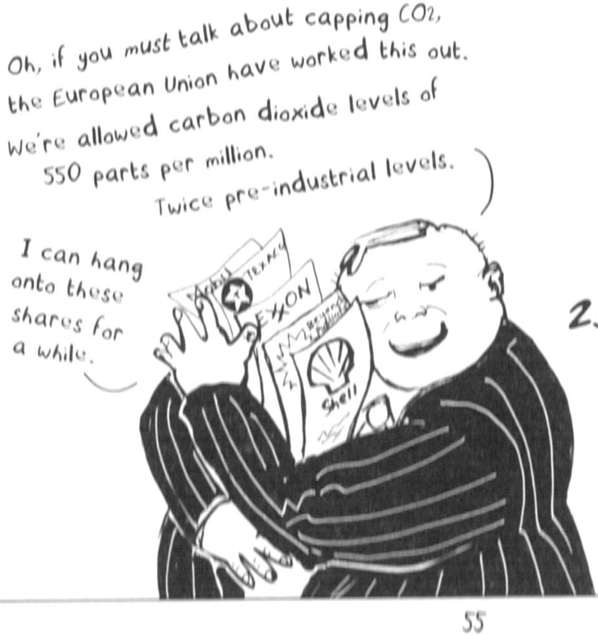
Oh, if you must talk about capping CO2, the European Union have worked this out. We're allowed carbon dioxide levels of 550 parts per million. Twice pre-industrial levels.
I can hang onto these shares for a while.
EXXON
Shell

THE EUROPEAN UNION HAS GOT ITS SUMS WRONG.[76] IF YOU TAKE **ALL THE PREDICTIONS** FROM **ALL THE MODELS**, AND **AVERAGE** THEM:

AT **550**ppm THERE'S A **75%** CHANCE THAT WARMING WILL EXCEED 2°C

AT **450**ppm THERE'S STILL A **50-50 CHANCE OF ARMAGEDDON**.

BUT IF WE LIMIT CO_2 CONCENTRATIONS TO **400**ppm THEN THERE'S **ONLY A 25% CHANCE OF (EXTREMELY) DANGEROUS CLIMATE CHANGE**. WHICH IS BETTER ODDS.

AT THE MOMENT, CO_2 LEVELS ARE NEARLY AT 380ppm. **WE'LL HAVE TO ACT FAST**.

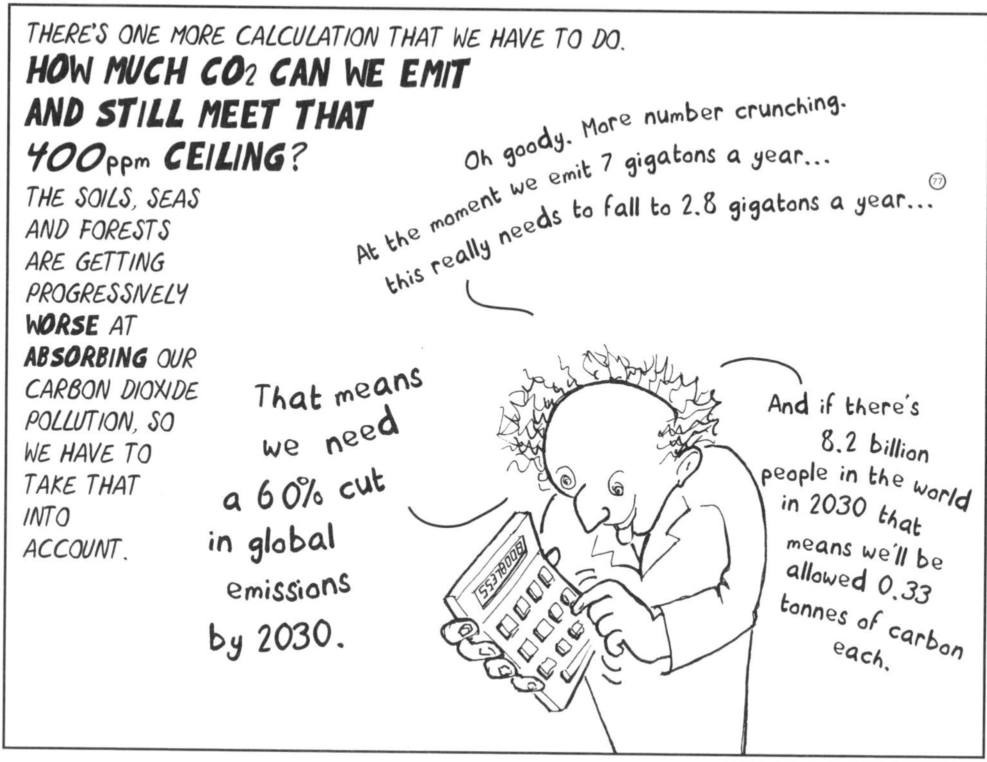
THERE'S ONE MORE CALCULATION THAT WE HAVE TO DO.
HOW MUCH CO_2 CAN WE EMIT AND STILL MEET THAT 400ppm CEILING?
THE SOILS, SEAS AND FORESTS ARE GETTING PROGRESSIVELY WORSE AT ABSORBING OUR CARBON DIOXIDE POLLUTION, SO WE HAVE TO TAKE THAT INTO ACCOUNT.
Oh goody. More number crunching.
At the moment we emit 7 gigatons a year...
this really needs to fall to 2.8 gigatons a year...[77]
That means we need a 60% cut in global emissions by 2030.
And if there's 8.2 billion people in the world in 2030 that means we'll be allowed 0.33 tonnes of carbon each.

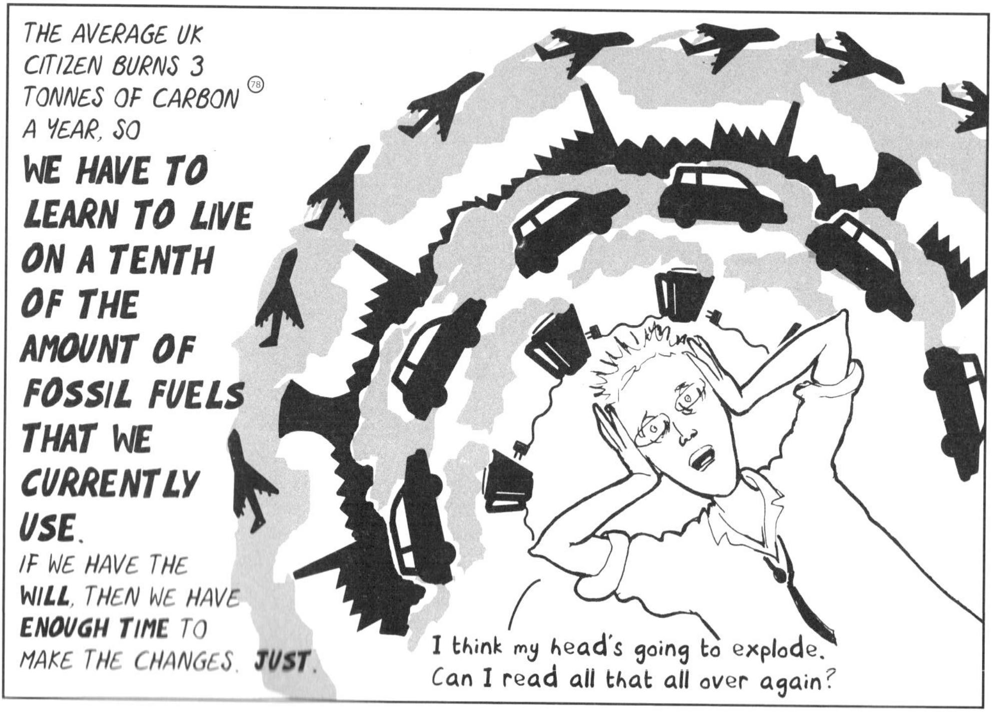
THE AVERAGE UK CITIZEN BURNS 3 TONNES OF CARBON[78] A YEAR, SO
WE HAVE TO LEARN TO LIVE ON A TENTH OF THE AMOUNT OF FOSSIL FUELS THAT WE CURRENTLY USE.
IF WE HAVE THE WILL, THEN WE HAVE ENOUGH TIME TO MAKE THE CHANGES. JUST.
I think my head's going to explode. Can I read all that all over again?

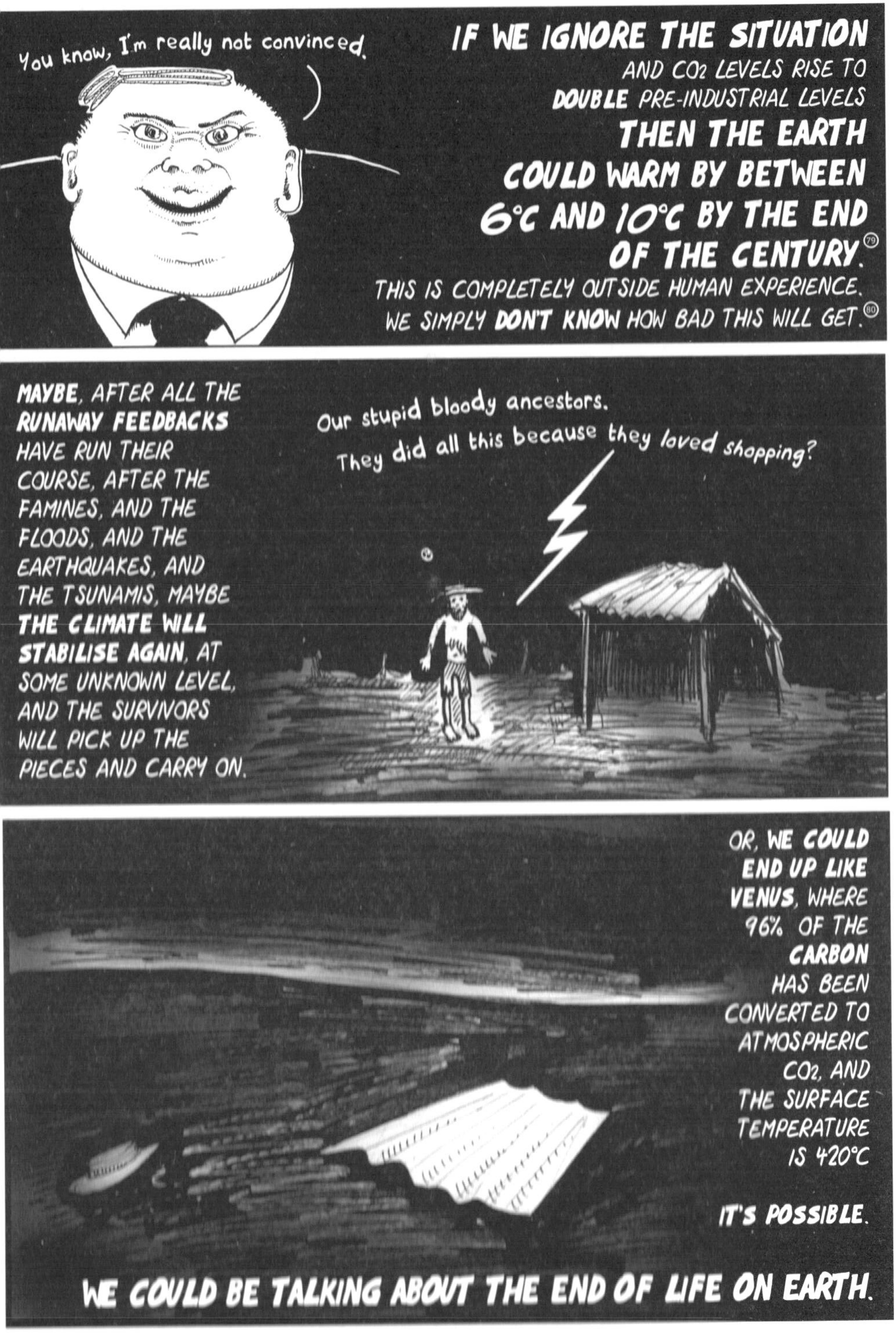

IF WE IGNORE THE SITUATION AND CO2 LEVELS RISE TO DOUBLE PRE-INDUSTRIAL LEVELS THEN THE EARTH COULD WARM BY BETWEEN 6°C AND 10°C BY THE END OF THE CENTURY.[79]
You know, I'm really not convinced.
THIS IS COMPLETELY OUTSIDE HUMAN EXPERIENCE. WE SIMPLY DON'T KNOW HOW BAD THIS WILL GET.[80]
MAYBE, AFTER ALL THE RUNAWAY FEEDBACKS HAVE RUN THEIR COURSE, AFTER THE FAMINES, AND THE FLOODS, AND THE EARTHQUAKES, AND THE TSUNAMIS, MAYBE THE CLIMATE WILL STABILISE AGAIN, AT SOME UNKNOWN LEVEL, AND THE SURVIVORS WILL PICK UP THE PIECES AND CARRY ON.
Our stupid bloody ancestors. They did all this because they loved shopping?
OR, WE COULD END UP LIKE VENUS, WHERE 96% OF THE CARBON HAS BEEN CONVERTED TO ATMOSPHERIC CO2, AND THE SURFACE TEMPERATURE IS 420°C
IT'S POSSIBLE.
WE COULD BE TALKING ABOUT THE END OF LIFE ON EARTH.

55) Carbon dioxide measurements, Mauna Loa Observatory, www.mlo.noaa.gov. This graph is an artistic representation.

56) "Global warming to speed up as carbon levels show sharp rise" *Independent on Sunday* 15/01/06.

57) Carbon sinks and emissions from B. Hare and M. Meinhausen *PIK Report* 93, 2004, Potsdam Institute for Climate Impact Research, reproduced in *The Cutting Edge: Climate Science to April 2005* Colin Forrest.

58) "Climate warning as Siberia melts" *New Scientist* 11/08/05.

59) "Vicious circle of emissions is speeding up climate change" *The Independent* 08/09/05 and "Soil may spoil UK's climate efforts" *New Scientist* 07/09/05.
See also M. Torn et al. of the Lawrence Berkely National Lab, US, who have factored the increase in soil emissions of CO2 into their climate models, and found that estimates of temperature rise by 3000 should be revised upwards to 7.7 degrees C. *Geophysical Research Letters*, reported in *The Guardian*, 23/05/06.

60) Peter Cox and Chris Jones, Hadley Centre etc.

61) Research by Jef Huisman et al. of the University of Amsterdam, published in *Nature* (*The Independent* 19/01/06)

62) "Fish numbers plummet in warming Pacific" *The Independent on Sunday* 13/11/05.

63) "Marine crisis looms over acidifying oceans" *New Scientist* 30/06/05, reporting research by John Raven of the University of Dundee, commissioned by the Royal Society.

64) CO2 solubility is basic physics.

65) Ram Oren et al, of Duke University, North Carolina, US, found that increasing CO2 levels stimulated trees to grow faster for around three years, but that after this period they reverted to normal rates of growth. (*New Scientist* 23/05/01)

66) Mark Maslin, *Global Warming*, p 62.

67) According to Peter Cox of the UK's Met Office Hadley Centre for Climate Prediction (*New Scientist* 22/11/03).

68) Mark Maslin, *Global Warming*, p 61.

69) The role of methane hydrates in the end-Permian extinctions is explored by palaeontologist Michael Benton in his book *When Life Nearly Died*. See also "Shadow of extinction" George Monbiot, *The Guardian,* 1/7/2003. "Also see the Palaeocene-Eocene Thermal Maximum (PETM) extinction, a short intense period of global warming about 55 million years ago when a huge amount of methane burped out of the ocean causing run-away global warming. An extra 5 degrees C was added to an already very very warm world. It took about 100,000 years for that extra carbon to be removed from the atmosphere." Mark Maslin, by email.

70) The Storegga slide, a massive, methane-hydrate induced tsunami, inundated the Shetland Isles with 20 metres of water 7080 years ago, wiping out settlements of Mesolithic people along the Scottish coast. (*New Scientist* 04/08/90)

71) "Record ice core gives fair forecast" *New Scientist* 09/06/04.

72) "Doomsday scenario", Fred Pearce, *New Scientist* 22/11/03. Verified by Mark Maslin.

73) A 2 degree C rise by 2150 is proposed in "Stabilising climate to avoid dangerous climate change - a summary of relevant research at the Hadley Centre" Jan 2005. 2 degrees C seems to be a common, unofficial 'best guess' amongst future climate scenarios for limiting global warming, although the timeframes for the projected 2 degree C rise vary.

74) "Scientific results from the Hadley Centre 2002" contains the calculation that, as of 2002, levels of greenhouse gases have committed the earth to 1.1 degrees C of warming by 2100, and 1.6 degrees C of warming overall, relative to pre-industrial times. I have subtracted the 0.8 degrees C of warming that has already occurred from the 1.6 degree C, long-term, overall figure.

75) Just to make it all extra confusing, some climate calculations talk about carbon dioxide levels, and some use a measure of the warming effect of all greenhouse gases, expressed as their equivalent as CO2 - "CO2 equivalent". I am talking about straight carbon dioxide here, and ignoring the other warming gases.

76) Calculations by Malte Meinshausen from the Swiss Federal Institute of Technology in Zurich, Switzerland. (*New Scientist* 03/02/05)

77) These calculations are from the summary of *The Cutting Edge: Climate Science to April 2005* by Colin Forrest.

78) There are two sets of figures regarding personal emissions too. Some authorities talk about tonnes of carbon dioxide emitted, which is heavier (the weight of the extra oxygen molecules). To convert carbon to carbon dioxide, multiply it by 44, then divide it by 12.

79) These figures greatly exceed the predictions of the last IPCC report in 2001. They are from three leading climatologists, Meinrat Andrae of the Max Planck Institute for Chemistry in Mainz, Germany, and Peter Cox and Chris Jones of the UK Met Office's Hadley Centre. The predictions are based on an analysis of the temporary cooling effect of aerosols currently in the atmosphere. If these are greater than previously estimated, then the warming effect when they disperse will be more severe. The study combines this assesment of aerosol cooling effect with an analysis of the the effect of the natural carbon cycle (reduced uptake of CO2 from trees, soils and oceans) to arrive at the higher end figure. (*Nature*, vol 435, 2005, reported in *New Scientist* 29/06/05)

80) In discussing the consequence of a greater than 6 C temperature rise, Meinrat Andrae commented that "It is so far outside the range covered by our experience and scientific understanding that we cannot with any confidence predict the consequences for the Earth" (source: as above).

Chapter 3
WHAT ARE WE DOING?

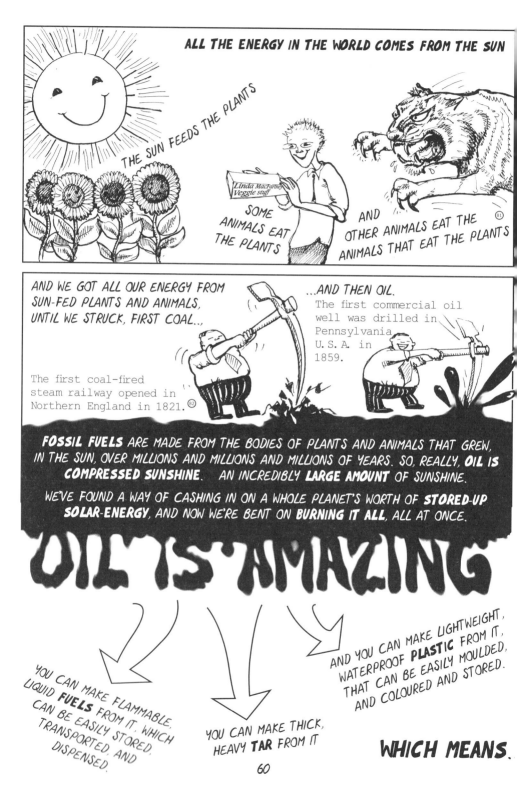

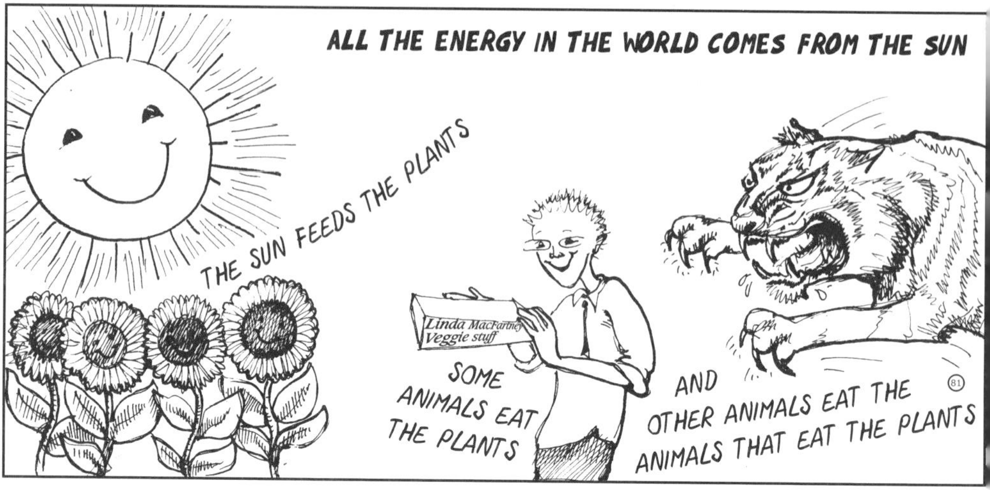
ALL THE ENERGY IN THE WORLD COMES FROM THE SUN
THE SUN FEEDS THE PLANTS
Linda MacCartney Veggie stuff
SOME ANIMALS EAT THE PLANTS
AND OTHER ANIMALS EAT THE ANIMALS THAT EAT THE PLANTS
81

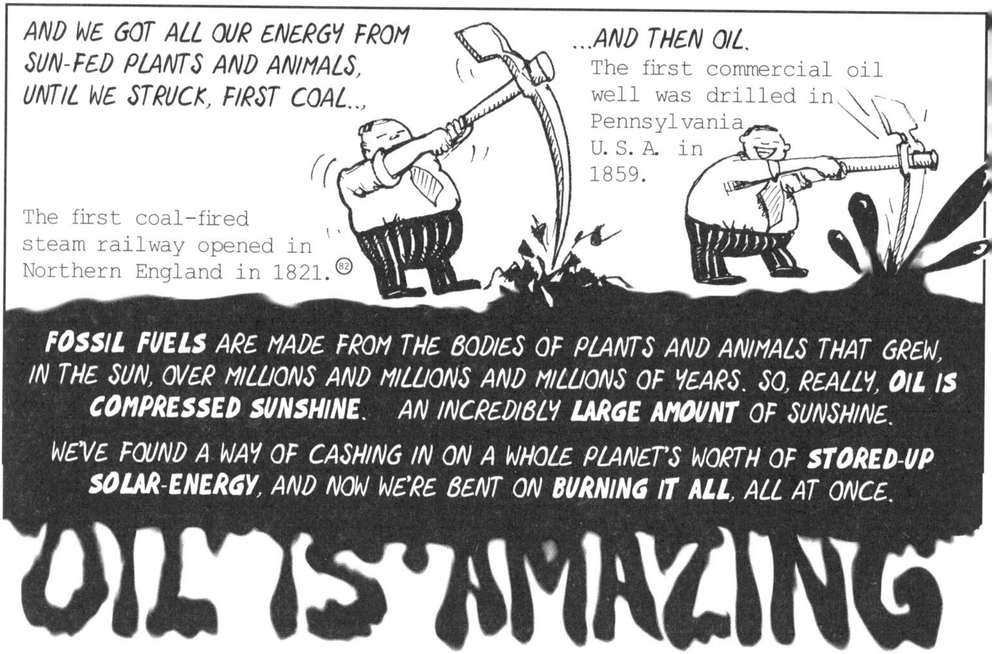
AND WE GOT ALL OUR ENERGY FROM SUN-FED PLANTS AND ANIMALS, UNTIL WE STRUCK, FIRST COAL..,
The first coal-fired steam railway opened in Northern England in 1821. 82
...AND THEN OIL.
The first commercial oil well was drilled in Pennsylvania U.S.A. in 1859.
FOSSIL FUELS ARE MADE FROM THE BODIES OF PLANTS AND ANIMALS THAT GREW, IN THE SUN, OVER MILLIONS AND MILLIONS AND MILLIONS OF YEARS. SO, REALLY, **OIL IS COMPRESSED SUNSHINE**. AN INCREDIBLY **LARGE AMOUNT** OF SUNSHINE.
WE'VE FOUND A WAY OF CASHING IN ON A WHOLE PLANET'S WORTH OF **STORED-UP SOLAR-ENERGY**, AND NOW WE'RE BENT ON **BURNING IT ALL**, ALL AT ONCE.

OIL IS AMAZING

YOU CAN MAKE FLAMMABLE, LIQUID **FUELS** FROM IT, WHICH CAN BE EASILY STORED, TRANSPORTED, AND DISPENSED.

YOU CAN MAKE THICK, HEAVY **TAR** FROM IT

AND YOU CAN MAKE LIGHTWEIGHT, WATERPROOF **PLASTIC** FROM IT, THAT CAN BE EASILY MOULDED, AND COLOURED AND STORED.

WHICH MEANS.

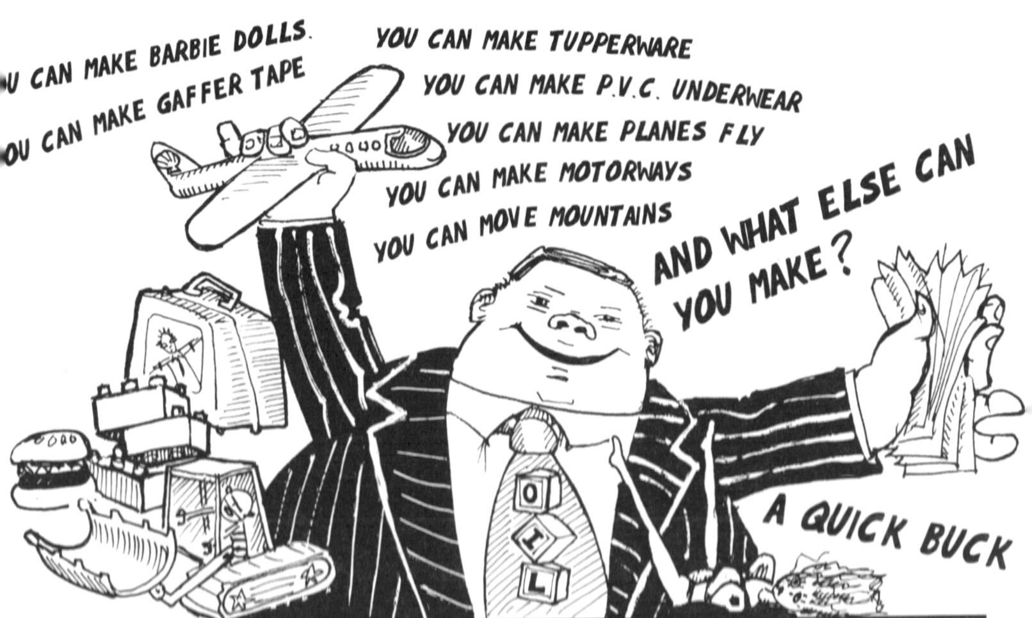

U CAN MAKE BARBIE DOLLS.
OU CAN MAKE GAFFER TAPE
YOU CAN MAKE TUPPERWARE
YOU CAN MAKE P.V.C. UNDERWEAR
YOU CAN MAKE PLANES FLY
YOU CAN MAKE MOTORWAYS
YOU CAN MOVE MOUNTAINS
AND WHAT ELSE CAN YOU MAKE?
A QUICK BUCK
OIL

BECAUSE OIL IS SO **USEFUL**, IT IS INCREDIBLY **PROFITABLE**. WHICH MEANS THAT OIL PRODUCING COMPANIES AND NATIONS ARE INCREDIBLY **RICH**, AND **POWERFUL**. AND THEY USE THAT POWER TO **CARRY ON GETTING RICHER**, BY **ENCOURAGING** OUR TENDENCY TO **USE**, AND TO **WASTE**, **MORE AND MORE OIL**.

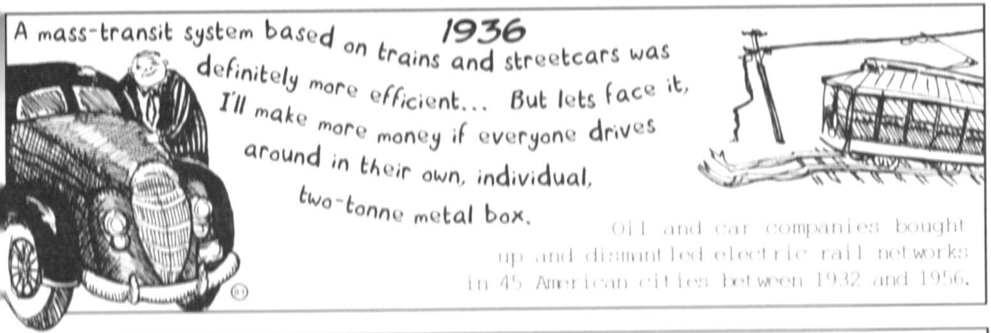

1936
A mass-transit system based on trains and streetcars was definitely more efficient... But lets face it, I'll make more money if everyone drives around in their own, individual, two-tonne metal box.
Oil and car companies bought up and dismantled electric rail networks in 45 American cities between 1932 and 1956.

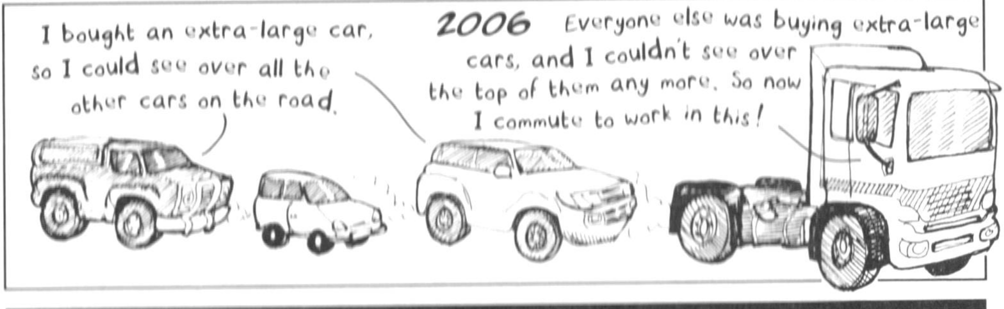

2006
I bought an extra-large car, so I could see over all the other cars on the road.
Everyone else was buying extra-large cars, and I couldn't see over the top of them any more. So now I commute to work in this!

WE'RE BURNING A **MILLION YEARS** WORTH OF STORED SOLAR ENERGY, **EVERY YEAR**. THIS **INCREDIBLE OIL BONANZA** HAS BEEN A LOT OF **FUN**, BUT IT'S **NOT EXACTLY SENSIBLE**.

2005 PROFITS - EXXON MOBIL: 36.13 BILLION DOLLARS... SHELL: 22.94 BILLION DOLLARS... BP: 19.31 BILLION DOLLARS... TOTAL: 14.6 BILLION DOLLARS... CHEVRON: 14 BILLION DOLLARS... CONOCOPHILLIPS: 13.5 BILLION DOLLARS.

OIL COMPANIES DON'T REALLY RUN THE WORLD.

WE LIVE IN A DEMOCRACY.

OIL AND GAS INDUSTRY DONATIONS TO U.S. POLITICAL PARTIES - 2000: DEMOCRATS $7,046,406 REPUBLICANS $26,794,056... 2002: DEMOCRATS $5,014,182 REPUBLICANS $19,899,682... [84] 2004: DEMOCRATS $5,014,182 REPUBLICANS $20,580839 2006: DEMOCRATS $1,663,027 REPUBLICANS $8,495,192 so far...

AND THE INTERNATIONAL COMMUNITY **HAS** MADE AN EFFORT TO ADDRESS THE PROBLEM OF CLIMATE CHANGE. IN 1992, THE **UNITED NATIONS FRAMEWORK CONVENTION ON CLIMATE CHANGE** WAS CREATED, AND IN 1997, INDUSTRIALISED NATIONS SIGNED UP TO

THE KYOTO PROTOCOL

THEY AGREED TO **FREEZE EMISSIONS** AT 1990 LEVELS, AND THEN, TO **REDUCE** THE RATE AT WHICH WE'RE EMITTING GREENHOUSE GASES BY A WHOPPING **5.4%** BY 2010. IT'S TAKEN NEARLY **TEN YEARS** FOR ENOUGH COUNTRIES TO RATIFY IT FOR IT TO ACTUALLY BECOME LEGALLY BINDING, BUT STILL, **IT'S A START**.

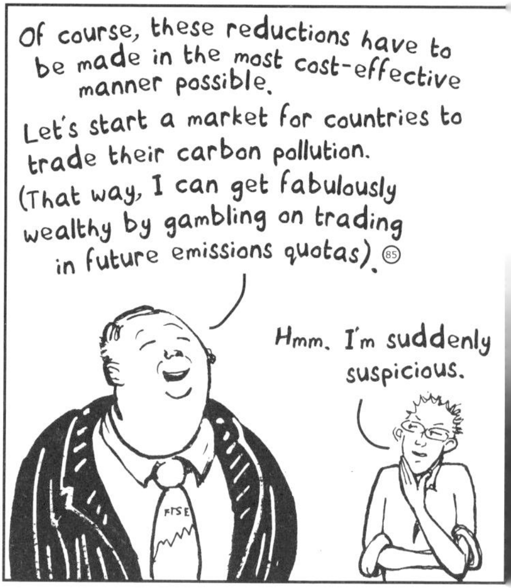
Of course, these reductions have to be made in the most cost-effective manner possible.
Let's start a market for countries to trade their carbon pollution.
(That way, I can get fabulously wealthy by gambling on trading in future emissions quotas). [85]
FTSE
Hmm. I'm suddenly suspicious.

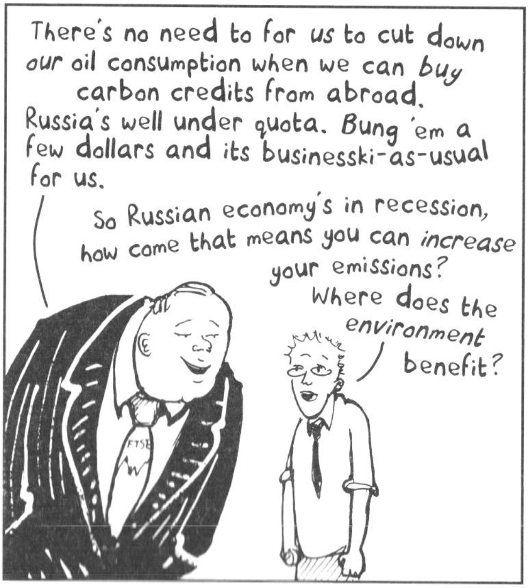
There's no need to for us to cut down our oil consumption when we can buy carbon credits from abroad.
Russia's well under quota. Bung 'em a few dollars and its businesski-as-usual for us.
So Russian economy's in recession, how come that means you can increase your emissions?
Where does the environment benefit?
FTSE

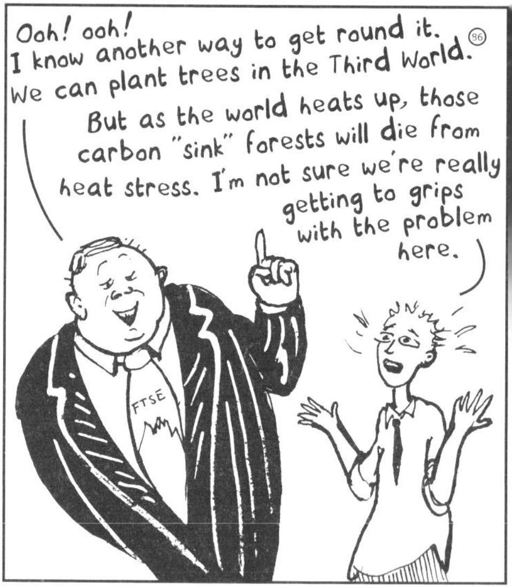
Ooh! ooh!
I know another way to get round it. [86]
We can plant trees in the Third World.
But as the world heats up, those carbon "sink" forests will die from heat stress. I'm not sure we're really getting to grips with the problem here.
FTSE

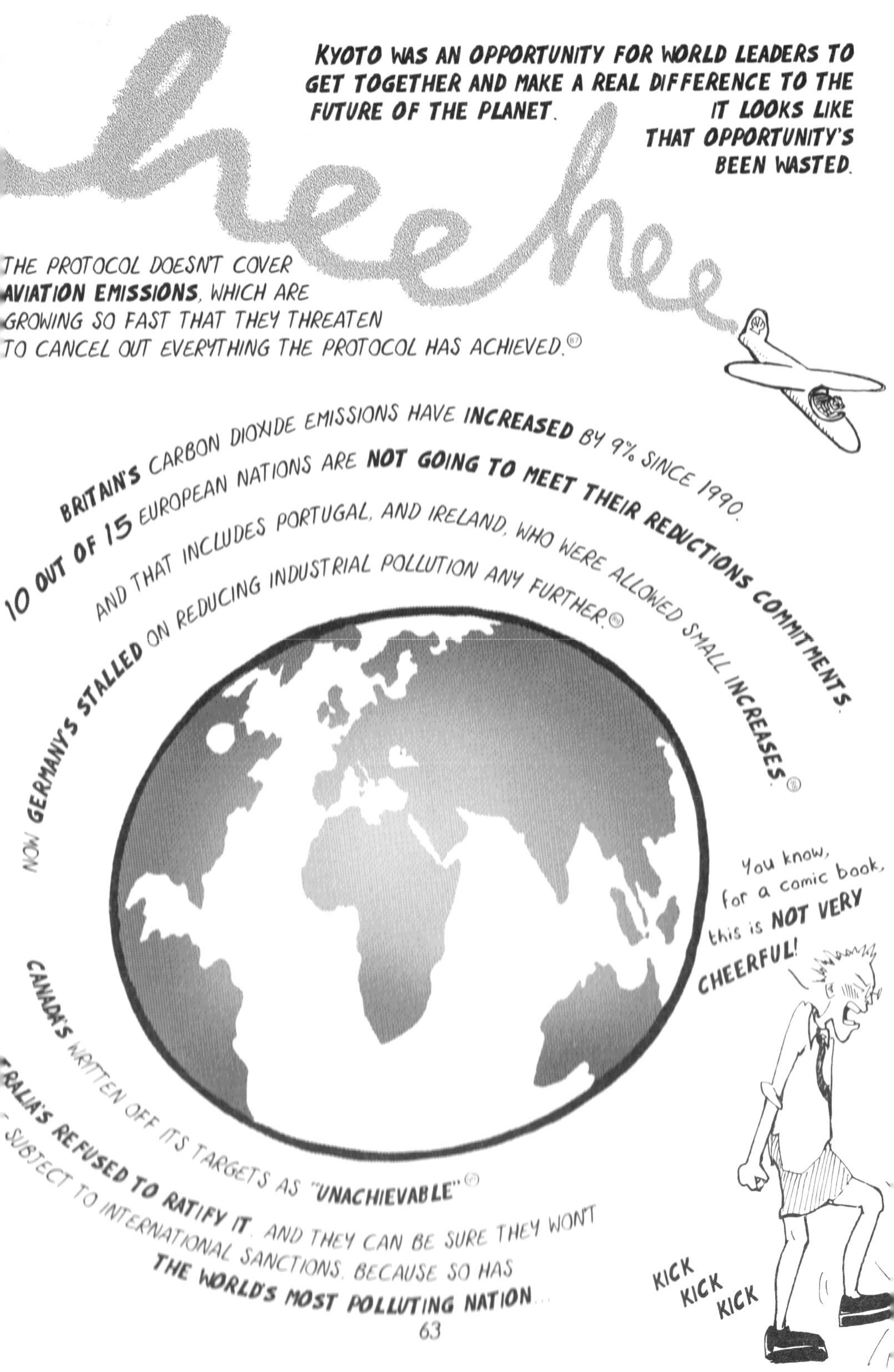
KYOTO WAS AN OPPORTUNITY FOR WORLD LEADERS TO GET TOGETHER AND MAKE A REAL DIFFERENCE TO THE FUTURE OF THE PLANET.
IT LOOKS LIKE THAT OPPORTUNITY'S BEEN WASTED.
heeheehee
THE PROTOCOL DOESN'T COVER **AVIATION EMISSIONS**, WHICH ARE GROWING SO FAST THAT THEY THREATEN TO CANCEL OUT EVERYTHING THE PROTOCOL HAS ACHIEVED.[87]
BRITAIN'S CARBON DIOXIDE EMISSIONS HAVE **INCREASED** BY 9% SINCE 1990.
10 OUT OF 15 EUROPEAN NATIONS ARE **NOT GOING TO MEET THEIR REDUCTIONS COMMITMENTS**.
AND THAT INCLUDES PORTUGAL, AND IRELAND, WHO WERE ALLOWED SMALL **INCREASES**.
NOW **GERMANY'S STALLED** ON REDUCING INDUSTRIAL POLLUTION ANY FURTHER.
CANADA'S WRITTEN OFF ITS TARGETS AS **"UNACHIEVABLE"**
TRALIA'S REFUSED TO RATIFY IT, AND THEY CAN BE SURE THEY WON'T
SUBJECT TO INTERNATIONAL SANCTIONS, BECAUSE SO HAS
THE WORLD'S MOST POLLUTING NATION...
You know, for a comic book, this is **NOT VERY CHEERFUL!**
KICK KICK KICK

THE UNITED STATES HAS 4% OF THE WORLD'S POPULATION AND EMITS 24% OF ITS GREENHOUSE GASES

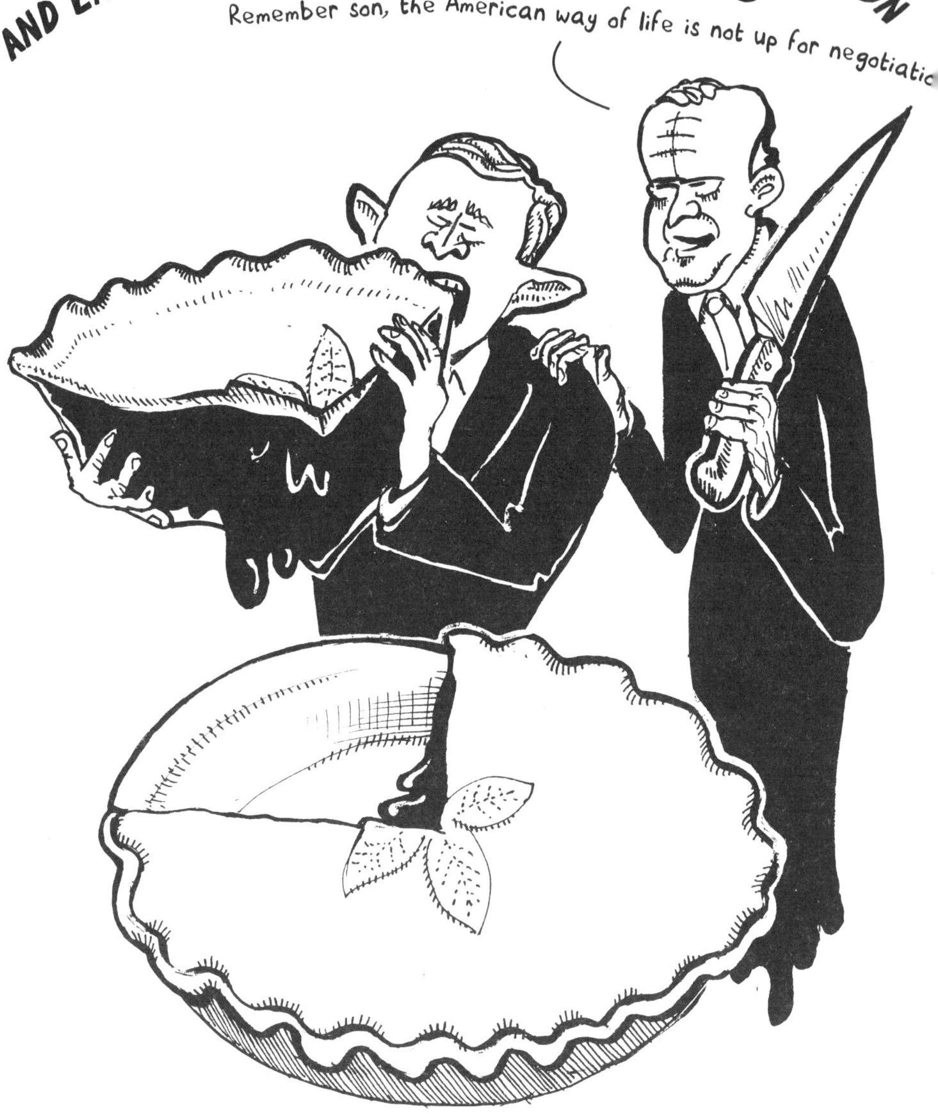
Remember son, the American way of life is not up for negotiatic

THE U.S. GOVERNMENT HAS RENOUNCED THE KYOTO PROTOCOL, AND REFUSES TO TAKE PART IN ANY NEGOTIATIONS WHICH WOULD LEAD TO NEW, BINDING COMMITMENTS.

AMERICA EXPECTS THE RATE AT WHICH IT PUMPS OUT CO_2 TO **INCREASE** BY MORE THAN A **THIRD** BY 2025.[93]

WHICH BEGS THE QUESTION,
WHY ARE THEY OCCUPYING **IRAQ**, ONE OF THE 3 MOST OIL-RICH COUNTRIES IN THE WORLD?

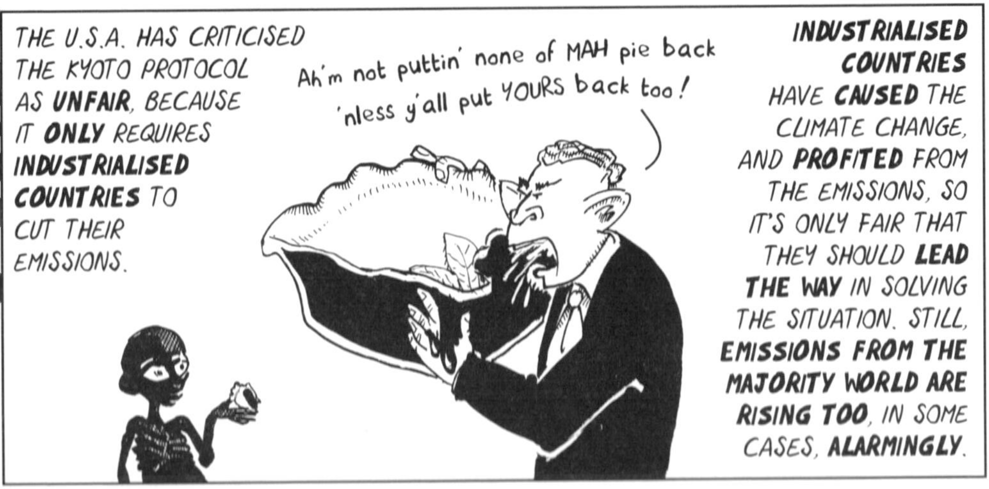
THE U.S.A. HAS CRITICISED THE KYOTO PROTOCOL AS UNFAIR, BECAUSE IT ONLY REQUIRES INDUSTRIALISED COUNTRIES TO CUT THEIR EMISSIONS.
Ah'm not puttin' none of MAH pie back 'nless y'all put YOURS back too!
INDUSTRIALISED COUNTRIES HAVE CAUSED THE CLIMATE CHANGE, AND PROFITED FROM THE EMISSIONS, SO IT'S ONLY FAIR THAT THEY SHOULD LEAD THE WAY IN SOLVING THE SITUATION. STILL, EMISSIONS FROM THE MAJORITY WORLD ARE RISING TOO, IN SOME CASES, ALARMINGLY.

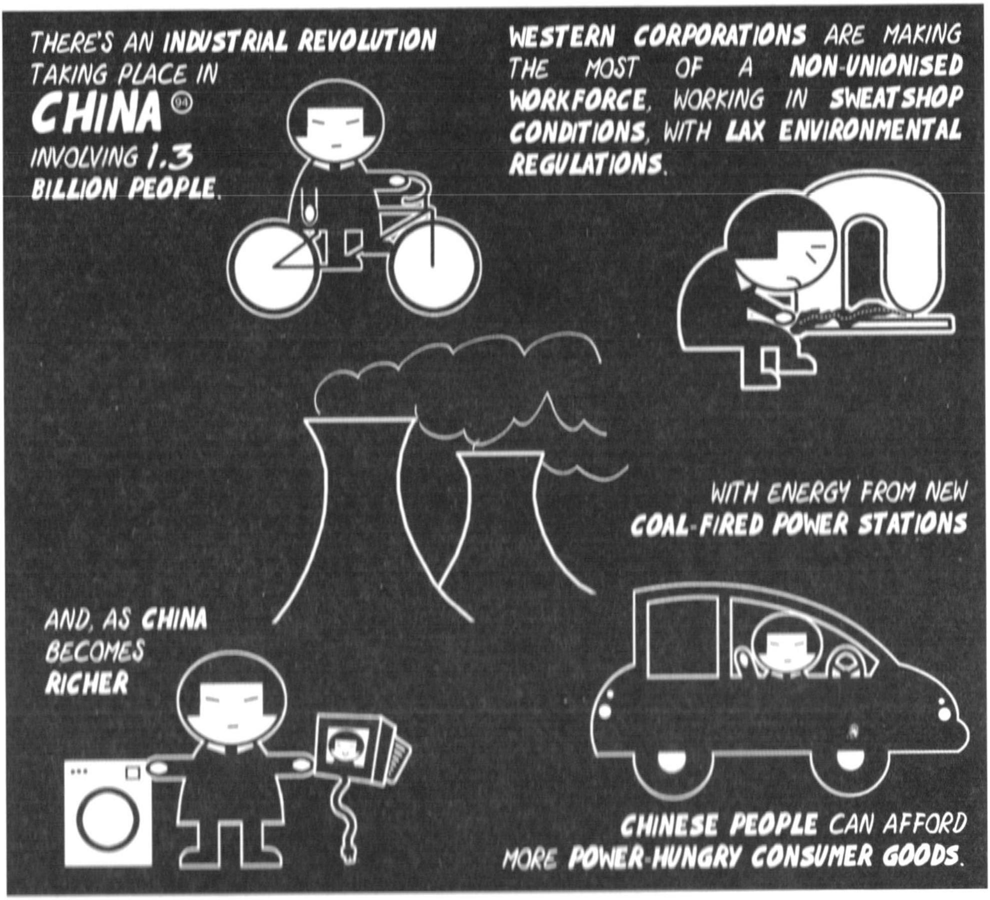
THERE'S AN INDUSTRIAL REVOLUTION TAKING PLACE IN CHINA [94] INVOLVING 1.3 BILLION PEOPLE.
WESTERN CORPORATIONS ARE MAKING THE MOST OF A NON-UNIONISED WORKFORCE, WORKING IN SWEATSHOP CONDITIONS, WITH LAX ENVIRONMENTAL REGULATIONS.
WITH ENERGY FROM NEW COAL-FIRED POWER STATIONS
AND, AS CHINA BECOMES RICHER
CHINESE PEOPLE CAN AFFORD MORE POWER-HUNGRY CONSUMER GOODS.

HILE WESTERN NATIONS ARE UNWILLING TO MEET THEIR LIMITED KYOTO COMMITMENTS, HERE IS THE INCENTIVE FOR OTHER COUNTRIES TO CURB FOSSIL-FUEL USE?

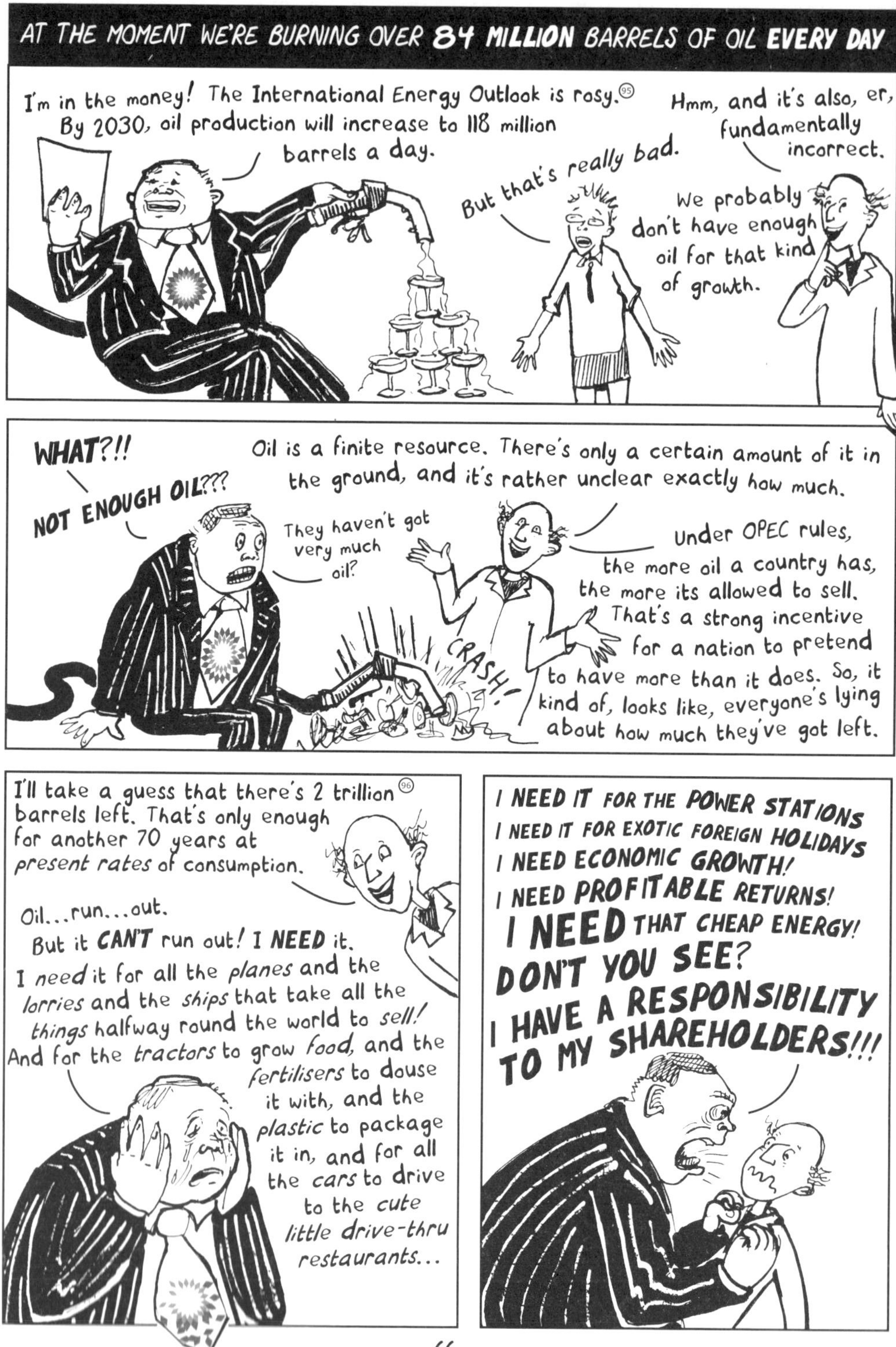
AT THE MOMENT WE'RE BURNING OVER 84 MILLION BARRELS OF OIL EVERY DAY
I'm in the money! The International Energy Outlook is rosy.[95] By 2030, oil production will increase to 118 million barrels a day.
But that's really bad.
Hmm, and it's also, er, fundamentally incorrect.
We probably don't have enough oil for that kind of growth.
WHAT?!!
NOT ENOUGH OIL???
Oil is a finite resource. There's only a certain amount of it in the ground, and it's rather unclear exactly how much.
They haven't got very much oil?
CRASH!
Under OPEC rules, the more oil a country has, the more its allowed to sell. That's a strong incentive for a nation to pretend to have more than it does. So, it kind of, looks like, everyone's lying about how much they've got left.
I'll take a guess that there's 2 trillion[96] barrels left. That's only enough for another 70 years at present rates of consumption.
Oil... run... out.
But it CAN'T run out! I NEED it.
I need it for all the planes and the lorries and the ships that take all the things halfway round the world to sell! And for the tractors to grow food, and the fertilisers to douse it with, and the plastic to package it in, and for all the cars to drive to the cute little drive-thru restaurants...
I NEED IT FOR THE POWER STATIONS
I NEED IT FOR EXOTIC FOREIGN HOLIDAYS
I NEED ECONOMIC GROWTH!
I NEED PROFITABLE RETURNS!
I NEED THAT CHEAP ENERGY!
DON'T YOU SEE?
I HAVE A RESPONSIBILITY TO MY SHAREHOLDERS!!!

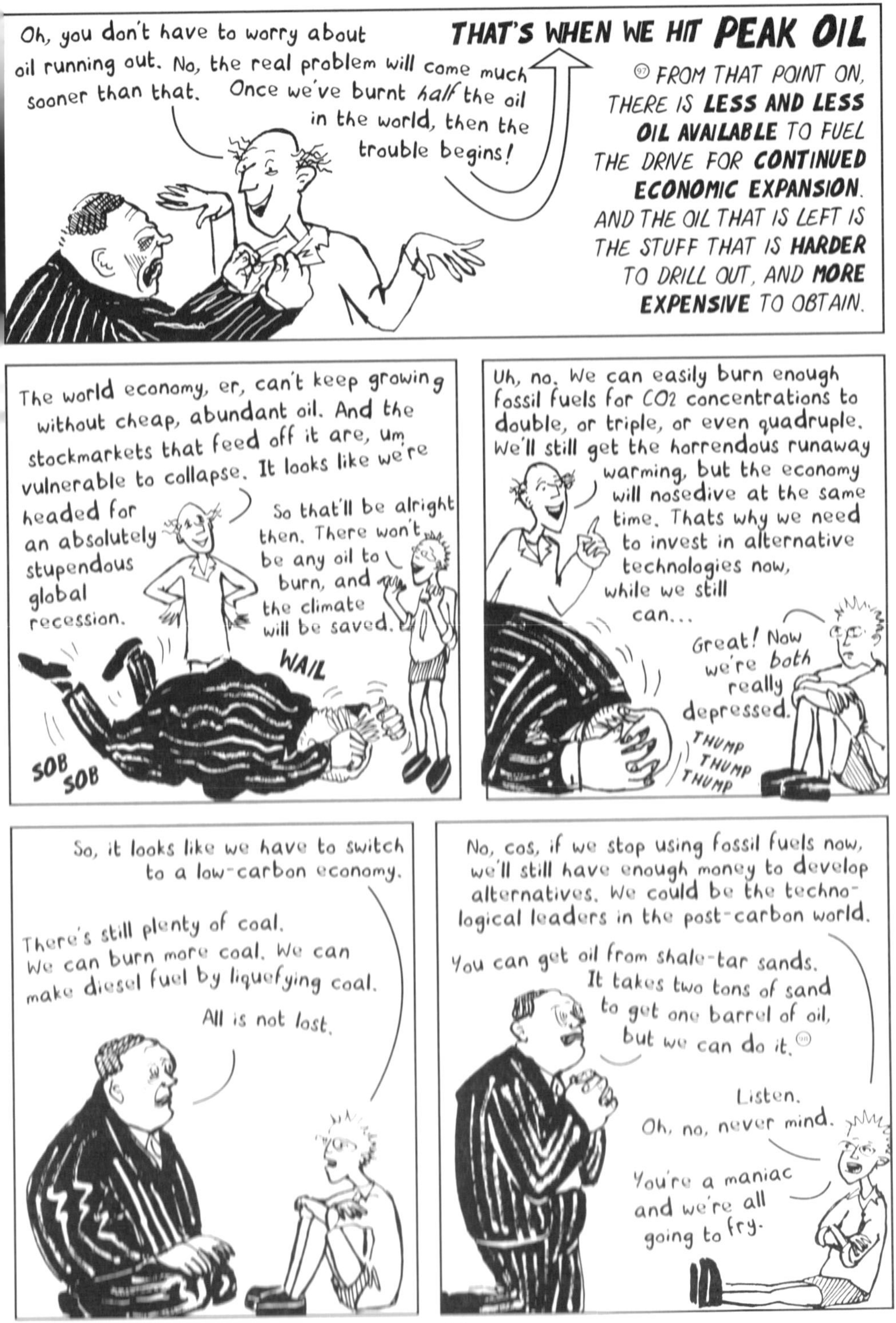

Oh, you don't have to worry about oil running out. No, the real problem will come much sooner than that. Once we've burnt *half* the oil in the world, then the trouble begins!
THAT'S WHEN WE HIT **PEAK OIL**
[97] FROM THAT POINT ON, THERE IS **LESS AND LESS OIL AVAILABLE** TO FUEL THE DRIVE FOR **CONTINUED ECONOMIC EXPANSION**. AND THE OIL THAT IS LEFT IS THE STUFF THAT IS **HARDER** TO DRILL OUT, AND **MORE EXPENSIVE** TO OBTAIN.
The world economy, er, can't keep growing without cheap, abundant oil. And the stockmarkets that feed off it are, um vulnerable to collapse. It looks like we're headed for an absolutely stupendous global recession.
So that'll be alright then. There won't be any oil to burn, and the climate will be saved.
WAIL
SOB SOB
Uh, no. We can easily burn enough fossil fuels for CO_2 concentrations to double, or triple, or even quadruple. We'll still get the horrendous runaway warming, but the economy will nosedive at the same time. Thats why we need to invest in alternative technologies now, while we still can...
Great! Now we're *both* really depressed.
THUMP THUMP THUMP
So, it looks like we have to switch to a low-carbon economy.
There's still plenty of coal. We can burn more coal. We can make diesel fuel by liquefying coal.
All is not lost.
No, cos, if we stop using fossil fuels now, we'll still have enough money to develop alternatives. We could be the techno-logical leaders in the post-carbon world.
You can get oil from shale-tar sands. It takes two tons of sand to get one barrel of oil, but we can do it. [98]
Listen.
Oh, no, never mind.
You're a maniac and we're all going to fry.

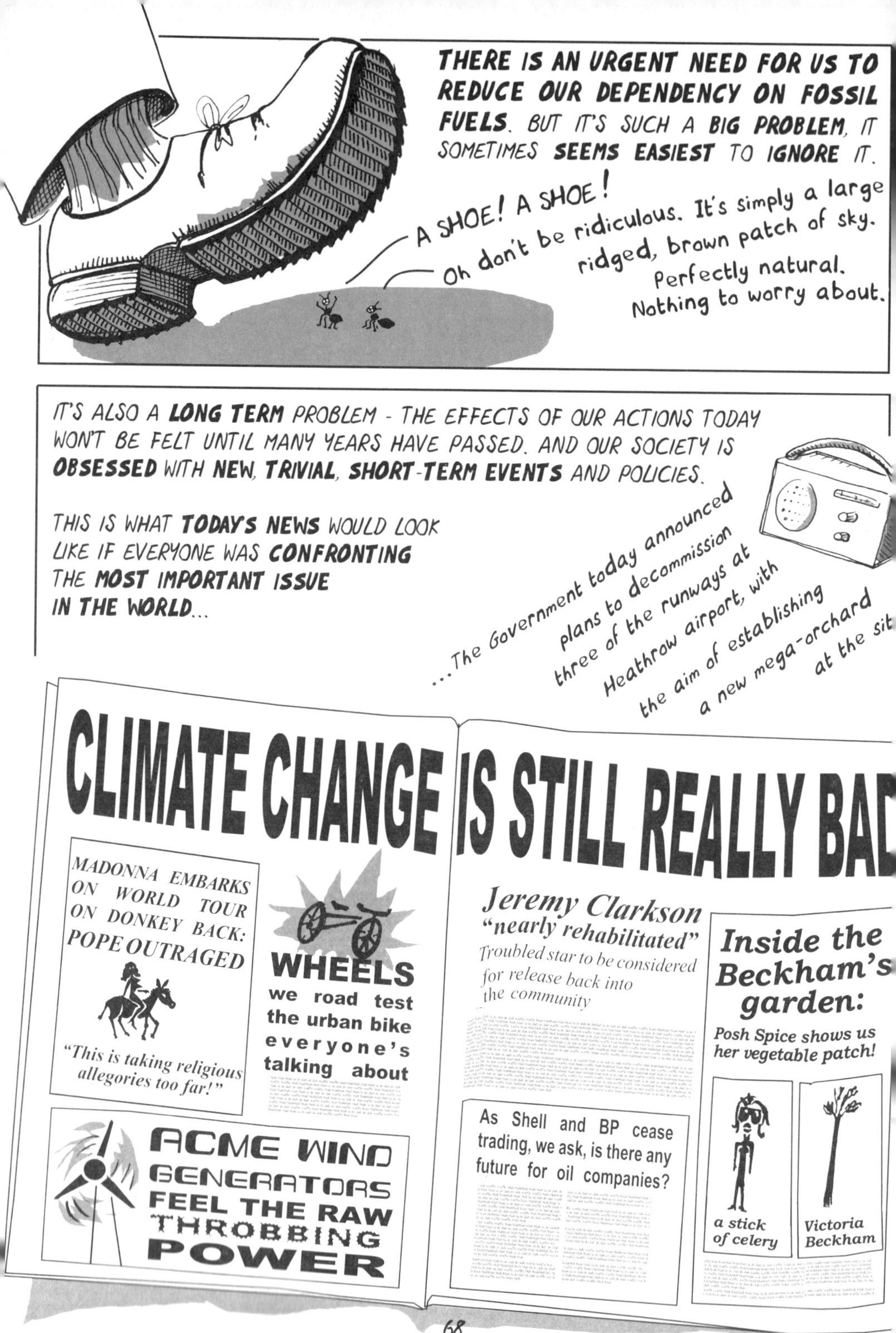
THERE IS AN URGENT NEED FOR US TO REDUCE OUR DEPENDENCY ON FOSSIL FUELS. BUT IT'S SUCH A BIG PROBLEM, IT SOMETIMES SEEMS EASIEST TO IGNORE IT.
A SHOE! A SHOE!
Oh don't be ridiculous. It's simply a large ridged, brown patch of sky. Perfectly natural. Nothing to worry about.
IT'S ALSO A LONG TERM PROBLEM - THE EFFECTS OF OUR ACTIONS TODAY WON'T BE FELT UNTIL MANY YEARS HAVE PASSED. AND OUR SOCIETY IS OBSESSED WITH NEW, TRIVIAL, SHORT-TERM EVENTS AND POLICIES.
THIS IS WHAT TODAY'S NEWS WOULD LOOK LIKE IF EVERYONE WAS CONFRONTING THE MOST IMPORTANT ISSUE IN THE WORLD...
...The Government today announced plans to decommission three of the runways at Heathrow airport, with the aim of establishing a new mega-orchard at the sit
CLIMATE CHANGE IS STILL REALLY BAD
MADONNA EMBARKS ON WORLD TOUR ON DONKEY BACK: POPE OUTRAGED
"This is taking religious allegories too far!"
WHEELS
we road test the urban bike everyone's talking about
ACME WIND GENERATORS FEEL THE RAW THROBBING POWER
Jeremy Clarkson "nearly rehabilitated"
Troubled star to be considered for release back into the community
As Shell and BP cease trading, we ask, is there any future for oil companies?
Inside the Beckham's garden:
Posh Spice shows us her vegetable patch!
a stick of celery
Victoria Beckham

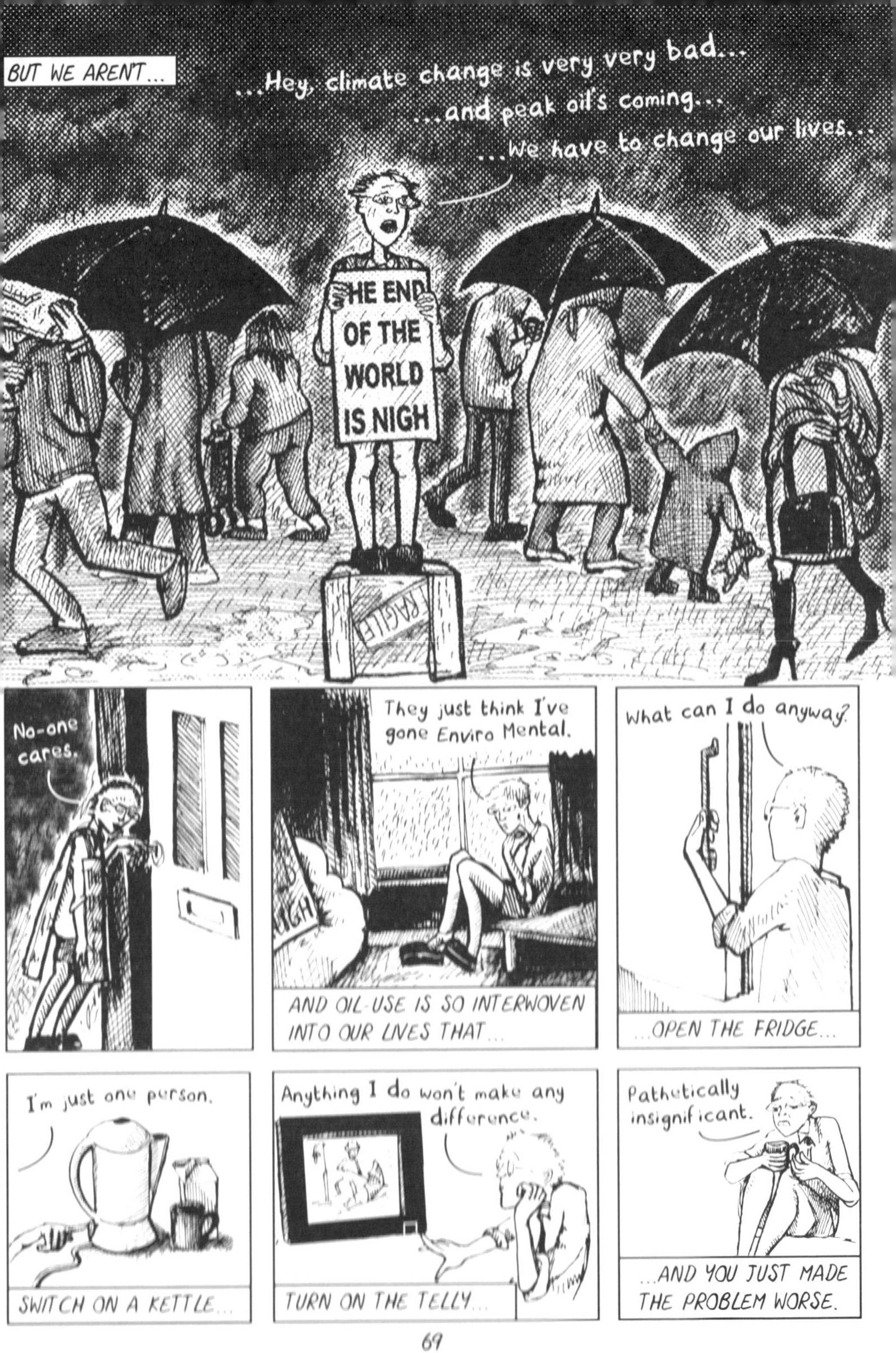
BUT WE AREN'T...
...Hey, climate change is very very bad...
...and peak oil's coming...
...We have to change our lives...
THE END OF THE WORLD IS NIGH
FRAGILE
No-one cares.
They just think I've gone Enviro Mental.
AND OIL-USE IS SO INTERWOVEN INTO OUR LIVES THAT...
What can I do anyway?
...OPEN THE FRIDGE...
I'm just one person.
SWITCH ON A KETTLE...
Anything I do won't make any difference.
TURN ON THE TELLY...
Pathetically insignificant.
...AND YOU JUST MADE THE PROBLEM WORSE.

81) *The Party's Over: Oil, War and the Fate of Industrial Societies* by Richard Heinberg pp 12-14.

82) On a small scale, humans have used oil and coal for heating and lighting for at least four thousand years. By the 17th century, coal had become essential to the English economy, and large-scale coal mining had begun. However, with the development of coal-fired railways, the coal-powered industrial revolution really picked up steam. *The Party's Over*, pp 50-53.

83) *The Party's Over*, p 66.

84) The Center for Responsive Politics. www.opensecrets.org

85) "Since Carbon Credits are tradable instruments with a transparent price, financial investors have started buying them for pure trading purposes. This market is expected to grow substantially, with banks, brokers, funds, arbitrageurs and private traders eventually participating. Emissions Trading PLC, for example, was floated on the London Stock Exchange's AiM market in 2005 with the specific remit of investing in emissions instruments." Entry on 'emissions trading' at Wikipedia.org.

There are several emissions trading markets in existence. The text here refers to a global market, in which first world countries buy credits from poorer nations. This means that a kind of carbon colonialism occurs, where richer countries buy up the easiest, cheapest options for reducing emissions abroad. Come the time when majority world countries try to reduce their own emissions, the cheapest options will have been snapped up.

There are also internal carbon markets, such as the one set up by the European Union. 12,000 European power plants and industrial sites have been issued with permits to pollute, which they can only trade between themselves. This system is more egalitarian, and should help markets to systematically reduce their carbon budget. Unfortunately, jockeying for quotas by national governments resulted in an overall allowance for carbon emissions that *exceeded* the amount that was actually being burnt. So as a tool for reducing emissions, the scheme has initially been astoundingly ineffective. "Governments accused of giving industries permisson to pollute" *The Guardian* 16/05/05.

86) The phrase "Third World" is used ironically here. The phrase "Majority World" is preferable, as it gives a more accurate impression of the proportion of the world that is impoverished.

87) "Adding fuel to the fire" John Vidal, The Guardian 30/06/05.

88) "Europeans missing their Kyoto targets" *The Independent* 27/12/05.

89) "Germany slams brakes on emissions targets" *New Scientist* 06/06/06.

90) "Canada may be caving in on Kyoto" *New Scientist* 27/05/06.

91) George Bush Snr said this before the 1992 Rio Earth Summit.

92) See "America's War with Itself" by George Monbiot (*The Guardian* 21/12/2004) for an account of the US administration's attempts to actively scupper climate negotiations.

93) The US Energy Information Administration projects an increase of between 30% and 47% between 2000 and 2025 ("Record US greenhouse gas emissions in 2004" *New Scientist* 21/12/05).

94) "Forget The Threat Of Terrorism. China Is About To Flick The Switch On A Global Energy Crisis And A Time Bomb That Will Bring Massive Destruction Worldwide" *The Sunday Herald* 25/07/04.

95) *International Energy Outlook 2006: World Oil Markets* from the Energy Information Administration of the US Government.

96) Kenneth Deffreyes, Princeton University Geophysicist, estimates remaining world oil reserves at 2.013 trillion barrels. 'Hubbert's Curve' entry at Wikipedia.org

97) Attempts to predict exactly when Peak Oil will hit are frustrated by the secrecy that surrounds remaining oil reserves. Kenneth Deffreyes reckons that is has already passed, in 2004. Geophysicist Colin Campbell gives 2010 as a likely date. The Association for the Study of Peak Oil give 2006-15 as the years in which it is most likely to occur. The peak will only be detectable retrospectively; a period of fluctuating prices at the peak itself will be followed by a steady, year-on-year price climb. See *The Party's Over* by Richard Heinberg, Chapter 3, for an analysis of Peak Oil predictions and naysayers.

98) *The Party's Over* by Richard Heinberg, Chapter 4 "Non-Petroleum Energy Sources" gives an analysis of the energy return over energy invested in oil substitutes.

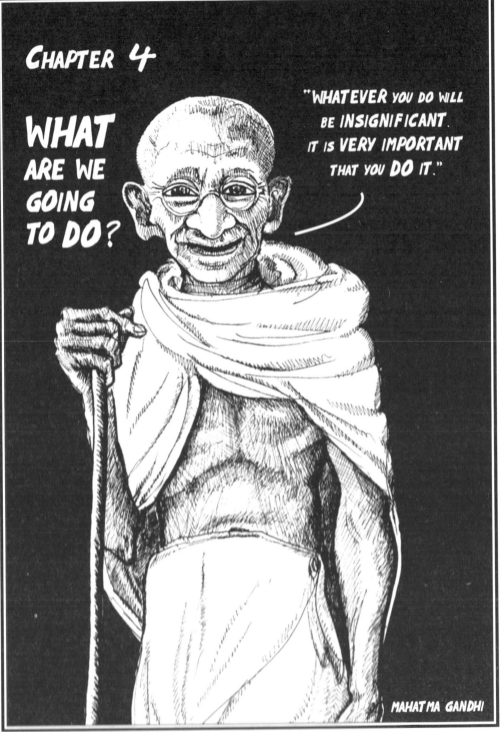

CHAPTER 4

WHAT
ARE WE
GOING
TO DO?

"WHATEVER YOU DO WILL BE INSIGNIFICANT. IT IS VERY IMPORTANT THAT YOU DO IT."

MAHATMA GANDHI

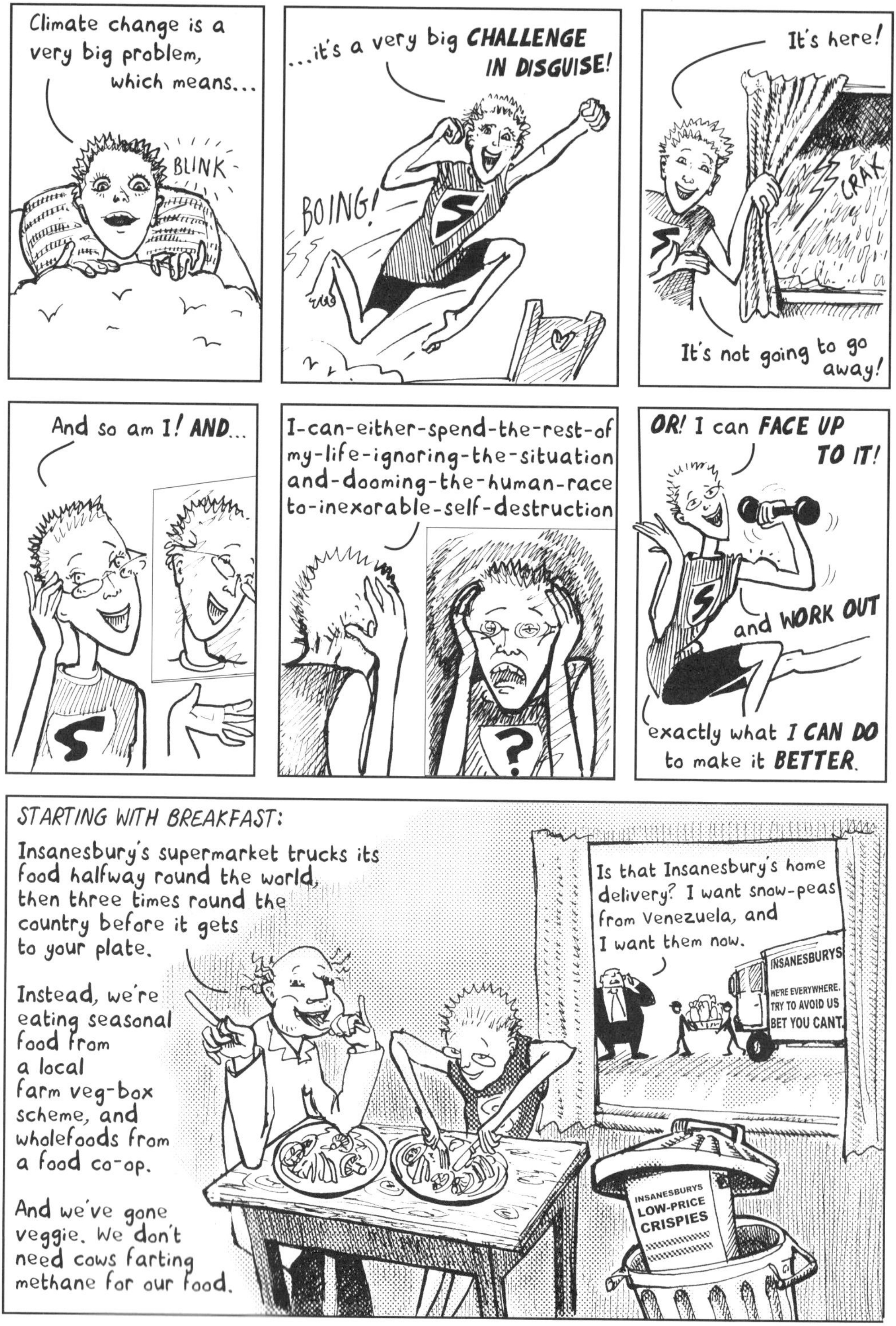

Climate change is a very big problem, which means...
BLINK
...it's a very big CHALLENGE IN DISGUISE!
BOING!
It's here!
CRAX
It's not going to go away!
And so am I! AND...
I-can-either-spend-the-rest-of my-life-ignoring-the-situation and-dooming-the-human-race to-inexorable-self-destruction
OR! I can FACE UP TO IT!
and WORK OUT
exactly what I CAN DO to make it BETTER.
STARTING WITH BREAKFAST:
Insanesbury's supermarket trucks its food halfway round the world, then three times round the country before it gets to your plate.
Instead, we're eating seasonal food from a local farm veg-box scheme, and wholefoods from a food co-op.
And we've gone veggie. We don't need cows farting methane for our food.
Is that Insanesbury's home delivery? I want snow-peas from Venezuela, and I want them now.
INSANESBURYS
WE'RE EVERYWHERE. TRY TO AVOID US BET YOU CANT.
INSANESBURYS LOW-PRICE CRISPIES

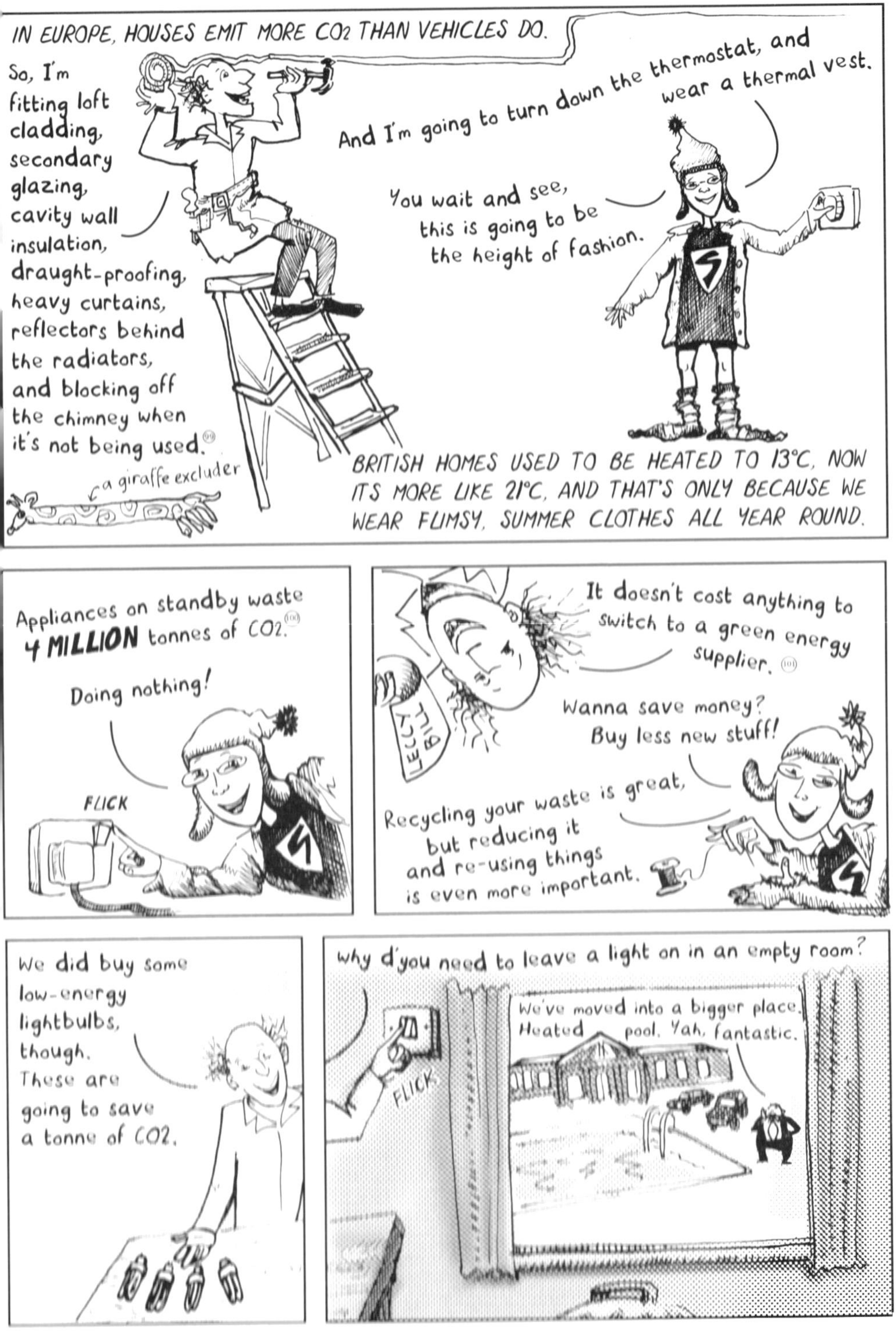
IN EUROPE, HOUSES EMIT MORE CO2 THAN VEHICLES DO.
So, I'm fitting loft cladding, secondary glazing, cavity wall insulation, draught-proofing, heavy curtains, reflectors behind the radiators, and blocking off the chimney when it's not being used.[99]
a giraffe excluder
And I'm going to turn down the thermostat, and wear a thermal vest.
You wait and see, this is going to be the height of fashion.
BRITISH HOMES USED TO BE HEATED TO 13°C, NOW ITS MORE LIKE 21°C, AND THAT'S ONLY BECAUSE WE WEAR FLIMSY, SUMMER CLOTHES ALL YEAR ROUND.
Appliances on standby waste **4 MILLION** tonnes of CO2.[100]
Doing nothing!
FLICK
It doesn't cost anything to switch to a green energy supplier.[101]
LECCY BILL
Wanna save money? Buy less new stuff!
Recycling your waste is great, but reducing it and re-using things is even more important.
We did buy some low-energy lightbulbs, though. These are going to save a tonne of CO2.
Why d'you need to leave a light on in an empty room?
FLICK
We've moved into a bigger place. Heated pool. Yah, fantastic.

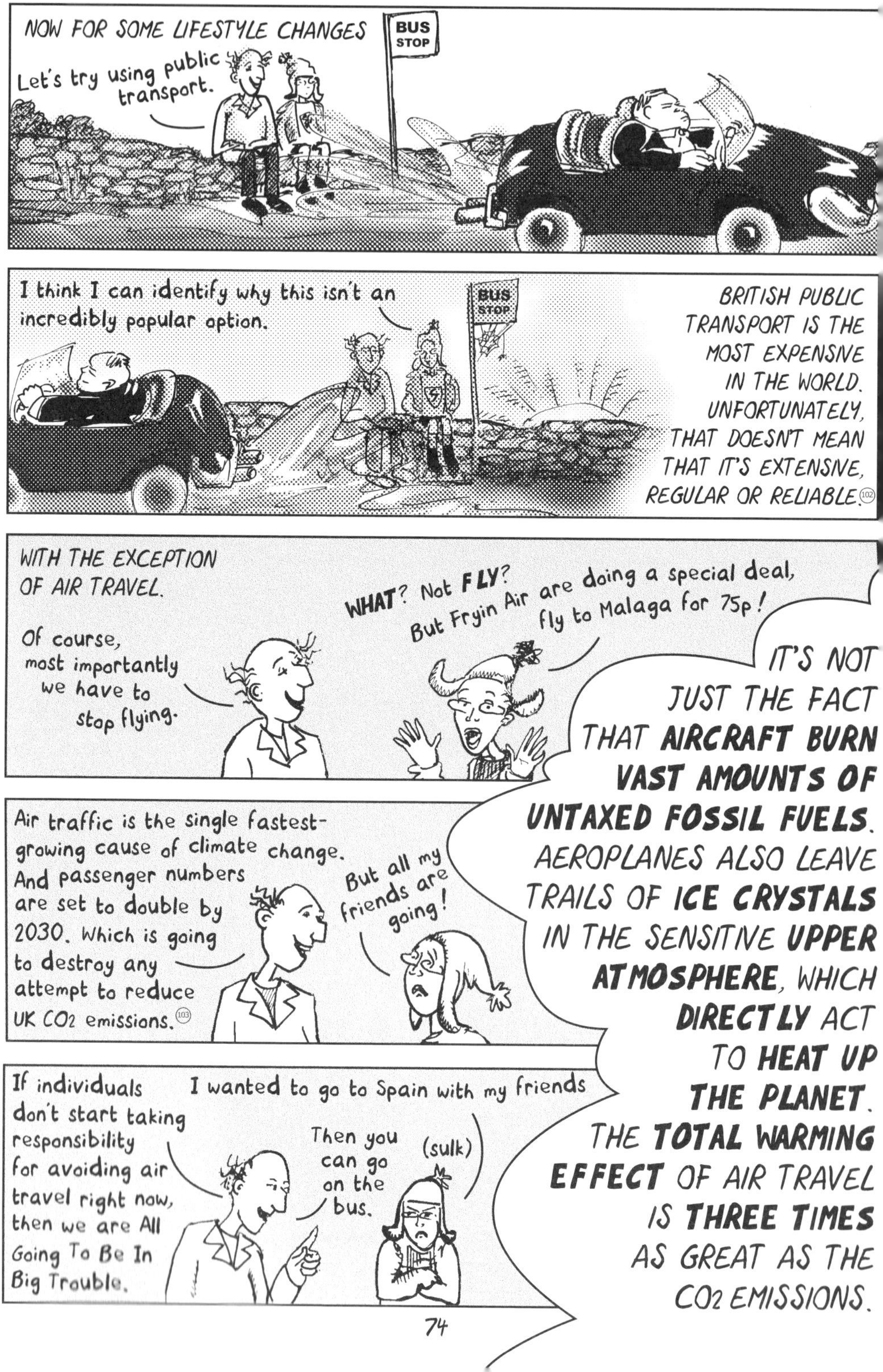
NOW FOR SOME LIFESTYLE CHANGES
Let's try using public transport.
BUS STOP
I think I can identify why this isn't an incredibly popular option.
BUS STOP
BRITISH PUBLIC TRANSPORT IS THE MOST EXPENSIVE IN THE WORLD. UNFORTUNATELY, THAT DOESN'T MEAN THAT IT'S EXTENSIVE, REGULAR OR RELIABLE. [102]
WITH THE EXCEPTION OF AIR TRAVEL.
Of course, most importantly we have to stop flying.
WHAT? Not FLY? But Fryin Air are doing a special deal, fly to Malaga for 75p!
IT'S NOT JUST THE FACT THAT AIRCRAFT BURN VAST AMOUNTS OF UNTAXED FOSSIL FUELS. AEROPLANES ALSO LEAVE TRAILS OF ICE CRYSTALS IN THE SENSITIVE UPPER ATMOSPHERE, WHICH DIRECTLY ACT TO HEAT UP THE PLANET. THE TOTAL WARMING EFFECT OF AIR TRAVEL IS THREE TIMES AS GREAT AS THE CO_2 EMISSIONS.
Air traffic is the single fastest-growing cause of climate change. And passenger numbers are set to double by 2030. Which is going to destroy any attempt to reduce UK CO_2 emissions. [103]
But all my friends are going!
If individuals don't start taking responsibility for avoiding air travel right now, then we are All Going To Be In Big Trouble.
I wanted to go to Spain with my friends
Then you can go on the bus.
(sulk)

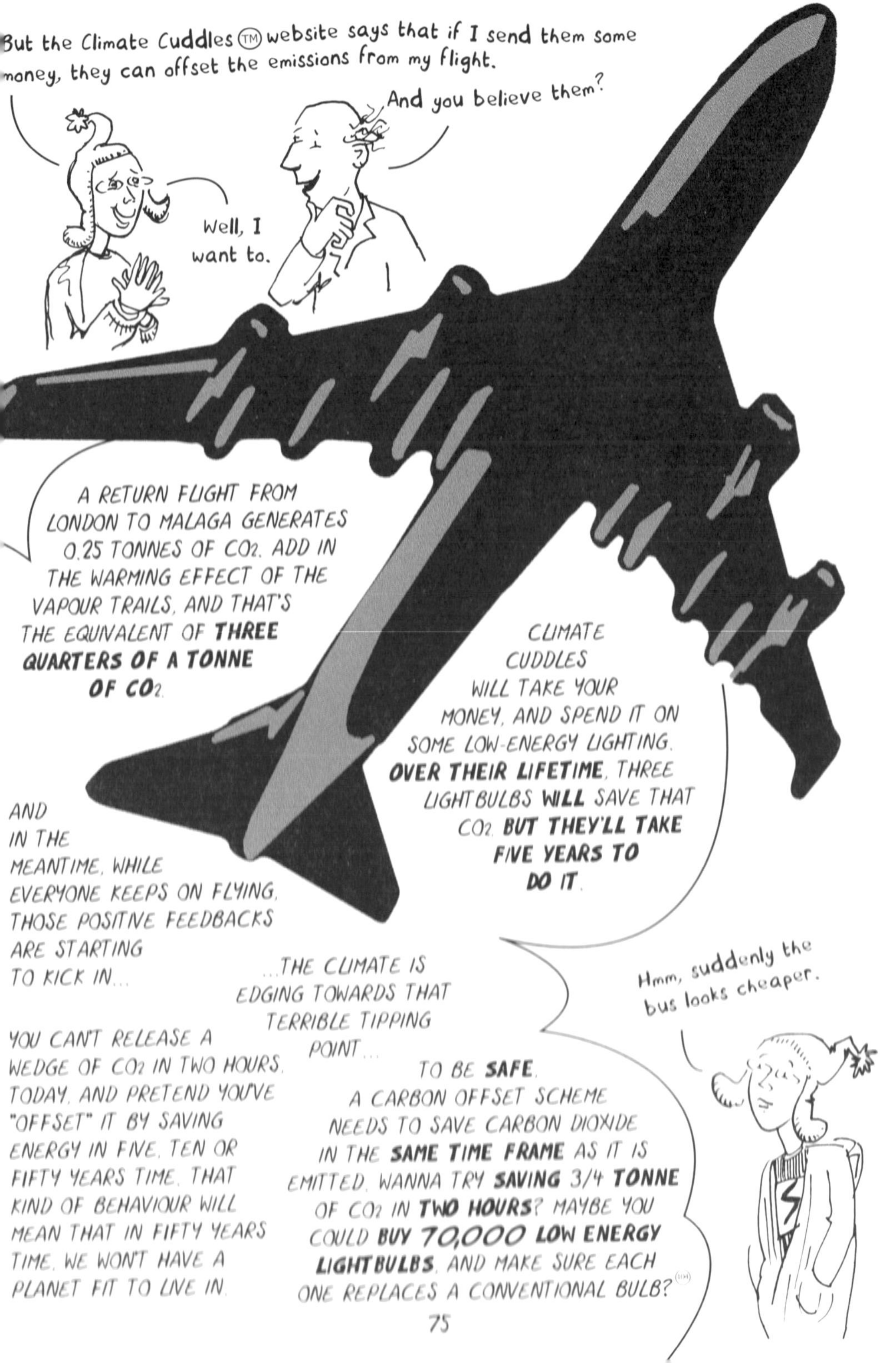

But the Climate Cuddles (TM) website says that if I send them some money, they can offset the emissions from my flight.
And you believe them?
Well, I want to.
A RETURN FLIGHT FROM LONDON TO MALAGA GENERATES 0.25 TONNES OF CO2. ADD IN THE WARMING EFFECT OF THE VAPOUR TRAILS, AND THAT'S THE EQUIVALENT OF **THREE QUARTERS OF A TONNE OF CO2**.
CLIMATE CUDDLES WILL TAKE YOUR MONEY, AND SPEND IT ON SOME LOW-ENERGY LIGHTING. **OVER THEIR LIFETIME**, THREE LIGHTBULBS **WILL** SAVE THAT CO2. **BUT THEY'LL TAKE FIVE YEARS TO DO IT**.
AND IN THE MEANTIME, WHILE EVERYONE KEEPS ON FLYING, THOSE POSITIVE FEEDBACKS ARE STARTING TO KICK IN...
...THE CLIMATE IS EDGING TOWARDS THAT TERRIBLE TIPPING POINT...
YOU CAN'T RELEASE A WEDGE OF CO2 IN TWO HOURS TODAY, AND PRETEND YOU'VE "OFFSET" IT BY SAVING ENERGY IN FIVE, TEN OR FIFTY YEARS TIME. THAT KIND OF BEHAVIOUR WILL MEAN THAT IN FIFTY YEARS TIME, WE WON'T HAVE A PLANET FIT TO LIVE IN.
TO BE **SAFE**, A CARBON OFFSET SCHEME NEEDS TO SAVE CARBON DIOXIDE IN THE **SAME TIME FRAME** AS IT IS EMITTED. WANNA TRY **SAVING 3/4 TONNE** OF CO2 IN **TWO HOURS**? MAYBE YOU COULD **BUY 70,000 LOW ENERGY LIGHTBULBS**, AND MAKE SURE EACH ONE REPLACES A CONVENTIONAL BULB? (104)
Hmm, suddenly the bus looks cheaper.

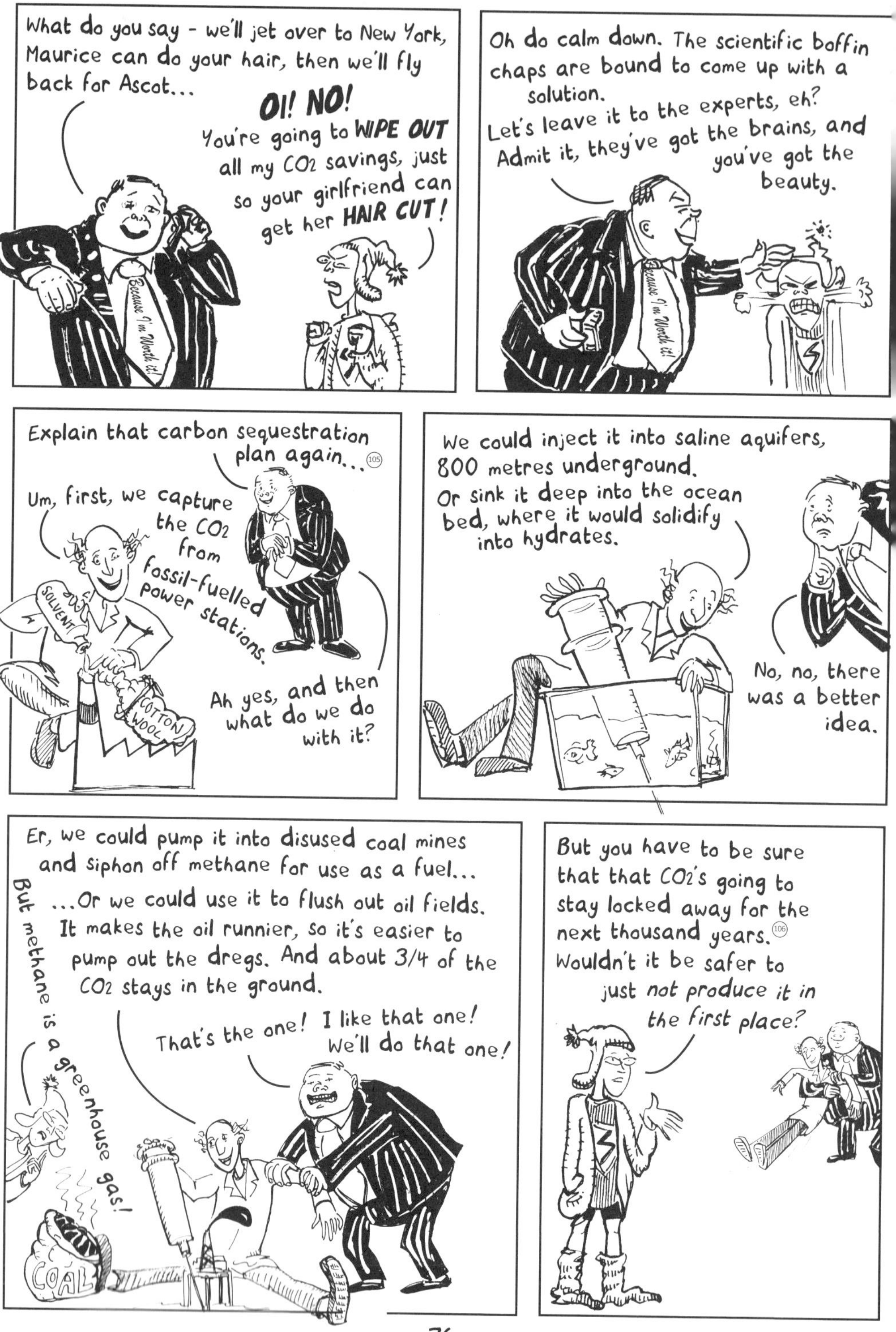
What do you say - we'll jet over to New York, Maurice can do your hair, then we'll fly back for Ascot...
OI! NO!
You're going to WIPE OUT all my CO_2 savings, just so your girlfriend can get her HAIR CUT!
Because I'm Worth it!
Oh do calm down. The scientific boffin chaps are bound to come up with a solution.
Let's leave it to the experts, eh?
Admit it, they've got the brains, and you've got the beauty.
Because I'm Worth it!
Explain that carbon sequestration plan again...[105]
Um, first, we capture the CO_2 from fossil-fuelled power stations.
SOLVENT
COTTON WOOL
Ah yes, and then what do we do with it?
We could inject it into saline aquifers, 800 metres underground.
Or sink it deep into the ocean bed, where it would solidify into hydrates.
No, no, there was a better idea.
Er, we could pump it into disused coal mines and siphon off methane for use as a fuel...
...Or we could use it to flush out oil fields. It makes the oil runnier, so it's easier to pump out the dregs. And about 3/4 of the CO_2 stays in the ground.
That's the one! I like that one! We'll do that one!
But methane is a greenhouse gas!
COAL
But you have to be sure that that CO_2's going to stay locked away for the next thousand years.[106]
Wouldn't it be safer to just *not produce it* in the first place?

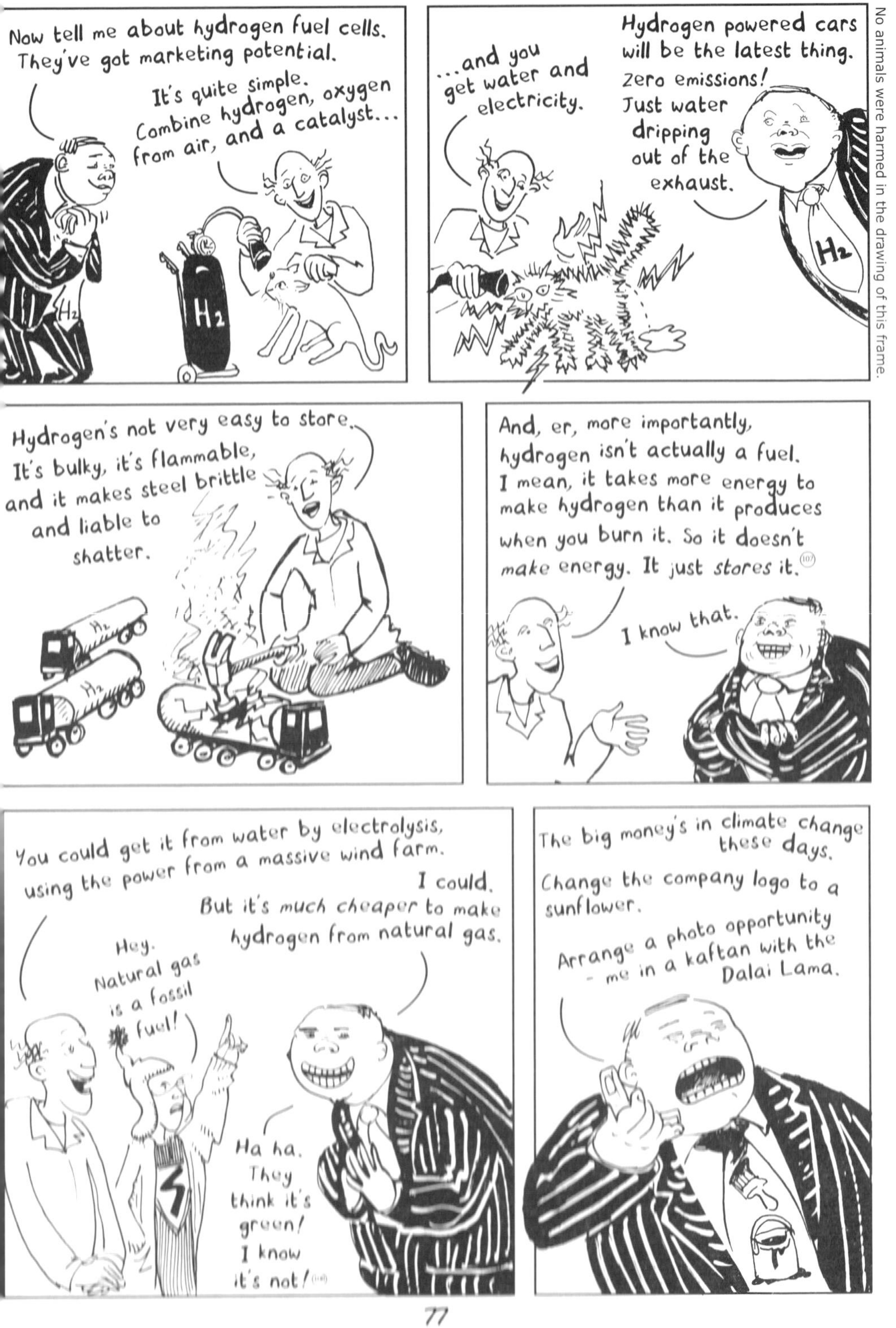
Now tell me about hydrogen fuel cells. They've got marketing potential.
It's quite simple. Combine hydrogen, oxygen from air, and a catalyst...
H_2
H_2
...and you get water and electricity.
Hydrogen powered cars will be the latest thing. Zero emissions! Just water dripping out of the exhaust.
H_2
No animals were harmed in the drawing of this frame.
Hydrogen's not very easy to store. It's bulky, it's flammable, and it makes steel brittle and liable to shatter.
H_2
H_2
And, er, more importantly, hydrogen isn't actually a fuel. I mean, it takes more energy to make hydrogen than it produces when you burn it. So it doesn't *make* energy. It just *stores* it. (107)
I know that.
You could get it from water by electrolysis, using the power from a massive wind farm.
I could. But it's *much cheaper* to make hydrogen from natural gas.
Hey. Natural gas is a fossil fuel!
Ha ha. They think it's green! I know it's not! (108)
The big money's in climate change these days.
Change the company logo to a sunflower.
Arrange a photo opportunity - me in a kaftan with the Dalai Lama.

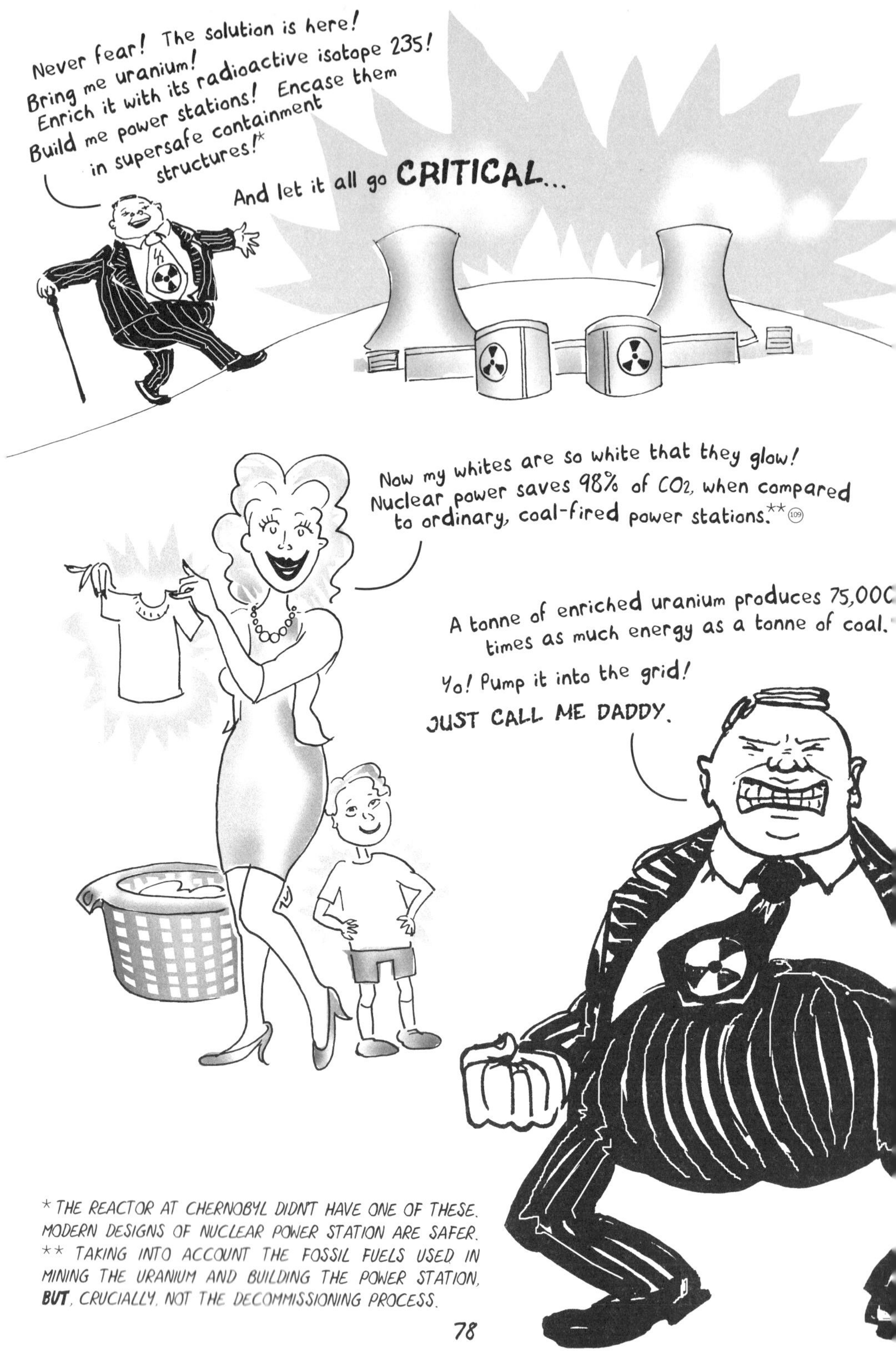
Never fear! The solution is here!
Bring me uranium!
Enrich it with its radioactive isotope 235!
Build me power stations! Encase them in supersafe containment structures!*
And let it all go CRITICAL...
Now my whites are so white that they glow!
Nuclear power saves 98% of CO2, when compared to ordinary, coal-fired power stations.** (109)
A tonne of enriched uranium produces 75,000 times as much energy as a tonne of coal.
Yo! Pump it into the grid!
JUST CALL ME DADDY.

* THE REACTOR AT CHERNOBYL DIDN'T HAVE ONE OF THESE. MODERN DESIGNS OF NUCLEAR POWER STATION ARE SAFER.

** TAKING INTO ACCOUNT THE FOSSIL FUELS USED IN MINING THE URANIUM AND BUILDING THE POWER STATION, **BUT**, CRUCIALLY, NOT THE DECOMMISSIONING PROCESS.

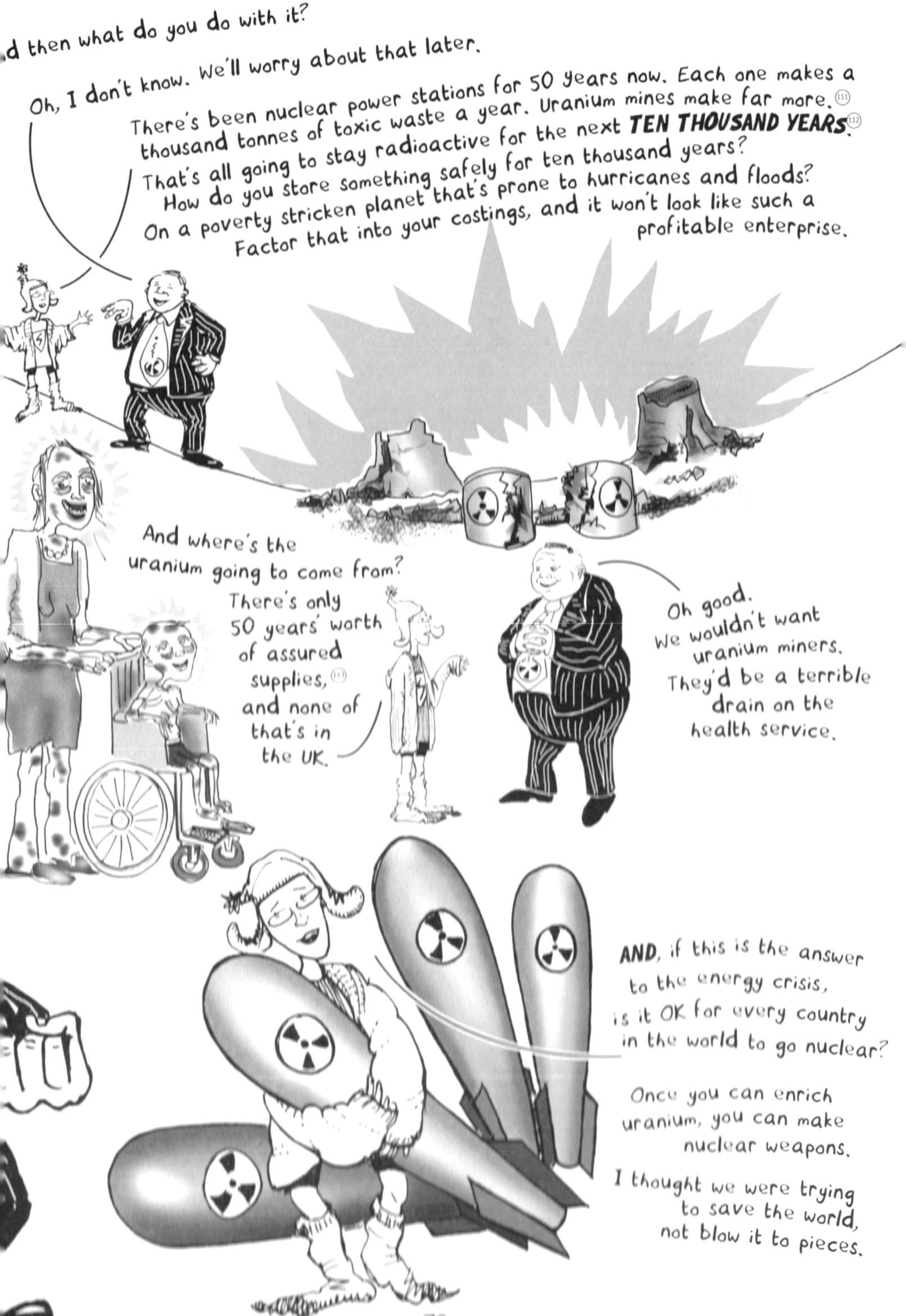
...d then what do you do with it?
Oh, I don't know. We'll worry about that later.
There's been nuclear power stations for 50 years now. Each one makes a thousand tonnes of toxic waste a year. Uranium mines make far more.[111]
That's all going to stay radioactive for the next **TEN THOUSAND YEARS**.[112]
How do you store something safely for ten thousand years?
On a poverty stricken planet that's prone to hurricanes and floods?
Factor that into your costings, and it won't look like such a profitable enterprise.
And where's the uranium going to come from?
There's only 50 years' worth of assured supplies,[113] and none of that's in the UK.
Oh good. We wouldn't want uranium miners. They'd be a terrible drain on the health service.
AND, if this is the answer to the energy crisis, is it OK for every country in the world to go nuclear?
Once you can enrich uranium, you can make nuclear weapons.
I thought we were trying to save the world, not blow it to pieces.

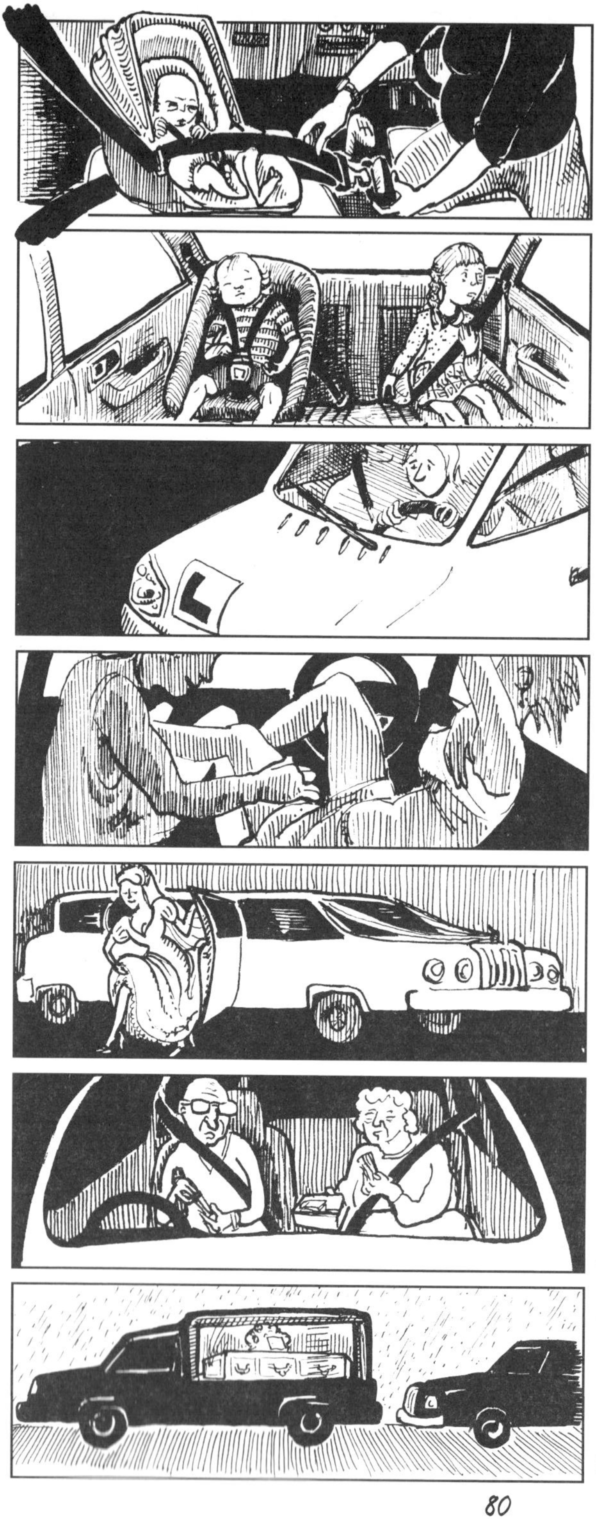

People think it's impossible. People think there's nothing we can do. But that's just because we're so used to living an energy intensive lifestyle, that we can't imagine it any other way.
Once you find out what the alternatives are, and start using them, they become real, and it all becomes possible.

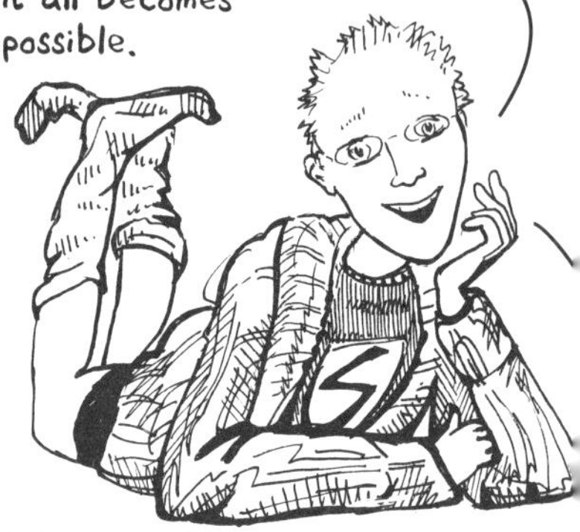

Take cars for example. We love them. We think we need them. Shame. There just isn't any way that we can keep on using cars in the way we do now.

Wanna run them on hydrogen? Looks like we'd need to double the capacity of the national grid to get enough electricity to make the fuel.

Biofuels sound like a nice idea. We could make petrol from sugar beet, and veg-oil diesel from rapeseed, and the plants soak up as much CO_2 as they give out when they're burned. But where're we going to grow them? We'd need 4 ½ times as much cropland to grow biodiesel as there is in the whole of the UK.[115]

So, we'll import it. Right now, people are starving in poorer countries, while their land is used to grow animal fodder so that we can eat roast beef. And next we're going to make them grow our petrol and diesel? I don't think so.
We need to get on our bikes.

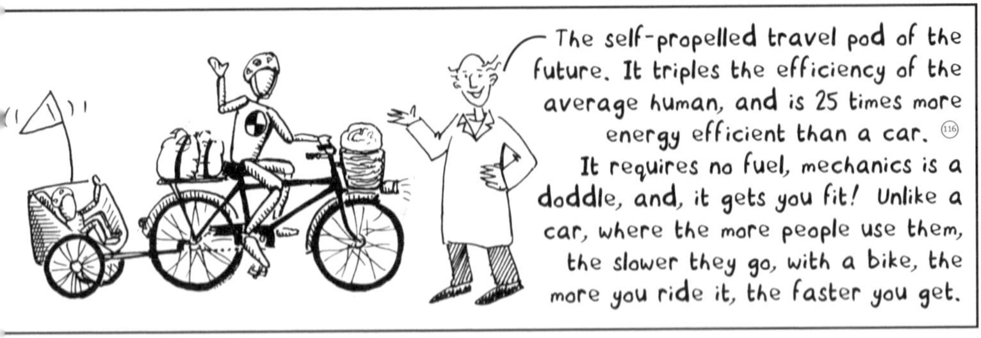
The self-propelled travel pod of the future. It triples the efficiency of the average human, and is 25 times more energy efficient than a car. [116]
It requires no fuel, mechanics is a doddle, and, it gets you fit! Unlike a car, where the more people use them, the slower they go, with a bike, the more you ride it, the faster you get.

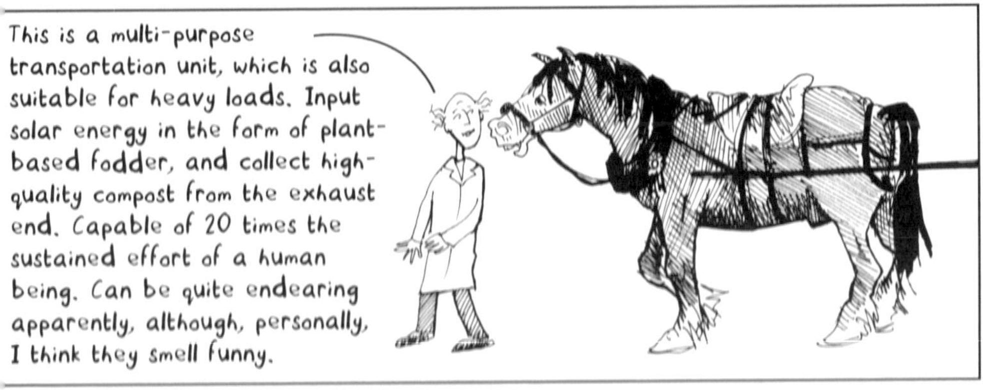
This is a multi-purpose transportation unit, which is also suitable for heavy loads. Input solar energy in the form of plant-based fodder, and collect high-quality compost from the exhaust end. Capable of 20 times the sustained effort of a human being. Can be quite endearing apparently, although, personally, I think they smell funny.

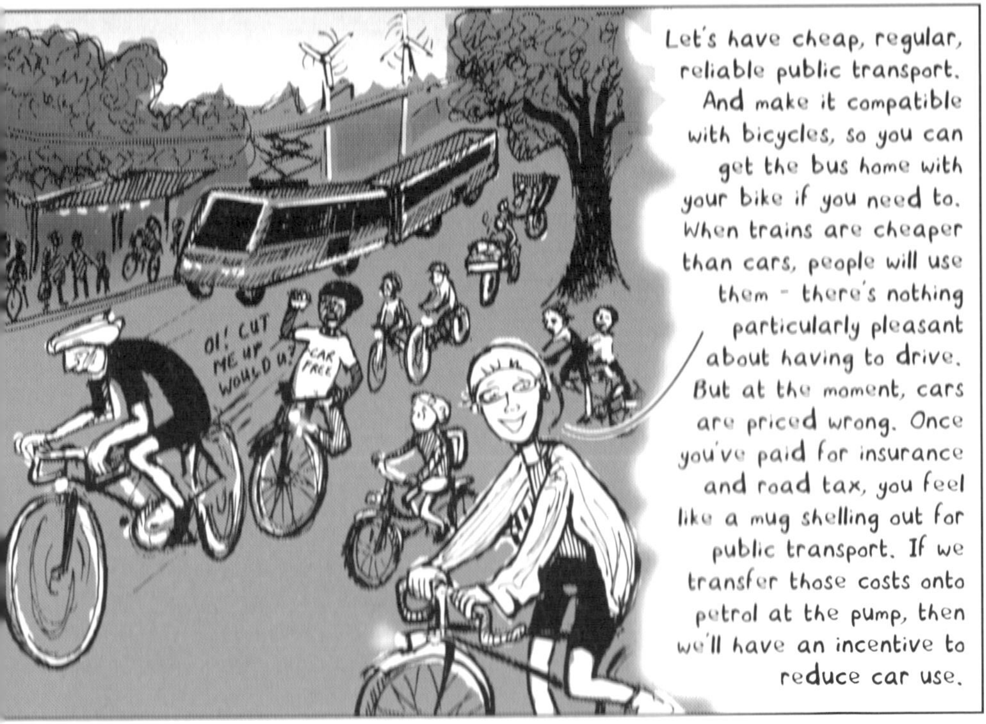
OI! CUT ME UP WOULD U?
CAR FREE
Let's have cheap, regular, reliable public transport. And make it compatible with bicycles, so you can get the bus home with your bike if you need to. When trains are cheaper than cars, people will use them - there's nothing particularly pleasant about having to drive. But at the moment, cars are priced wrong. Once you've paid for insurance and road tax, you feel like a mug shelling out for public transport. If we transfer those costs onto petrol at the pump, then we'll have an incentive to reduce car use.

Why don't we reorganise our towns? The planning system in this country is powerful and well-organised. Easy. Analyse new building projects in terms of their carbon emissions, and only allow the most sustainable developments. We could reunite areas of work and housing, so we can walk to work. We'll have car-free streets and city centres. Housing co-ops could get 100% mortgages, and we'll see the rebirth of functioning communities.[117] With "passive house" building standards, new homes can heat themselves with sunshine.[118] The technology's there, we can just start using it.

As for the energy crisis. At the moment, we're *wasting* energy, and its cooking the planet. Duh! The current energy debate is all about meeting projections of increased demand. But what's the point in keeping the lights on, when most of them aren't illuminating anything?

Centralised energy generation is criminally inefficient. The national grid wastes $2/3$ of the energy that it generates.[119] So, we cut down the amount of power available on the national grid, and then people can start powering themselves.

Oi, keep cycling, I'm nearly onto the next level.

GRAND THEFT PUSHBIKE

Carbon rationing makes sense. When you restrict the electricity that's available, then people use it efficiently. You just don't leave the telly on standby if it means there won't be any power left to watch your favourite programme later on.

If you want more power, then you'll get a wind generator, or a solar panel. And, for when its neither windy or sunny, a cycle generator. We're all going to have fantastically toned thighs.

The most energy-efficient businesses will be the new market leaders. Low energy appliances will be in vogue. And we could grow biomass on urban spaces to power generators for hospitals and schools.

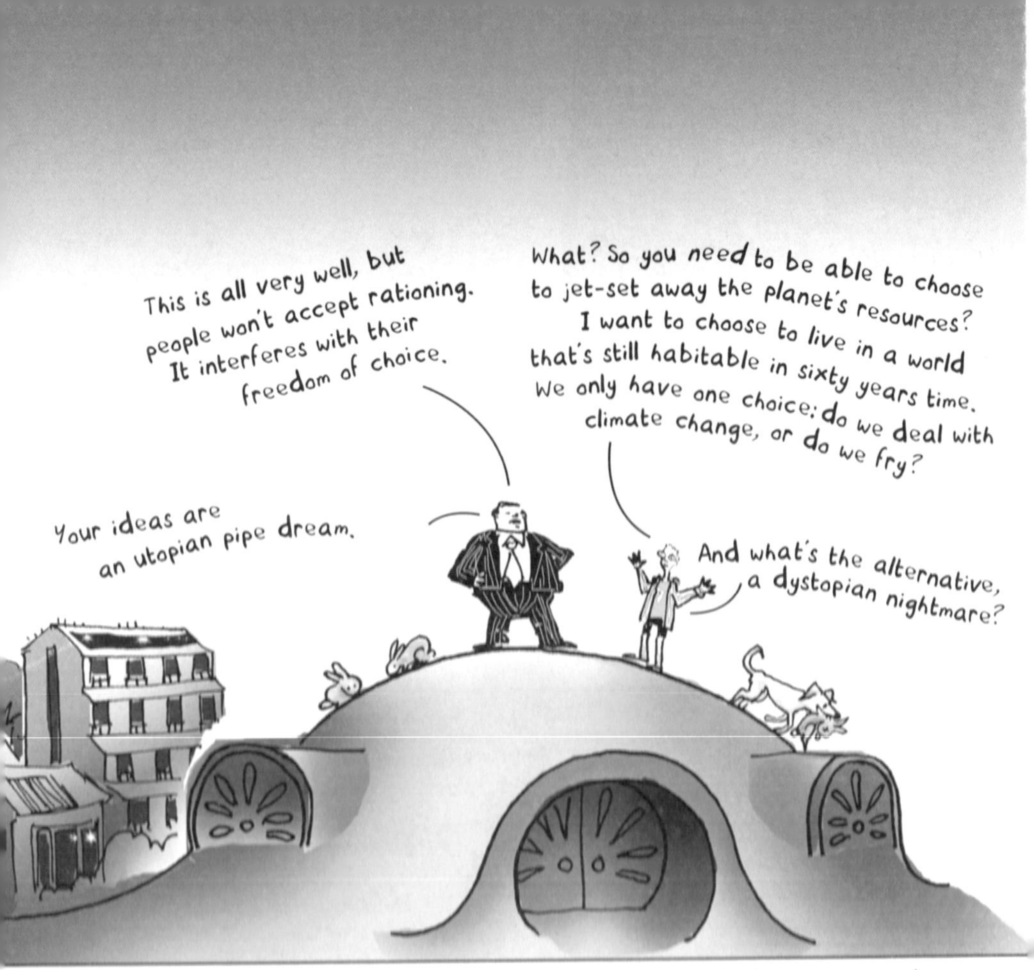
This is all very well, but people won't accept rationing. It interferes with their freedom of choice.
What? So you need to be able to choose to jet-set away the planet's resources? I want to choose to live in a world that's still habitable in sixty years time. We only have one choice: do we deal with climate change, or do we fry?
Your ideas are an utopian pipe dream.
And what's the alternative, a dystopian nightmare?

Hey, modern high-energy living isn't that great. Depression and obesity are endemic. We might just enjoy coming together for a common cause. And since we have to scale down our energy-use at some point, the sooner we do it, the easier it's going to be.

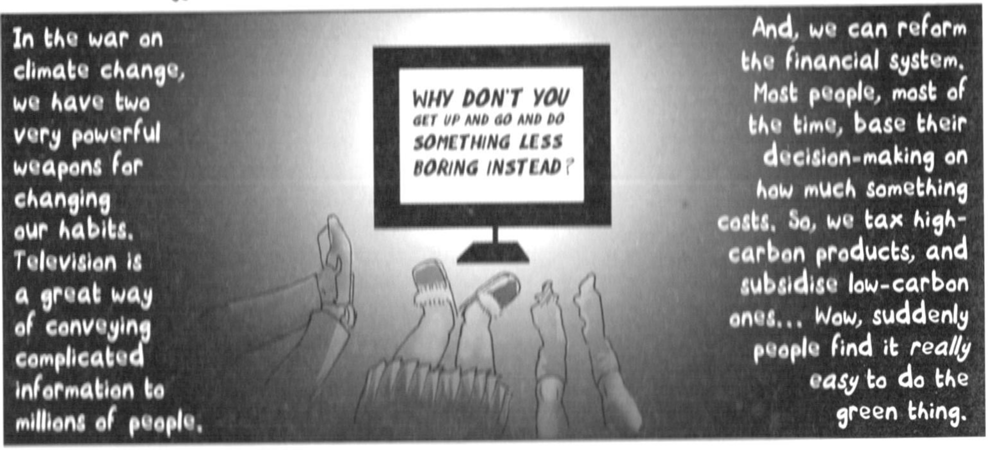
In the war on climate change, we have two very powerful weapons for changing our habits. Television is a great way of conveying complicated information to millions of people.
WHY DON'T YOU GET UP AND GO AND DO SOMETHING LESS BORING INSTEAD?
And, we can reform the financial system. Most people, most of the time, base their decision-making on how much something costs. So, we tax high-carbon products, and subsidise low-carbon ones... Wow, suddenly people find it *really easy* to do the green thing.

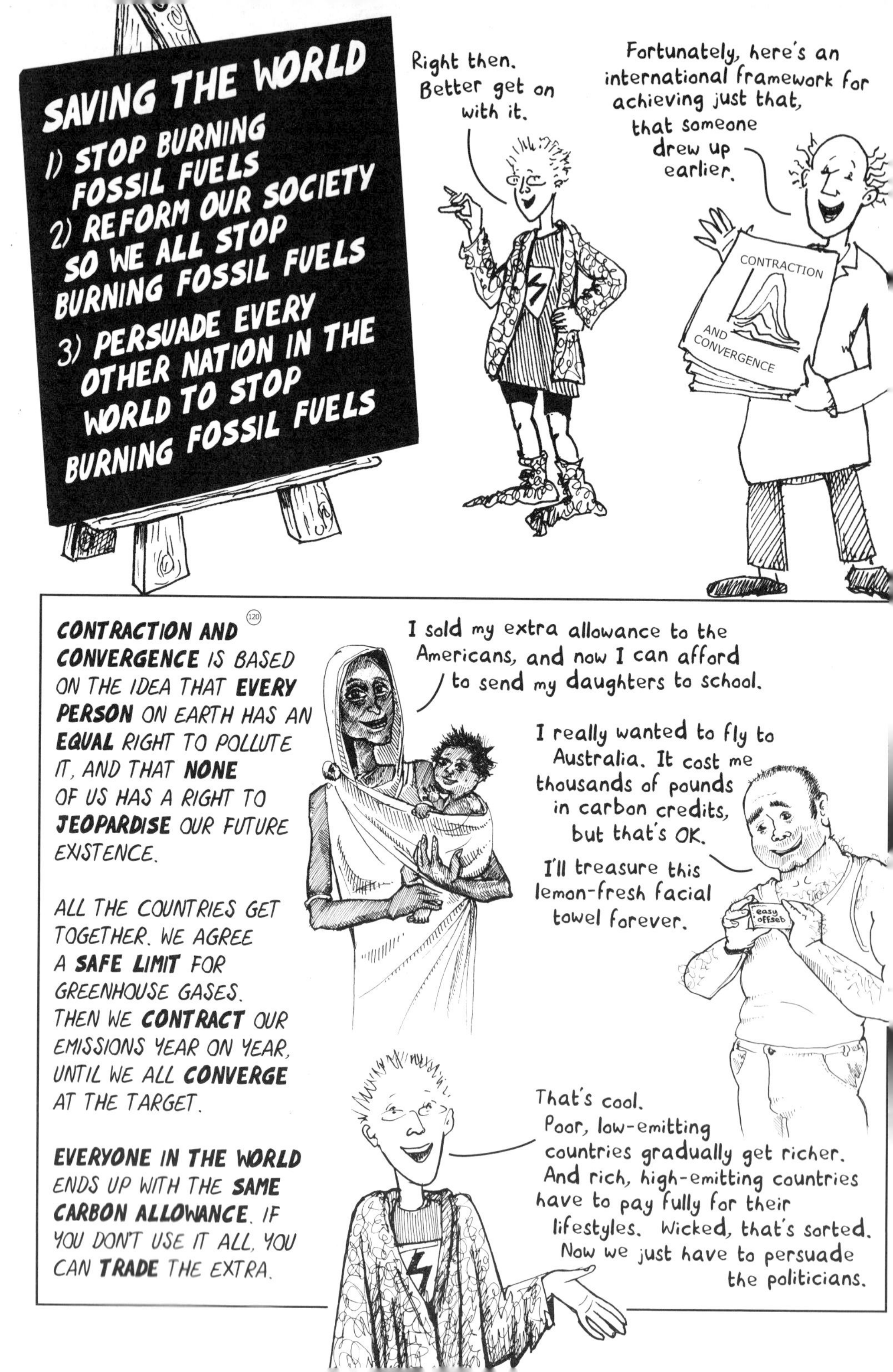
SAVING THE WORLD
1) STOP BURNING FOSSIL FUELS
2) REFORM OUR SOCIETY SO WE ALL STOP BURNING FOSSIL FUELS
3) PERSUADE EVERY OTHER NATION IN THE WORLD TO STOP BURNING FOSSIL FUELS
Right then. Better get on with it.
Fortunately, here's an international framework for achieving just that, that someone drew up earlier.
CONTRACTION AND CONVERGENCE
CONTRACTION AND CONVERGENCE [120] IS BASED ON THE IDEA THAT EVERY PERSON ON EARTH HAS AN EQUAL RIGHT TO POLLUTE IT, AND THAT NONE OF US HAS A RIGHT TO JEOPARDISE OUR FUTURE EXISTENCE.
ALL THE COUNTRIES GET TOGETHER. WE AGREE A SAFE LIMIT FOR GREENHOUSE GASES. THEN WE CONTRACT OUR EMISSIONS YEAR ON YEAR, UNTIL WE ALL CONVERGE AT THE TARGET.
EVERYONE IN THE WORLD ENDS UP WITH THE SAME CARBON ALLOWANCE. IF YOU DON'T USE IT ALL, YOU CAN TRADE THE EXTRA.
I sold my extra allowance to the Americans, and now I can afford to send my daughters to school.
I really wanted to fly to Australia. It cost me thousands of pounds in carbon credits, but that's OK.
I'll treasure this lemon-fresh facial towel forever.
easy offset
That's cool. Poor, low-emitting countries gradually get richer. And rich, high-emitting countries have to pay fully for their lifestyles. Wicked, that's sorted. Now we just have to persuade the politicians.

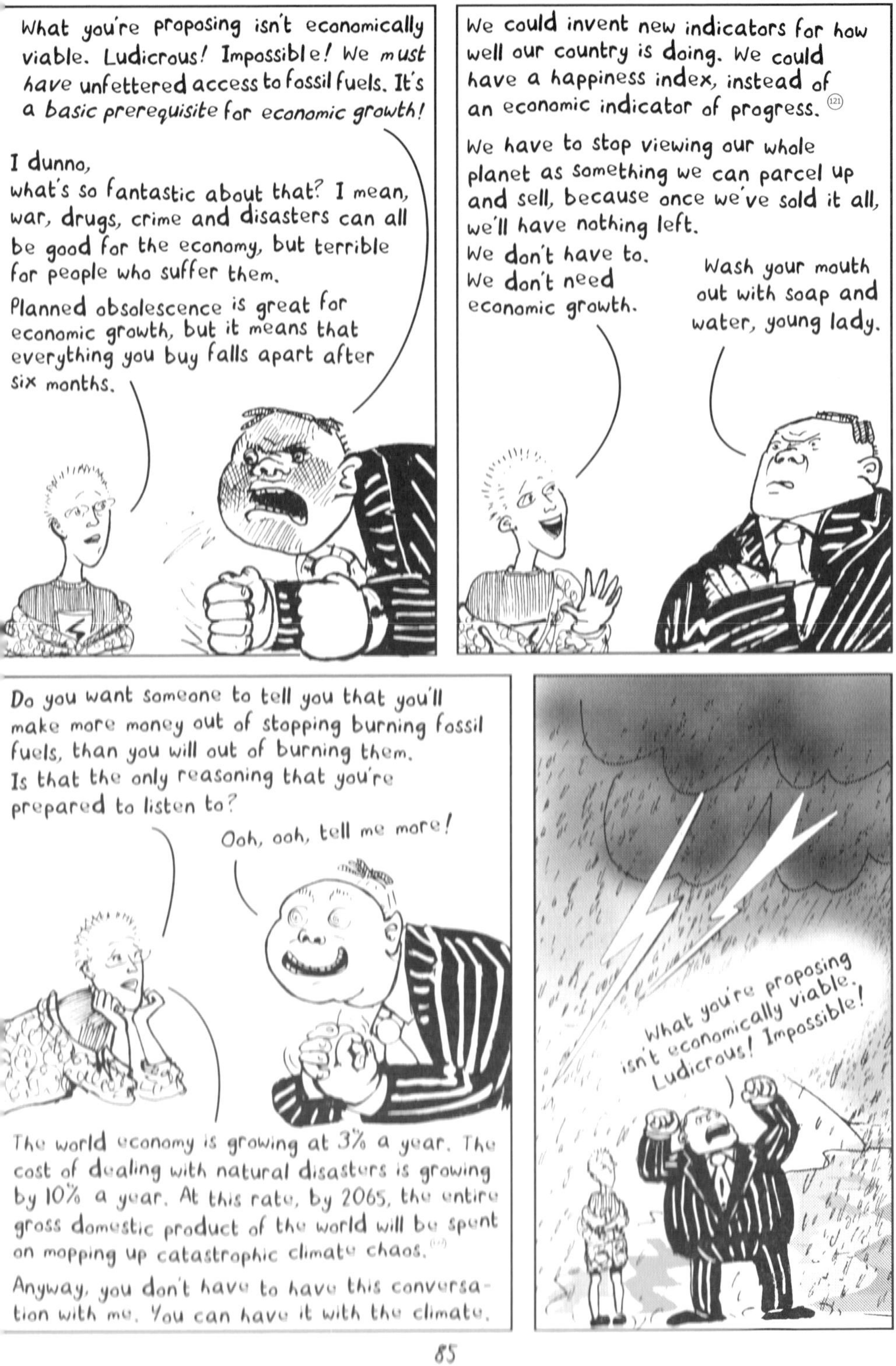

What you're proposing isn't economically viable. Ludicrous! Impossible! We *must have* unfettered access to fossil fuels. It's a *basic prerequisite* for *economic growth!*
I dunno, what's so fantastic about that? I mean, war, drugs, crime and disasters can all be good for the economy, but terrible for people who suffer them.
Planned obsolescence is great for economic growth, but it means that everything you buy falls apart after six months.
We could invent new indicators for how well our country is doing. We could have a happiness index, instead of an economic indicator of progress. [121]
We have to stop viewing our whole planet as something we can parcel up and sell, because once we've sold it all, we'll have nothing left.
We don't have to. We don't need economic growth.
Wash your mouth out with soap and water, young lady.
Do you want someone to tell you that you'll make more money out of stopping burning fossil fuels, than you will out of burning them. Is that the only reasoning that you're prepared to listen to?
Ooh, ooh, tell me more!
The world economy is growing at 3% a year. The cost of dealing with natural disasters is growing by 10% a year. At this rate, by 2065, the entire gross domestic product of the world will be spent on mopping up catastrophic climate chaos.
Anyway, you don't have to have this conversation with me. You can have it with the climate.
What you're proposing isn't economically viable. Ludicrous! Impossible!

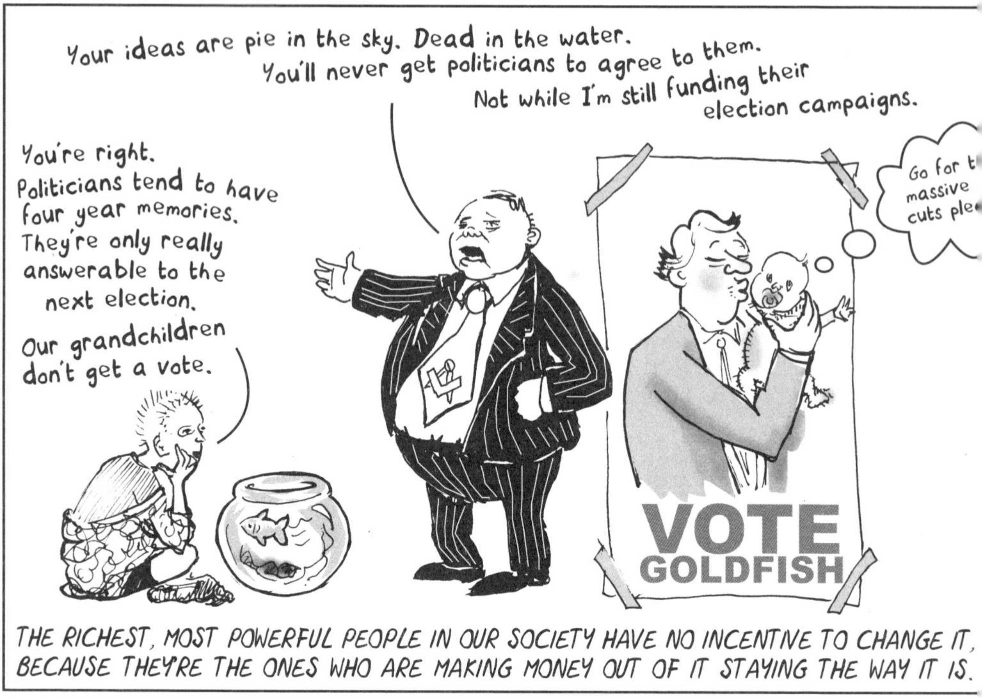
Your ideas are pie in the sky. Dead in the water.
You'll never get politicians to agree to them.
Not while I'm still funding their election campaigns.
You're right.
Politicians tend to have four year memories.
They're only really answerable to the next election.
Our grandchildren don't get a vote.
massive
VOTE
GOLDFISH
THE RICHEST, MOST POWERFUL PEOPLE IN OUR SOCIETY HAVE NO INCENTIVE TO CHANGE IT, BECAUSE THEY'RE THE ONES WHO ARE MAKING MONEY OUT OF IT STAYING THE WAY IT IS.

So what do we do? What are you going to do? Pretend it isn't happening? Are you going to forget you've read all this? Can you go back to not knowing, and not caring?

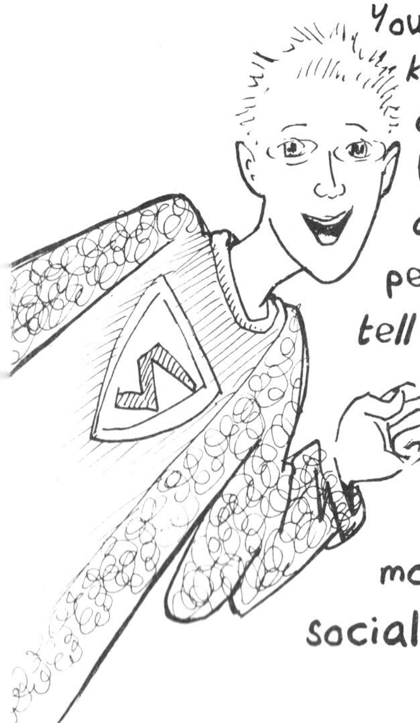

You see, the more people who *know* about climate change, and who *realise* that they can do something about it, the more people they *talk to*, and *tell* about it, the closer we'll get to our *own tipping point*... An unstoppable movement for social change.

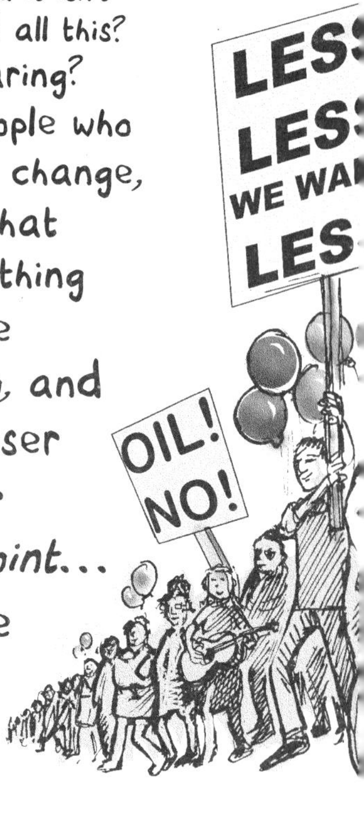
OIL!
NO!

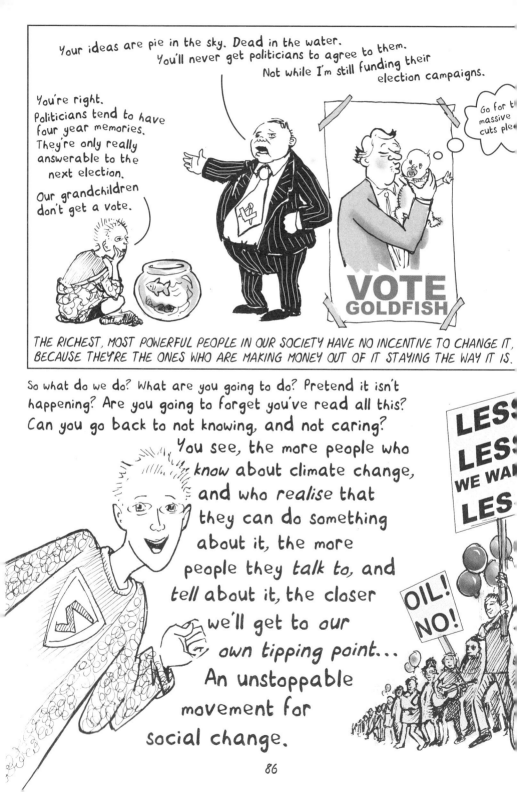

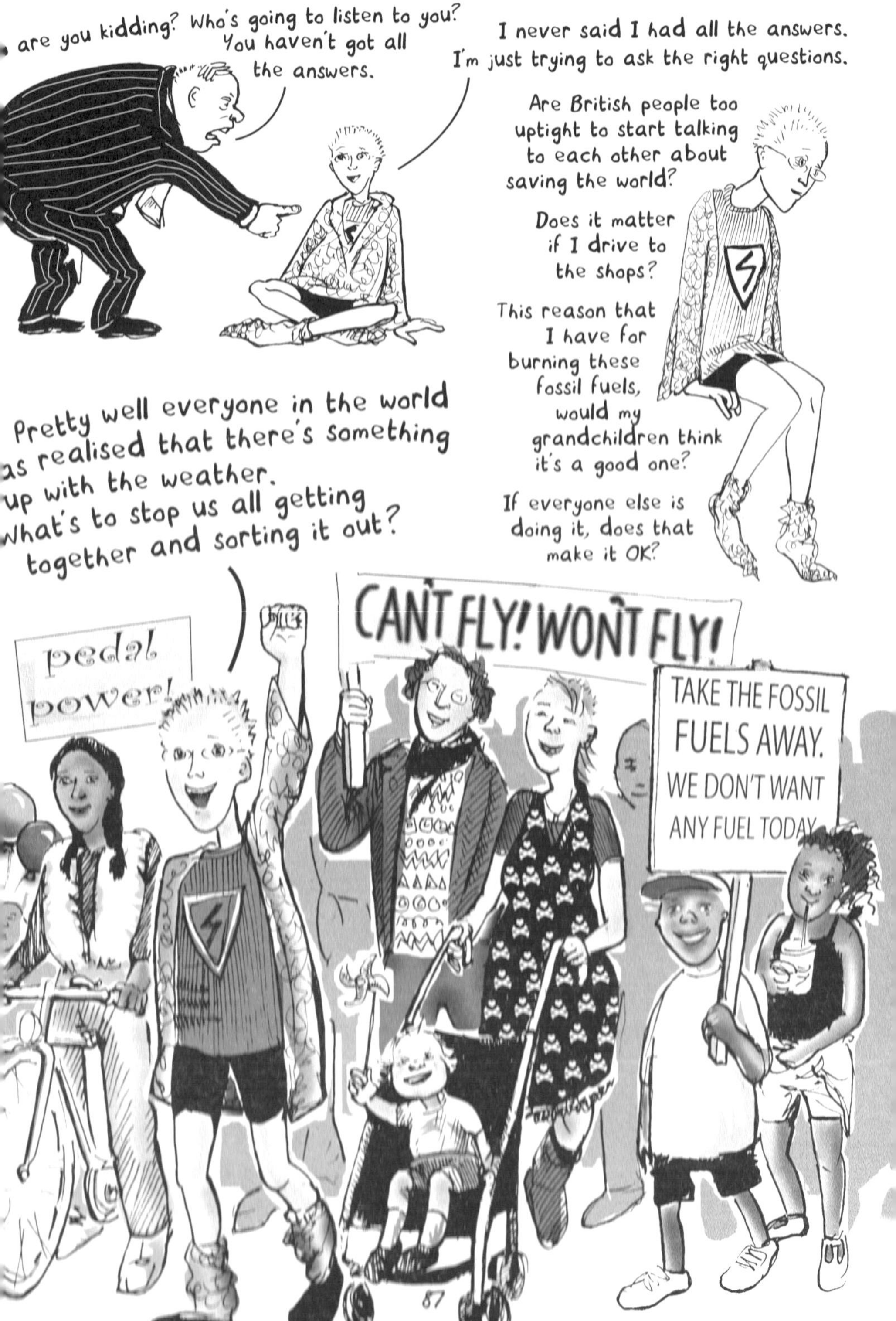
are you kidding? Who's going to listen to you? You haven't got all the answers.
I never said I had all the answers. I'm just trying to ask the right questions.
Are British people too uptight to start talking to each other about saving the world?
Does it matter if I drive to the shops?
This reason that I have for burning these fossil fuels, would my grandchildren think it's a good one?
If everyone else is doing it, does that make it OK?
Pretty well everyone in the world as realised that there's something up with the weather. What's to stop us all getting together and sorting it out?
pedal power!
CAN'T FLY! WON'T FLY!
TAKE THE FOSSIL FUELS AWAY. WE DON'T WANT ANY FUEL TODAY

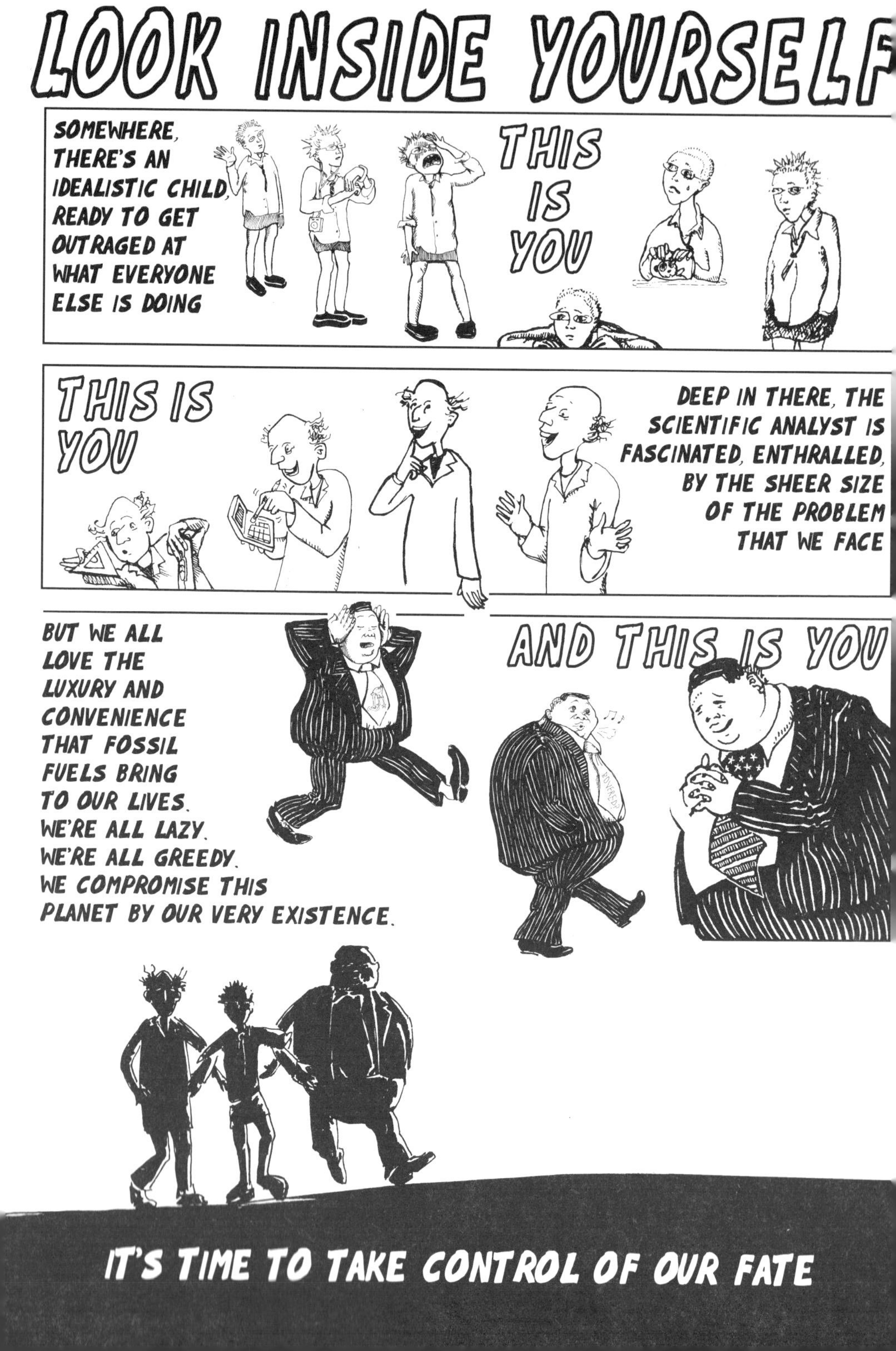
LOOK INSIDE YOURSELF
SOMEWHERE, THERE'S AN IDEALISTIC CHILD, READY TO GET OUTRAGED AT WHAT EVERYONE ELSE IS DOING
THIS IS YOU
THIS IS YOU
DEEP IN THERE, THE SCIENTIFIC ANALYST IS FASCINATED, ENTHRALLED, BY THE SHEER SIZE OF THE PROBLEM THAT WE FACE
BUT WE ALL LOVE THE LUXURY AND CONVENIENCE THAT FOSSIL FUELS BRING TO OUR LIVES. WE'RE ALL LAZY. WE'RE ALL GREEDY. WE COMPROMISE THIS PLANET BY OUR VERY EXISTENCE.
AND THIS IS YOU
IT'S TIME TO TAKE CONTROL OF OUR FATE

NOTES TO CHAPTER 4. PAGES 71 TO 88

99) See *www.est.org.uk* to find out what grants are available for home insulation in your area.

100) "Thanks, but we still don't need it" George Monbiot *The Guardian* 11/06/06.

101) This statement is slightly misleading. Subscribing to a renewable energy tariff is currently slightly more expensive than buying fossil fuel and nuclear derived electricity. However, it doesn't actually cost anything to switch supplier.

102) "Goodbye Carmageddon" George Monbiot, *The Guardian*, 15/09/99.

103) "Everyone's carbon dioxide emissions must go to zero to allow for aviation pollution reveals major analysis of UK climate change targets" Tyndall Centre Media Release 21/09/05.

104) Letter by Duncan Law to *The Independent*, 03/04/06. Carbon offset firms can underestimate the warming effects of flights, by calculating emissions per seat (aeroplanes have an average occupancy of 80 percent), and by using a lower multiple for the warming effect than the 2.7 that I have used.

105) "Clean energy special: Going underground" *New Scientist* 03/09/05 and "Deep sea graveyard for CO2" *New Scientist* 08/08/06.

106) It takes 1000 years for the planet to fully heat up, therefore, CO2 must be locked away for many thousands of years in order to not contribute to anthropogenic warming. Large scale leaks of CO2 from underground stores could suffocate people and animals.

107) *The Party's Over*, Richard Heinberg, pp 146-9.

108) Reforming natural gas or coal into hydrogen and using it in a fuel cell results in fewer greenhouse gas emissions than if the fossil fuels are burnt directly. So the technology is green, maybe only light green, but still green (*The Party's Over* p 147). However oil companies are currently advertising hydrogen-powered initiatives as "zero emissions", which is also misleading. Currently, hydrogen is commercially produced almost entirely from fossil fuels. Hydrogen is an inefficient and problematic solution to the forthcoming energy crisis, see *The Long Emergency* by James Kunstler, and *The Party's Over*, ibid.

109) "4.4tC/Gwh [nuclear], compared to 243tC/Gwh for coal and 97tC/Gwh for gas." The Sustainable Development Commission: *The role of nuclear power in a low carbon economy*, p 5, March 2006.

110) UK Department of Trade and Industry figures, "Thanks, But We Still Don't Need It" George Monbiot, *The Guardian*, 20/08/06.

111) Each nuclear power station is also responsible for the annual production of 100,000 tonnes of radioactive uranium tailings from the mining process. Richard Heinberg, *The Party's Over*.

112) The United States Environmental Protection Standards estimates that after 10,000 years, spent nuclear fuel will no longer pose a threat to public health and safety.

113) There are concerns that demand for uranium-235 may start to outstrip supply as early as 2020. "Human health may be the cost of a nuclear future" *New Scientist* 10/06/06, see also "On the road to ruin" Michael Meacher, *The Guardian*, 07/06/06. Fast breeder reactors utilise uranium-238, which is far more abundant than uranium-235. However, these types of reactors create plutonium, which is extremely hazardous, and can be used for nuclear weapons. There is currently only one fast breeder reactor in operation. www.wikipedia.org.

114) Based on **US** figures for car use and electricity production, **not UK**. "A Different Kind of Revolution" George Monbiot, *The Guardian*, 26/04/05.

115) "Feeding Cars, Not People", George Monbiot, *The Guardian* 23/11/04, see also, "Worse Than Fossil Fuel" by George Monbiot, *The Guardian*, 06/12/05. Biofuels are not carbon neutral, as fossil fuels are used intensively in agricultural production. Recycled vegetable oil can be regarded as a truly green alternative to diesel, but there is only enough spare chip fat to fuel 1/380th of the current UK fleet of vehicles.

116) "The conventional bicycle is among the most efficient means of human locomotion. To travel one kilometre by bike requires approximately 5-15 watt/hours (w/h) of energy, while the same distance requires 15-20 w/h by foot, 30-40 w/h by train, and over 400 in a singly occupied car." *The Energy Cost of Human and Electric Powered Bicycles*, p 2, Justin Lemire-Elmore, www.ebikes.ca/sustainability.

117) Sounds far fetched? The government used to issue favourable rate 100% mortgages for housing co-ops, until Margaret Thatcher abolished the scheme in 1979. Promotion of housing co-ops would solve both the energy inefficiency, and the social isolation suffered by single-parent and single occupier households.

118) The Passive House, or Passivhaus, is a German design of house where the insulation and draught proofing are to such a high standard that the house can heat itself by passive solar gain. They are being constructed across Germany and Austria for as little as 8% over conventional construction costs.

119) "The Energy Review (Facts Included)" Greenpeace advertisement, *The Independent*, 21/06/06.

120) Contraction and Convergence was formulated by Aubrey Meyer, and is promoted by the Global Commons Institute. www.gci.org.uk. Under C+C rules, carbon trading still occurs, but unlike with the Kyoto protocol, every country in the world is obliged to reduce their fossil fuel use. This prevents "carbon colonialism", where rich nations cherrypick the cheap carbon offset deals from the Majority World. Instead all nations institute their own indigenous carbon reduction programmes, and surplus capacity is traded for a fair price.

121) The New Economics Foundation is conducting research into using a 'happiness index' as an indicator for national progress.

122) Study by Munich Re, the worlds largest reinsurance firm, quoted by Dr Andrew Dlugoecki, the Chairman of the UNEP Insurance Industry Initiative at http://www.saka-consul.com/Mita/dr ad.html

TAKE ACTION:

Climate Outreach and Information Network (COIN) 16B Cherwell Street, Oxford, OX4 1BG, UK. Tel: +44 (0)1865 727911. Comprehensive advice on all aspects of climate change education and personal carbon emissions reduction. Speakers available, including Kate Evans, author of this book. http://coinet.org.uk

Risingtide 62 Fieldgate St, London, E1 1ES, phone +44 (0)7708794. UK branch of an international movement, linking individuals and organisations to take action to halt climate chaos. http://risingtide.org.uk

Campaign against Climate Change Top Floor, 5 Caledonian Road, London N1 9DX, UK, Tel: +44 (0)20 7833 9311 Co-ordinates national and local demonstrations about climate change, to keep the issue in the public consciousness. www.campaignCC.org

Stop Climate Chaos The Grayston Centre, 28 Charles Square, London, N1 6HT, UK. Tel: +44 (0)20 7324 4750. Umbrella group working to build a popular mandate for political action. www.stopclimatechaos.org

Schnews.org.uk Uncompromising weekly free-sheet giving details of environmental and ethical protest in the UK and around the world. Search their web database for other action groups that may be of interest.

Friends of the Earth 26-28 Underwood Street, London, N1 7JQ, UK. Tel +44(0)20 7490 1555 Local groups provide an approachable way to start networking on environmental issues. www.foe.co.uk

Greenpeace Canonbury Villas, London, N1 2PN. Tel: +44 (0)20 7865 8100 Co-ordinated media-friendly direct action through regional groups, and cybercampaigning that you can do at home. You can even get a Greenpeace Visa Card. www.greenpeace.org.uk.

STUDENT:

People and Planet 51 Union Street Oxford OX4 1JP, UK. Tel: +44 (0)1865 245678 Campaigns on the environment, world poverty and human rights. www.peopleandplanet.org

FAITH-BASED:

Christian Ecology Link Multi-denominational Christ-ian environmental organisation. www.christian-ecology.org.uk

Quaker Green Action Promotes a low-impact lifestyle. www.quakergreenaction.org.uk

Islamic Foundation for Ecology and Environment Sciences www.ifees.org 93 Court Road, Balsall Heath, Birmingham, B12 9LQ, UK. Tel: 44 (0)121 440 3500. Works to articulate and disseminate Islamic environmentalism.

ETHNIC MINORITY:

The Black Environment Network Works to encourage participation by and inclusion of ethnic minorities in environmental initiatives. www.ben-network.co.uk

POLITICS:

The Green Party 1a Waterlow Road, London, N19 5NJ, UK. Tel: +44 (02)0 7272 4474. Aims to create a sustainable and equitable society, primarily through the electoral system. www.greenparty.org.uk

People's Global Action Decentralised international organisation linking resistance to, and nurturing alternatives to, global capitalism. www.agp.org

LOW-IMPACT LIVING:

The Centre for Alternative Technology, Machynlleth, Powys, SY20 9AZ, UK. Tel +44 (0)1654 705950 Researches and promotes methods for low-impact living. Their factsheets provide practical information on everything from solar hot water heating to compost toilets, and their residential courses are excellent. www.cat.org.uk

The Low Impact Living Initiative. Redfield Community, Winslow, Bucks, MK18 3LZ, UK. Tel: +44 (0)1296 714184. Original ideas and products to reduce your carbon impact, together with useful direct links to relevant websites. www.lowimpact.org.

Choose to not fly. Sign the Gold pledge at www.flightpledgeorg.co.uk. Don't worry, its only for a year. If you really can't bring yourself to do that, you can go for their Silver Pledge, where you're allowed two short-haul or one long-haul flight, and presumably the environment won't mind.

The Man in Seat Sixty-One knows how to get there without flying. Follow his complicated, but comprehensible advice for cross-continental travel by rail and boat. www.seat61.com

KEEP UP WITH CLIMATE CHANGES:

www.climatewire.net Website detailing climate-related news summaries from around the world.

www.climatechangenews.org Similar, but better. Essential articles are highlighted, to save you from information overload.

The Ecologist Magazine *www.theecologist.org*. Available at newsagents or, paper-free, online. Investigative journalism on environmental issues. Their 1999 climate issue was the inspiration for the first, 16 page version of this "Funny Weather" cartoon.

The Environmental Change Institute at Oxford University pioneers research into the climate, ecosystems, and low-carbon futures. Also fosters collaboration between artists and climate scientists. *www.eci.ox.ac.uk*

The Hadley Centre is the UK Meteorolgical Office's climate change research unit. It models current and future climate trends. *www.metoffice.com/research/hadleycentre*

The Intergovernmental Panel on Climate Change publishes its Assessment Reports online at *www.ipcc.ch*

New Scientist magazine Available at newsagents or online at *www.newscientist.com*. Includes comprehensive coverage of climate science.

www.realclimate.org Climate science by climate scientists. Interesting online comment and debate.

The Tyndall Centre Cross-disciplinary academic body which develops sustainable responses to climate change. *www.tyndall.ac.uk*

INTERACTIVE ONLINE GAMES:

Greena the Worrier Princess presents a fun introduction to the issues at *www.abc.net.au/science/planetslayer/* Very silly.

Also check out the ***Climate Challenge*** online computer game, which can be played at *www.bbc.co.uk/sn/*

RECOMMENDED FURTHER READING:

The Atlas of Climate Change by Kirsten Dow and Thomas E Downing. Maps the impact of climate change around the world. A pictoral assesment of the global situation. *www.myriadeditions.com*

Boiling Point by Ross Gelbspan. Reveals how fossil fuel industries have directed US domestic and foreign policies, together with a roadmap for economic adjustment to climate change. *www.heatisonline.org*

Climate Change: A Very Short Introduction by Professor Mark Maslin. Comprehensive and readable, with a thoughtful analysis of the arguments of climate change "sceptics".

Heat: How to stop the planet burning by George Monbiot explores ways and means to make a 90% cut in CO2 emissions by 2030 a reality. *www.monbiot.com*

How We Can Save the Planet by Mayer Hillman with Tina Fawcett. Dense, fact-filled overview of climate change, and solutions for the UK, including carbon rationing.

High Tide by Mark Lynas gives a personal account of current climate crises, and his forthcoming book ***Six Degrees*** (out March 2007) explores what's in store if we don't sort it out. *www.marklynas.org*

I Have Waited and You Have Come by Martine McDonagh. Novel set in a climate-changed future. Its really good, and I'm not just saying that because we share a publisher.

The Last Generation: How Nature will take her Revenge for Climate Change by Fred Pearce. Punchy, pacy book, with a thorough exploration of positive feedback mechanisms.

The Little Earth Book by James Bruges. Succinct, fascinating account of current financial and social structures, and their alternatives. *www.fragile-earth.com*

The No-Nonsense Guide to Climate Change by Dinyar Godrej. Interesting introduction to the subject, with good Majority World perspectives.

The Party's Over: Oil, War and the Fate of Industrial Society by Richard Heinberg. Thorough analytical explanation of peak oil and the forthcoming energy shortfall. *www.richardheinberg.com*

Saving the Planet Without Costing the Earth: 500 Simple Steps to a Greener Lifestyle by Donnachadh McCarthy, provides help with auditing your environmental impact, and plenty of ideas for improvement.

Stormy Weather: 101 Solutions to Global Climate Change by Guy Dauncey with Patrick Mazza. Packed with practical suggestions.

HOW MUCH CARBON DIOXIDE DO YOU EMIT IN A YEAR?

Grab a calculator, a sheet of paper and a pencil. And probably, an eraser.

AT HOME
Check your fuel bills, then choose from these options:

GAS Look for the units on all your bills, and add them together.
EITHER KWh x 0.19
OR cubic metres × 1.77
OR Therms x 5.5 = kg CO_2

COAL Kgs of coal × 2.4 = kg CO_2
OIL litres of heating oil ×3 = kg CO_2

BOTTLED GAS Kgs of butane x 1.74
OR Kgs of propane x 1.95 = litres of gas
THEN litres of bottled gas x 1.5 = kg CO_2

ELECTRICITY - nothing! if you use a green supplier like **ECOTRICITY** or **GREEN ENERGY**. **OTHERWISE** annual KWh x 0.5 = kg CO_2 A key meter will tell you a total figure for numbers of KWhs used. Take one reading, then another a week later. Average weekly readings through the year, for accuracy.

WOOD kgs burnt x 1.03 = kg CO_2, but then, you can divide this by half, because the trees will grow back in the next 25 years. Hopefully.

DIVIDE YOUR TOTAL by the number of adults in the household. **The average UK citizen scores 2800kg.** How did you do?

TRAVEL
This is a big one, but there're plenty of ways to change it.

BY CAR Get your annual mileage by comparing your MOT certificates. If it has an:
under 1.4 litre engine x 0.28
under 2.1 litre engine x 0.36
over 2.1 litre engine x 0.43 = kg CO_2
OR litres of petrol/diesel x 2.5 = kg CO_2
DIVIDE YOUR TOTAL by the number of adults using the car.   Recycled biodiesel scores nil.

Miles travelled on **PUBLIC TRANSPORT**:
by **RAIL** x 0.1 = kg CO_2
by **CITY BUS** or **SUBWAY** x 0.17 = kg CO_2
by **LONG DISTANCE BUS** x 0.08 = kg CO_2

Miles travelled by **FERRY** x 0.75
Days at sea on **CRUISE SHIP** x 230 = kg CO_2

The average UK citizen emits 1600kg from land travel. Do you?

FLYING
Human beings probably aren't meant to fly. A return trip to:
Western Europe = 700 kg CO_2
East Coast USA = 4249 kg CO_2
West Coast USA = 5700 kg CO_2
East Asia = 6400 kg CO_2 and
Australia = 11000 kg CO_2, which is more than most people's total annual emissions! A one-way flight to New York is worse than driving a car for a year. Ooops.

SHOPPING
Add on some more CO_2 to compensate for your place in the consumer economy:

"I own a car" + 555 kg CO_2

THINGS: "I buy second-hand wherever possible" + 600 kg CO_2
OR "I buy new things when I need them" + 2000 kg CO_2
OR "I love shopping" + 3000 kg CO_2

FOOD "I eat meat" + 1200 kg CO_2
AND EITHER "I grow all my own fruit and veg" + 0 kg CO_2
OR "I eat organic UK fruit and veg" + 400 kg CO_2
OR "I eat non-organic fruit and veg" +800 kg $CO2$

The average UK shopper consumes 4000kg of $CO2$. Can you beat that?

Add up your totals, and what have you got?
Average UK annual emissions = 10.371kg

You want to aim for 2500kg of CO_2 a year. Yikes. And that's still *twice* what we'll be allowed in 2030, if there are 8.2 billion people by then. Double yikes. This is a radical lifestyle change. We need root and branch reform to be able to meet it. Still, doing the sums will give you an idea of which areas of your life are most energy hungry, and help you to see how to change them. Set yourself realistic targets. Tackle some of the big figures, like flights and commuting. Low-carbon living will help you to see how we need to change our society to save the world.

This calculator is amalgamated from *www. resurgence.org/carboncalculator,* which you can complete online, and from *coinet.org/projects/ challenge/measure.*

INDEX

www.cartoonkate.co.uk

ABOUT THE AUTHOR:

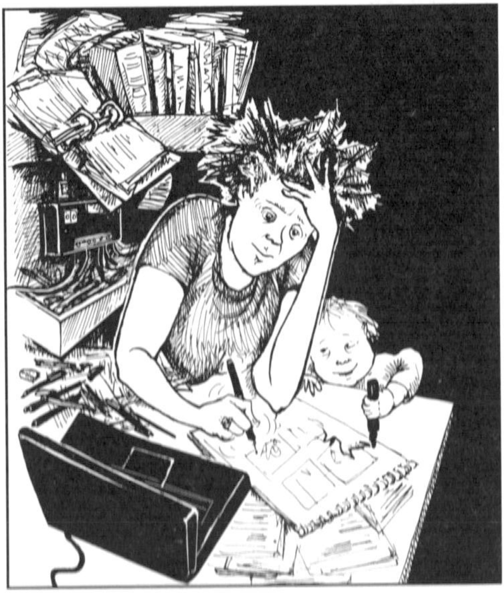

KATE EVANS IS A CARTOONIST AND ENVIRONMENTALIST WHO CURRENTLY LIVES IN A HEDGE JUST OUTSIDE BATH. SHE SPENDS HER TIME ALTERNATELY WORRYING ABOUT THE STATE OF THE PLANET AND CONTRIBUTING TO THE OVER-POPULATION PROBLEM.

THE PRODUCTION OF THIS BOOK WAS PREDOMINATELY POWERED BY A SOLAR PANEL AND A 350 WATT WIND GENERATOR. IT WAS HEATED BY A WOOD-BURNING STOVE, PASSIVE SOLAR HEATING, AND THE WEARING OF SKI-ING SALOPETTES. GIVE THAT WOMAN A BLUE PETER BADGE.

THIS BOOK WAS WRITTEN, RESEARCHED, ILLUSTRATED AND LAID OUT BY KATE EVANS. SHE HAS PREVIOUSLY WRITTEN (RESEARCHED, ILLUSTRATED, LAID OUT AND PUBLISHED) *COPSE: THE CARTOON BOOK OF TREE PROTESTING* ABOUT HER EXPERIENCES AS AN ENVIRONMENTAL ACTIVIST. *THE FOOD OF LOVE - BREASTFEEDING YOUR BABY* IS NEXT, PROBABLY FOLLOWED BY SOMETHING ON PREGNANCY AND BIRTH. SHE IS THE AUTHOR OF NUMEROUS STRIP CARTOONS AND FULL-LENGTH COMIC FEATURES INCLUDING *WHAT'S REALLY GOING ON IN THERE?* ABOUT FERTILITY AWARENESS, AND *BIG BROTHER* AN EXPLORATION OF UK CIVIL LIBERTIES (SOMETIMES REALITY IS SCARIER THAN REALITY TV). MORE ON THE WEBSITE - CHECK IT OUT.

SHE CAN ALSO DO A MEAN ILLUSTRATED LECTURE ON CLIMATE CHANGE, IF YOU NEED SOMEONE TO BRIGHTEN UP YOUR DISCUSSIONS OF DOOM AND GLOOM.

www.funnyweather.org

MANY THANKS TO DONACH, DUNCAN LAW, GEORGE MARSHALL, MARK BROWN, GEORGE MONBIOT, FRED PEARCE, ANEETA, COLIN FORREST, CHRIS JONES, MARK MASLIN AND EVERYONE AT TIPPING POINT FOR ADADEMIC INPUT, CORINNE PEARLMAN AND CANDIDA LACEY FOR BELIEVING IN CARTOONS, CHARLES AND ELEANOR ANDERSON FOR LAUNDRY SERVICES, ROSIE EVANS AND ADAM MARSHALL FOR FINANCIAL SUPPORT, SHARON FOR CARING, MIKE HOLDERNESS FOR WEB GEEKERY, MIPSY FOR ARTISTIC INSPIRATION AND LOUDEN FOR BEING CUTE. APOLOGIES TO TONY AND SU. IF YOU'RE NOT ONE OF THE PEOPLE MENTIONED ABOVE, THAT WAS PROBABLY QUITE BORING. ANYWAY, GET IN TOUCH WITH ME AT kate@cartoonkate.co.uk AND TELL ME WHAT YOU THINK OF THE BOOK.

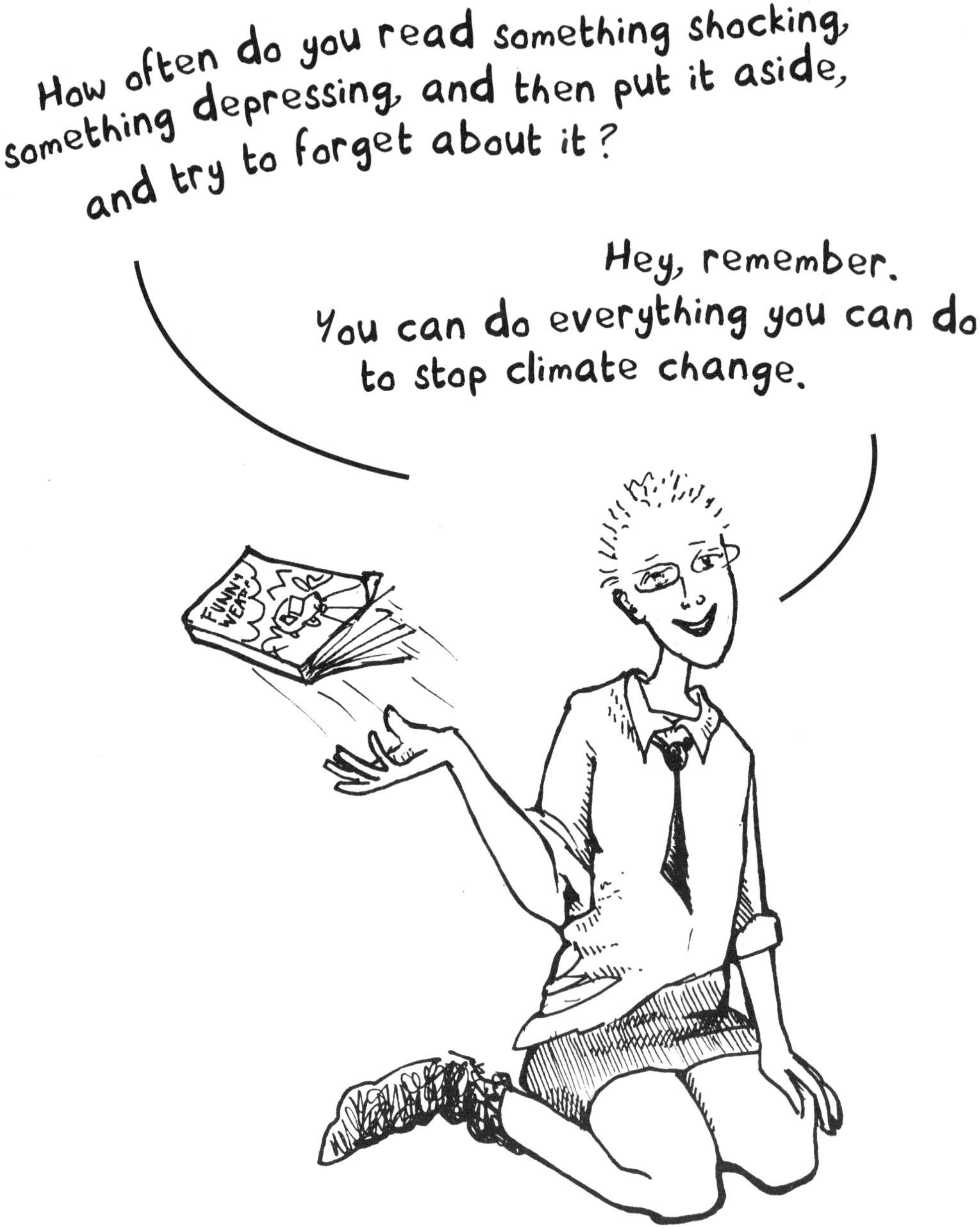
How often do you read something shocking, something depressing, and then put it aside, and try to forget about it?
Hey, remember. You can do everything you can do to stop climate change.